Intelligent Infrastructure

INTELLIGENT INFRASTRUCTURE

ZIP CARS, INVISIBLE NETWORKS, AND URBAN TRANSFORMATION

EDITED BY   T. F. TIERNEY

University of
Virginia Press
Charlottesville
and London

University of Virginia Press
© 2016 by the Rector and Visitors of the University of Virginia
All rights reserved
Printed in the United States of America on acid-free paper

First published 2016

9 8 7 6 5 4 3 2 1

Library of Congress Cataloging-in-Publication Data

Names: Tierney, Thérèse, editor.
Title: Intelligent infrastructure : zip cars, invisible networks, and urban
    transformation / edited by T. F. Tierney.
Description: Charlottesville : University of Virginia Press, 2017. | Includes
    bibliographical references and index.
Identifiers: LCCN 2016020646| ISBN 9780813939414 (cloth : alk. paper) | ISBN
    9780813939483 (pbk. : alk. paper) | ISBN 9780813939421 (ebook)
Subjects: LCSH: Intelligent transportation systems. | Transportation—
    Technological innovations. | Urban transportation. | Infrastructure
    (Economics)
Classification: LCC TE228.3 .I555 2017 | DDC 388.4—dc23
LC record available at https://lccn.loc.gov/2016020646

Cover art: City of the Future, Urbaneering Brooklyn 2110. (© Mitchell Joachim/
Terreform ONE)

Contents

Acknowledgments   vii

Introduction: Infrastructural Intelligence—Connective Systems for a
Postcarbon City   1

Part I. Soft Systems   37

The Conceptual Roots of Infrastructure   39
  Mitchell Schwarzer

Tinkering toward (A)utopia: Telecommunications and Transit in the
Twentieth-First-Century City   63
  Anthony Townsend

Phantom Tollbooth Plaza   71
  Jordan Geiger

Part II. Mashed Systems   85

Mobile Networks as Tactical Transportation   87
  *T. F. Tierney with Ben Feldman, Katherine Handy, Tyron Marshall, Dinesh
  Perera, and Gerald Tierney*

(Driver)less Is More   100
  Bjarke Ingels and Kai-Uwe Bergmann

Ubiquitous Multimodality: A Vision for Urban Mobility in the (Near) Future   109
   Carlo Ratti, Nashid Nabian, and Christine Outram

The Future of Personal Urban Mobility: An Engineer's Perspective   121
   Sven Beiker

Part III. Hard Systems   133

The Automobile, the City, and the New Urban Mobilities   135
   Frederic Stout

Rethinking Urban Utopias: A Manifesto for Self-Supported Infrastructure, Technology, and Territory   159
   Mitchell Joachim

Urban Mobility in the Informal City   173
   Alfredo Brillembourg and Hubert Klumpner

The Paradox of Urban Mobility and the Spatialization of Technological Utopia   186
   Chamee Yang

Conclusion: Networked Urbanism and Everyday Mobility in the City   209

Selected Bibliography   223

Notes on Contributors   239

Index   245

Acknowledgments

First and foremost, I thank the many authors who contributed to this volume. If it were not for the intellectual generosity and professionalism of those scholars, engineers, designers, and architects, this volume would not exist.

Intelligent Infrastructure is the synthesis of more than ten years of research on networked urbanism. Many of the ideas within this volume began with William Mitchell at Massachusetts Institute of Technology media lab. Mitchell's boundless vision of a connected city inspired all who studied with him. I am also grateful for John Maeda's courage and immeasurable patience to adopt a humanities scholar, as well as for the collegiality he fostered in his lab. I would like to thank Burak Arikan, Hilary Karls (now with Uber), Kelly Norton, Noah Passel, Carlos Rocha, and Marc Schwartz for their encouragement. Within MIT's Course 4 Design + Computation Group there were many who listened to my formative concepts about networks and offered invaluable suggestions: Saeed Arida, Mitchell Joachim (whose work is featured in this volume), Axel Kilian, Yani Loukissas, JunSik Moon, and Neri Oxman. I am also very grateful to Ryan Chin, who continued to advance Mitchell's legacy with City Science Initiative.

After returning to San Francisco in 2009 to complete my dissertation, Peter Zellner at Southern California Institute for Architecture (SciArc) launched his influential competition, "New Infrastructure: Transit Solutions for Los Angeles." Thanks to Peter, along with Dana Cuff, Kevin Daly, Neil Denari, Greg Lynn, Tom Mayne, Eric Owen Moss, Stephen Phillips, and others who have been advancing innovative urban thinking in a particularly challenging urban environment. I am particularly indebted to my LA_REDcar collaborators: Katie Handy and Dinesh Perrera of Format Design and Ben Feldman, Tyrone

Marshall, and Gerry Tierney of 510 Collective. Without their inspired efforts and perseverance, neither the Mobility and the City Colloquium (2010) nor this volume would have been possible. I also wish to thank Ila Berman and David Meckel at California College of the Arts, the American Institute of Architects, and Architect's Newspaper for their support of the colloquium.

I owe a debt of gratitude to several institutions and organizations for their support while I was developing the manuscript. Thomas Deschamps, consulate general of France in San Francisco, sponsored my travels to France to study smart cities at a formative time in my writing. The tour was an exceptional opportunity to meet other researchers from academia, industry, startups, as well as government representatives—and share ideas on smart and sustainable cities. During the Futur en Seine Conference, workshop panels emphasized a strong link between policy, sustainability, and technological development. I wish to thank the Paris Region Lab, PRIME, Christophe Arnaud with IER Responsible Ligne d'activite, Lieux Publics. Thanks also to Vincent Roumeas for sharing his knowledge on infrastructural planning. Special thanks go to our hosts: Pierrick Bouffaron, Basile Bouquet, and Marie-Perrine Durot, and to Caroline Nowacki, now at Stanford University. I also wish to thank my fellow delegates for our lively discussions—Jonathan Reichental, Rajiv Bhatia, Jose Campos, Patrick Dempsey, Mark Gibb, Peter Hirshberg, Danielle Murray, Sean Ness, and Paul Wright.

I am grateful to University of Virginia Press for making their belief in this publication clearly evident, most especially for Boyd Zenner's advocacy for the project and for steering this book through every stage with confidence. Much appreciation also goes to Mark Saunders, Ellen Satrom, and the entire staff at the Press, to Jane Curran for copyediting, as well as to the reviewers, who remain unnamed.

Investigating the questions of this book was only possible with guides willing to help me become a more rigorous researcher. At University of California Berkeley, I am very grateful to Jean-Pierre Protzen, Nezar Alssayad, Ken Goldberg, and Eleanor Rosch for their intellectual generosity. I am thankful for the guidance of Sanford Kwinter, Mitchell Schwarzer, and Mabel O. Wilson, who provided the conceptual foundations for this book. A special acknowledgment goes to Mark Wigley and Saskia Sassen at Columbia for their important work on the Audi Future Initiative. I also wish to thank Reinhold Martin, who has been a guiding force in critical thinking about networked urbanism. Wigley,

Martin, and Saskia's unilateral encouragement toward a younger generation of scholars is immeasurable. Anthony Townsend and Greg Lindsey at NYU Rudin Center for Transportation Policy—thank you for your strategic advice when I had difficulty moving forward. And to the many others who are doing important research in this area: Sartac Karaman, Katja Schechtner, Meejin Yoon and Eric Howler, Janette Sadik-Khan, Susan Shaheen at UC Berkeley, Geoffrey Thün, Kathy Velikov, Dan McTavish, and Sue Zielinski at University of Michigan.

At UIUC, I wish to thank Edward Feser, Dianne Harris, and Peter Mortensen for their unqualified support and for fostering a vibrant intellectual climate. It is their continual insistence on the importance of interdisciplinary research that makes teaching here worthwhile. Indeed, thanks goes to Kathleen Harleman and the entire faculty at FAA, to my colleagues at Center for People and Infrastructure: Kevin Hamilton, Karrie Karahalios, Cedric Langbort, Christian Sandvig (now at University of Michigan), and also to Dan Work and Brian Deal; they provide the inestimable gift of solidarity. I am grateful to William Buttlar, Roy Campbell, Alan Craig, and Kevin Franklin at NCSA, and to my colleagues at the School of Architecture. Special thanks to Areli Marina for reading my drafts and making constructive comments, and to Barbara Diller-Young and Leslie Til, whose keen intelligence and editorial rigor were essential to this project. I am very grateful to the following friends and colleagues who provided valuable feedback and advice on this subject: Sean Ahlquist, Kathryn Anthony, Kai Bergmann, Regan Bice, Kory Bieg, Marshall Brown, Anthony Burke, Ravi Choksombatchai, Cynthia Davidson, Lynne Dearborn, Elen Deming, Alexander Eisenschmidt, Gustav Fagerstrom, Sara Bartumeus Ferre, Stewart Hicks, Lisa Iwamoto, Craig Hodgetts, Mitch Joachim and Melanie Fessel, Dr. Kenneth Graham, Adam Greenfield, Ellen Hartman, David Hays, Gabe Klein, Jason Kelly Johnson, Robert LaFrance, Jung Hoon Lee, Ana María León, Nik Luka, Sandy and Rob Ludlow, Susana Macarron, Joy Malnar, Mary Pat Mattson McGuire, Brandon McGlone, Nicholas Negroponte, Allison Newmeyer, Luke Ogrydziak and Zoë Prillinger, Jeffery Poss FAIA, Stephen Sears, Amita Sinha, Cara Stepp, Bill Sullivan, Ken Tracy and Christine Yogiaman, Deke Weaver, Andrew Weiss, and Pengjun Zhao.

I am deeply indebted to University of Illinois at Urbana-Champaign Campus Research Board, the College of Fine and Applied Arts Creative Research Award, the American Institute of Architects, the Architects Newspaper, California College of the Arts, Field Paoli Architects, and Perkins + Will Architecture. Without their generous support, this volume would never have reached completion.

As to all of the seemingly endless detail involved in collecting material for the manuscript, I am very grateful to my graduate research assistants. Special thanks for the arduous work involved with obtaining permissions goes to Maria Dorofeeva, who maintained a cheerful countenance throughout the process. Thanks also to Braulio Soto, Anthony Dombrowski, Stephanie Morganthaler, Yang Yu, and the entire communications team at Bjarke Ingels Group, especially Aiden Bowman and Daria Pahhota, and to Daniel Schwartz at Urban–Think Tank for their timely assistance, and to Iwan Baan for granting permission to reproduce his exquisite photographs in this book.

Finally, I thank my entire family, especially my parents, Frances and Julius, and my aunt Mary, who supported my explorations from the beginning.

Introduction

Infrastructural Intelligence—Connective
Systems for a Postcarbon City

The concept of the city as we know it is undergoing an enormous reformation. As high-speed networks, locative technologies, and environmental sensor systems converge in physical space, new organizational logics are reshaping the geography and conditions of urban living.[1] Concurrently, confronting climate change urgently demands new policies governing carbon emissions, nuclear power, and the protection of specific natural resources.[2] As urban governance contends with these challenges, the incentives to investigate alternative solutions proliferate. Governments and industries must develop not only cleaner mobility strategies but also the means to implement them: new forms of energy production, allocation, and infrastructure, as well as a more reliable and equitable system of resource distribution.

Although climate change is the most immediate of the threats, a host of lesser but nevertheless potentially destabilizing problems accompany and intersect with it. Internal and external factors, such as migration and population growth, materially influence contemporary urban form. In rapidly growing cities such as Los Angeles, Mexico City, and Manila, seven hundred or more new residents arrive every day.[3] While increased density may be seen as a temporary solution to urban growth, some critics cite planning policies themselves as problematic.[4] Formal, rigidly modernist agendas, established during a time of relative stasis, were not designed to respond nimbly to complex, constantly shifting problems. One solution proposed by social geographer Edward Soja suggests that, rather than focusing on built forms, architects and engineers study the connections and infrastructural systems that bind cities together, thus creating an advanced framework for improved growth and change.[5]

The late William Mitchell, architect, writer, and director of the MIT Media

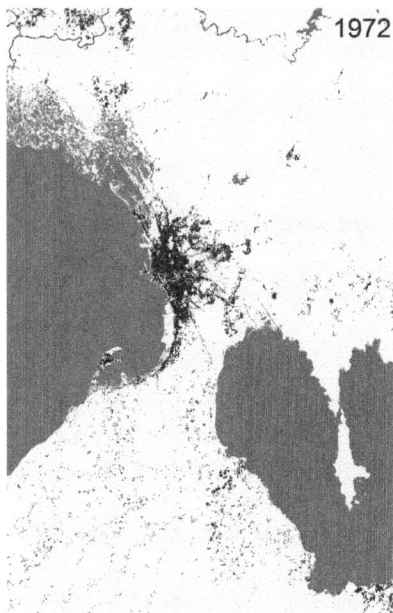

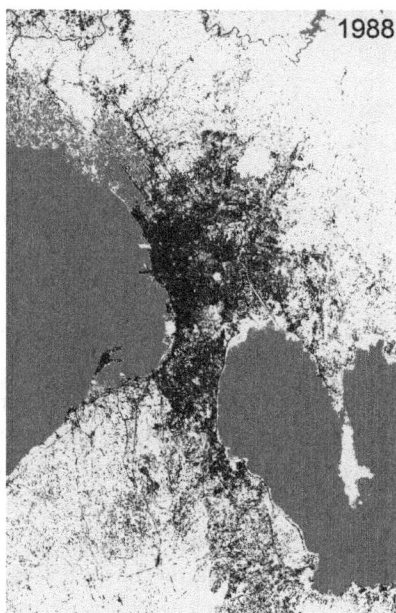

Figs. 1–3. Urban growth analysis in the example of Manila, Philippines, from 1972 to 2010. (H. Taubenböck, T. Esch, A. Felbier, M. Wiesner, A. Roth, and W. Dech, "Monitoring of Mega-Cities from Space," *Remote Sensing of Environment* 117 [2012]: 171)

Lab from 2002 to 2006, adopted one such approach.[6] He conceptualized the modern city as an interconnected network of systems, an intelligent and responsive infrastructure imbued with self-awareness through sensors and computing. Questioning the primacy of personal automobiles, Mitchell proposed designing cars to suit a sustainable vision of the city, rather than designing the city to suit the arbitrary specifications of the car. *Reinventing the Automobile: Personal Urban Mobility for the 21st Century* documents his research and outlines the ways a postcarbon landscape could reshape urban transportation practices. The sustainable city he, along with coauthors Chris Borroni-Bird and Lawrence Burns, imagined would integrate connected e-cars, mobility-on-demand systems, smart electric grids, and dynamically priced markets. With Mitchell's book as the launching point, *Intelligent Infrastructure: Zip Cars, Invisible Networks, and Urban Transformation* represents the combined thoughts of designers, engineers, and scholars, some of whom studied with Mitchell and are now continuing his legacy. Our objective in this book is to focus on one key concept, *connection*, as it relates to the impact of information and communication technologies (ICTs) on urban infrastructure, particularly mobility systems. Other topics, such as urban sociology, human-computer interaction, fuel-efficient automobiles, resilience and renewable energy, while worthy of further study, are discussed only as subsets of the primary intelligent cities framework.

Roadmap

The purpose of this introductory chapter is to present the overall thesis and theoretical background of the collection. First, the term *intelligent infrastructure* is defined. Second, the theoretical framework of the collection is set forth. In this section, intelligent infrastructure and mobility systems are positioned within a larger conversation related to "smart cities" by examining existing literature on the technologically augmented city, such as environmental issues, resource sharing, and network culture. The background, scope, and direction of the book thus presented, its organization is then outlined. Finally, each chapter is described briefly and placed in context with the overall objectives of the book.

Although the field of urban studies is responding to rapid advancements in information and communication technologies (ICT), the literature has not yet fully addressed the impact of wireless infrastructure on reformulating urban space.[7] Significant sociological research has emerged on the topic;[8] however, it has mostly been confined to empirical studies, and consequently the findings are not aimed at urban design and planning. Examinations of sensor-enabled environments exist,[9] but the implications of such environments have not been fully theorized. Other studies analyze transportation and sustainability but are addressed exclusively to policy makers.[10] Some studies consider the territorial implications of global economies and free trade zones,[11] while still others address specific developments in technologies of transportation but fail to integrate these into a wider theoretical perspective on mobility and urbanism.[12] More importantly, previous research assumed fixed use of the Internet and was carried out before the widespread adoption of mobile technologies and the "Internet of Things" (also known as Internet of Everything or Cloud of Things, or IoT), defined as the integration of Web 2.0, mobile communication, and sensing technologies.[13] Overall, what is lacking in the literature is an updated and synthesized approach to the subject of networked urban mobility.

Even Mitchell omits many of the ways in which people and cities will also change from his outline of the myriad ways automobile design will change in the future. Although he introduces the "Mobility Internet" and how it could become a unified delivery mechanism for previously separated data streams and services, the topic is only touched on, not fully developed.[14] Similarly, the description of how such capabilities can enable automobiles to be integrated into urban-scale networked computing and control (NCC) systems—merging traffic flow, road safety space, vehicle fleets, and electrical supply—omits discussion of the important social overlay.[15]

By enfolding social practices into transportation infrastructure, *Intelligent Infrastructure* stakes out a holistic position in the debate by investigating how cities are being reordered through new kinds of urban logic, technical systems, and discursive relations. The volume offers one of the first empirically based and theoretically informed narratives on the Internet of Things—what we are calling *intelligent infrastructure*. Contributors focus on the ways in which the human dimensions of networked infrastructure can be instrumental in shaping everyday mobility in urban space: how wireless technologies are being employed to connect transportation, commerce, and architecture, effectively reshaping the contemporary urban condition. In accord with Stephen Graham and Simon Marvin's notion that cities are sociotechnical processes,[16] we investigate the iterative effect of communication technologies: how social practices are enabled by technology and how technology in turn shapes new social practices. Sharing a belief that infrastructural networks are the ideal integrators of urban spaces, we propose ways in which they can bind cities and regions together into political wholes.

What Is Intelligent Infrastructure?

Anthony Townsend defines intelligent cities as "cellular networks and cloud computing tying together the complex choreography of mega-regions of tens of millions of people."[17] A quotidian example of intelligent infrastructure is a wireless mobile communication device (smartphone), which connects people, places, and practices within an urban context. Other types of intelligent platforms cover the spectrum—from networked traffic signals that can be adjusted from afar to electric grids that respond to usage to location-aware apps such as Foursquare, which (among other things) combines restaurant reviews with health inspection data. In Seoul, a "T-money card" or, in Hong Kong, an "Octopus card" (electronic money card) offers access to wide variety of goods and services. In Zaragoza, Spain, a "citizen card" (electronic pass card) offers free citywide Wi-Fi, municipal bike sharing, museum and library privileges, and free public transport anywhere.[18] In Paris, networked resource sharing includes the electric Autolib' car-sharing system. Vehicles can be reserved via mobile device or online by credit card; they can also be unlocked and allotted parking spaces. Other informal modes collectively known as mobility-on-demand systems (MoD) include Lyft, Uber, and car2go, and more services are emerging weekly.

In addition to networked programs initiated by government institutions or private start-ups, intelligent infrastructure also comprises participatory practices. In this category we include civic hacking, crowdsourcing, urban games, and the open source/open data movement. Although space does not allow us to go into all aspects of the phenomena, it is important to note that individuals and groups are creating their own platforms specific to their culture and locale. Coders volunteer hundreds of hours of their time in hackathons, designing and developing open source applications for public use. Relevant to the discussion are transit apps, which leverage open public data; for example, Roadify and Waze.

Other critical applications have been realized for communities under crisis in disaster or emergency situations. Currently, many humanitarian groups and NGOs are developing mobile platforms; for example, the Digital Humanitarian Network (DHN), a group of sixteen volunteer technology organizations, acts as an interface between those groups and conventional humanitarian organizations. The DHN brings together expertise in geographical information systems, online mapping, data analysis, and statistics to help hundreds of thousands of people find information, supply aid, and assist with disaster and recovery efforts—all through their mobile devices. In addition to nonprofit ventures, collective coding groups such as Code For America enlist volunteer developers to partner with contractors, entrepreneurs, and municipalities, in some cases leading to the creation of start-up companies. Ad hoc software platforms, developed by volunteers, allow citizen users to combine best practices into user-friendly social media toolkits for risk mitigation and community response.[19] One of the best known is Ushahidi, a data management system and platform that utilizes Short Message Service (SMS) messaging and proved highly effective during the earthquake in Haiti and Hurricane Sandy.[20]

These bottom-up efforts by ordinary citizens and coders are some of the more exciting aspects of intelligent infrastructure. Described as DIY (do-it-yourself) urbanism, these projects include installation of free neighborhood Wi-Fi, as with the Detroit Digital Stewards, or community wireless educational toolkits that aim to foster equal access to networked infrastructure. DIY efforts may overlap with other movements, including Internet activism; some of the best known are Indymedia and the Occupy movement. DIY differs in that, although networked technologies may be employed for organizational purposes, the objective is to seek to change directly within a neighborhood. These networked efforts may strengthen community and democratic efforts.[21]

Networked urbanism simultaneously encourages a reassessment of institutional foundations in planning and decision making. In addition to using infrastructure-focused sites such as Fix My Street or Fill That Hole, city governments are increasingly embracing networked technologies (online interfaces and smartphone applications) for involving constituents in land use planning and control. The prevalence and ease of use of these platforms offer citizens opportunities to voice their concerns and provide informational input to land use control through political participation. Crowdsourcing discussion and decision making may avoid unexpected or unwanted land use changes. "The point is not to turn over land use authority outright to the public," says Lee Anne Fennell, "but rather to find better ways to elicit, aggregate, coordinate, and channel the preferences, intentions, and experiences of current and future land-users. . . . Planners must begin shifting their focus from the top-down regulation of land use to the development of information platforms for coordinating land use."[22]

As efficient and innovative as these new communication strategies are, they do not yet get us to the smart city. So how will a smart city work? Social practices enabled by intelligent infrastructure—known as *near-field communication*—allow wireless radio communication between such things as phones, transit cards, and readers. These networked interactions can enable payments through Google Wallet, Clipper Card, or other bank and credit cards; they can also support data sharing—location information, songs, or photos. Such interactions are now common practice in everyday life, where, effectively, the smartphone has become the urban interface in OECD (Organisation for Economic Co-operation and Development) countries. In the developing world, where governments are slow or reticent to invest in fixed infrastructure, mobile phones have emerged as the primary method of data communication.[23] In place of expensive fixed transportation routes or linear communication systems, residents use mobile phones (and attendant connection to the Internet) to access political, consumer, and health information. Mobile technologies are being employed for everyday interactions: banking, making and receiving payments, and even medical consultations.[24]

Such a system is supported by four components: (1) software: Internet Protocol version 6 (IPv6), enabling the previously mentioned IoT, where any object can access (and be accessed through) the Internet; (2) long-range broadband wireless connectivity: what used to be called radio communication;[25] (3) processing/transmission hardware: device connectivity via built-in radio communication;[26] and (4) sensors: mechanical devices sensitive to environmental conditions that transmit signals to measuring or control instruments.[27] This new experience of technology in the everyday is called *intelligent infrastructure.*

While the Internet has been in everyday use for decades, what is distinct about intelligent infrastructural systems is self-awareness. While the smartphone, the most ubiquitous intelligent device, incorporates sensors such as an accelerometer, compass, and GPS, the high cost of these sensors formerly prevented them from being used indiscriminately in the environment. That has changed. The recent affordability of sensors allows their widespread use in machines, devices, transportation, and even on individuals (an example is the Apple Watch). Increasingly, inexpensive wireless sensors will be embedded in the urban environment, creating sophisticated large-scale sensor networks. Within these networks, smartphones will effectively act as wireless hubs for other devices, connecting the Internet of Things (IoT) at the urban scale.[28] Autonomous cars with embedded sensors will be capable of perceiving other cars, pedestrians, and road position, in addition to intracar communication. Whether sensors are mobile or fixed, they are examples of infrastructural intelligence, enabling citizens and infrastructure to become hyperconnected to each other and their environment.[29]

In the context of that conversation between people and devices, IoT describes an urban society enmeshed with technology in what social scientist Bruno Latour calls a *sociotechnical system*—a complex assemblage of human, computational, and physical resources.[30] More recently, philosopher Graham Harman proposed a framework known as object-oriented ontology (OOO). He reinterpreted the sociotechnical assemblage by focusing on relationships between entities by ascribing equal agency to things and beings.[31] Further, OOO argues that objects such as robots or other devices exist independently of human perception, and thus all relations, human and nonhuman, are said to exist on equal ontological footing with one another. While OOO disavows any totalizing thesis such as Latour's actor network theory (ANT), these notions need not be seen as contradictory. Considering the world and the interdependence of all its entities, a philosophical position such as OOO can undergird a broad ecological position frequently championed by Timothy Morton, which I am calling "equality among entities" or EaE. One important realization is that each of the increasingly critical topics in today's environments—sustainable resources, mobility issues, social practices, communication networks, public space, and data privacy—can no longer be understood considered in isolation.

Theoretical Background

Along with the discussion of sensors and telecommunication devices, a larger theoretical conversation concerns land use and nonrenewable resources. Design disciplines recognize a shift exemplified by intensified discourse on sustainable practices, upon which Mitchell Joachim elaborates in his essay, "Rethinking Urban Utopias." A body of theories, largely subsumed under the term *landscape urbanism*, is accelerating an expansion in both the scope and scale of projects by designers of the built environment. Informed by postmodern, poststructuralist sensibilities, landscape urbanism suggests that the contemporary urban condition is too complex for any singular disciplinary perspective. While the origins of landscape urbanism lie in critiques of modernist architecture and planning, architect and theorist Stan Allen argues that landscape urbanism has fallen short of its promise.[32] Projects built under its banner have primarily been large parks; in that sense, what is considered "urban" has been left out of the equation. In contrast, *ecological urbanism*, as advanced by Mohsen Mostafavi, dean of the Harvard Graduate School of Design, "searches for a new basis of a performative urbanism that emerges from the bottom up, geared to the technological and ecological realities of the postindustrial world."[33] Mostafavi's directive is straightforward. It recognizes that climate change is related to carbon emissions produced by burning fossil fuels; thus, if we want to limit warming, those emissions have to be phased out.[34] Designers, whether architects, planners, or engineers, must address that fact in their research and practice.

Ecological urbanism participates in the discussion on urban resiliency by examining the city under duress. It encompasses the unexpected, heterogeneous, and climatic and leverages them as a means of projecting future opportunities. Ecological urbanism favors holistic design solutions that meaningfully integrate the mechanisms for exchange across—and transgression of—disciplinary boundaries. For the purposes of this book, ecological urbanism becomes instrumental when it addresses context, whole systems, top-down versus bottom-up planning, and social equality. While the essays here adopt a theoretical position grounded in ecological urbanism, the objective is to expand that position in new and more interesting ways, first by employing holistic strategic thinking, and second by applying tactical prototypes. Our focus is on projects that are well researched, practical, and implementable.

Design possibilities notwithstanding, we cannot presume that ICTs are a wholesale solution to complex urban issues. The development of more individualized and flexible forms of engagement within networked environments may actually counter the connective potential of the networks themselves by enabling a personal infrastructure that stands in contrast with public works.[35] While personal does not always undermine public, infrastructure, as a metastructure, is generally understood to be universally accessible and thus related to social equity. In addition to debate over the proliferation of sensors and telecommunication devices, a larger and more important discussion involves economics, policy making, and governance of this technology. Policy makers express guarded optimism that ICTs, including large-scale data analysis, can bring increased understanding and order to urban processes. Before we can examine that proposition, we must ask who (or what) is behind smart cities initiatives. The smart city conversation is currently driven almost exclusively by large IT organizations such as Cisco, IBM, GE, and Siemens—corporations that are motivated to implement their optimization strategies in economically challenged cities.[36] Other corporations keen to participate in the connected car discussion specifically are well known: Google, Apple, Audi, Ford, GM, Tesla, and others that are attracted to the massive data collection opportunities—and the lucrative selling of that data to third parties.[37] Cities, however, are not corporations.

Serious questions about data collection and data sharing remain unanswered. Networked technologies, by their very structure, allow citizens to be tracked.[38] In addition, sensor networks record information about everyday sociality, as the metadata collected through user-generated content running on proprietary applications can also be commercially or politically valuable.[39] I have written elsewhere about warranted concern over the surveillance of individual and collective actions.[40] The implications for individual privacy are clear.[41] If cities are to be reconfigured, both as physical structures and mediated environments, it is crucial that as we move to network urban processes in response to energy-related or other concerns, we also give serious attention to the unintended consequences that intelligent infrastructure could hold for a democratic society.

History of the Smart City

Smart cities appear to be a recent phenomenon, but is that actually the case? The essays in the first section, "Soft Systems," consider the historical development of the technologically augmented city and reflect on its formation. While the interweaving of engineering technologies with the planning and construction of cities dates back to classical antiquity, the postwar period of the OECD countries is particularly relevant to our concerns.[42]

The late 1950s and early 1960s were a lively period of experimental design and infrastructural innovation. In both the United States and the UK, modernist planning efforts were responding to challenges similar to those we face today, such as managing population density and distribution through new transportation models. A brief historical survey brings to light numerous experimental proposals describing techno-utopian expectations and midcentury social biases. It also demonstrates that built projects represented only a few possibilities within a much broader range of options. What emerged in each case was a visionary engagement with original ideas that were subsequently discarded, however valuable. A careful review of those earlier proposals could point the way to mobility strategies applicable today.

During the 1950s, the rapid rate of technological change characteristic of postindustrial societies called for new methods of organizing space that would facilitate an integrated flow of objects and information. At the 1958 Delos Summit, the Greek architect and planner C. A. Doxiadis launched the field of Ekistics (a complex term signifying settlement within ecological balance). In concert with architect Buckminster Fuller and cultural theorist Marshall McLuhan, he proposed an "invisible extension of the physical."[43] The intention was to design at the largest possible scale by analyzing vast amounts of global information, what today we would call big data. Without access to computers, but inspired by systems theory, Doxiadis, Fuller, and McLuhan believed that spatial patterns could be detected in patterns emerging from flows of information. Their visionary proposals initiated a form of urban planning dependent upon a grid of networks and special-interest communities[44]—all predating the Internet.[45]

The 1960s also marked a theoretical transition away from the notion of urban space as a neutral container and toward an understanding of it as a conductive medium for the movement of people, information, and objects. Spatial theorists envisioned relational structures as topologies that could be projected onto physical social space. In particular, urban planner Melvin Webber's notion of "city as a communication system"[46] and architectural critic Reyner Banham's "autopia"[47] contributed to an increased understanding of the urban condition determined by mobility systems. A vigorous discussion emerged out of the College of Environmental Design at University of California, Berkeley, where Webber theorized that communication technologies would begin to define an urban realm that "is neither urban settlement nor territory, but heterogeneous groups of people communicating with each other through space."[48] Moreover, he argued, "'A city is not described by the buildings, but by the social relations which bind the city together." Indeed, a community is defined by its social overlay—the interweaving of social relations and communications.[49] A city, then, is a spatial adaptation to social practices and information exchange.[50] To borrow Webber's phrase, the contemporary city can be understood as an "information system" and conceptualized as a second-order abstraction in which the forces behind the form play a role in producing the form. Whereas technological determinists perceived change as originating from modern advances in technology, spatial theorists examined the specific economic and geographic forces driving those occurrences. Those theoretical frameworks positioned space as inherently caught up in social relations, thus producing and consuming them.

Webber's urban theories were influential not only in San Francisco but also in the planning of the new town of Milton Keynes, in the UK (coincidentally, a test location for today's self-driving car).[51] The history of the 1960s subsequently documents an escalating complexity in transportation policy and in the decision-making processes necessary to achieve change.[52] As postwar trends placed increasing pressure on the historical English city, the demographic shift from rural to suburban was producing its own challenges. Paradoxically, while the 1960s witnessed the automobile's rise to dominance as a means of personal mobility, in the UK the decade also saw the proliferation of critiques of the car and a search for alternatives. Rail lines, especially futuristic monorails, were viewed as the solution to increased auto traffic, and perhaps also (implicitly) as a remedy to the presumed moral laxity of the postwar social environment.[53] In the United States, however—specifically, in Los Angeles—the opposite trend developed: rail lines were removed and then replaced by freeways, furthering individualized transit methods.[54] As the decade progressed, unrestrained freeway construction would come under fire for its impact on both communities and the environment. By the late 1960s, in cities as diverse as Milwaukee and San Francisco, the unilateral support for freeways began to erode.[55]

Alternative Visions

In addition to engendering pragmatic planning proposals, architectural discourse in the 1960s broached the topic of visionary cities.[56] Because new cities arose through contested processes and governance, town planners had limited ability to realize their schemes. Utopic designers, however, had no such obstacles. For example, Geoffrey Jellicoe's future town of Motopia embodied a radical approach to the issue of division between pedestrian paths and car roads. For the proposed town of thirty thousand inhabitants, roads would be located on roofs of buildings, leaving the ground plane a vast pedestrian park.[57] In France, working on the principles for the Ville Spatiale, Yona Friedman sought to provide maximum flexibility through huge superstructures over existing cities and other locations. Future inhabitants of l'Architecture Mobile were free to construct their dwellings within these structures.[58]

In the United States, Disney Realty Company prepared plans for Project X, an experimental prototype community of tomorrow (E.P.C.O.T.) in 1966 (prior to the theme park of the same name). Project X was a designed community dedicated to advancing industrial research and development of new ideas. According to urban planner Sam Gennawey, Disney was inspired by Stanford Industrial Park (built in 1951) located in Palo Alto, California.[59] Stanford University had developed the property to exploit its intellectual and applied research ac-

Fig. 4. A model of Motopia: Glass City of the Future, where automotive transportation is carried at roof-top level, leaving the ground below free for pedestrians. Geoffrey Jellicoe, architect, commissioned by Pilkington Brothers, 1959. (Film still courtesy of British Pathé Ltd.)

Fig. 5. Project X:
Conceptual Site
Plan, delineating
the city center and
transportation hub.
Marvin Davis, 1966.
Colored pencil,
watercolor, felt pen on
brownline, pasted to
cardboard. (© 1966
Disney)

tivities in science and technology. The university combined two things that at
the time seemed antithetical: industry and parkland, thereby inventing a new
hybrid land use. And similar to many present-day start-ups, the community
was envisioned as an entrepreneurial enterprise. According to Disney, "(Project
X) will take its cue from the new ideas and new technologies that are emerging
from the forefront of American industry. It will be a community of tomorrow
that will never be completed. It will always be showcasing and testing and
demonstrating new materials and new systems."[60]

One peculiarity was that Project X residents were to be assigned dual roles of both researcher and experimental subject. Each resident was essentially a test subject, trying out various urban and industrial inventions during the course of his or her everyday activities—a relationship that might be difficult to legislate in the present. Disney's conservative politics notwithstanding significant controversies,[61] certain elements of the scheme seem to resonate today: the residences, offices, and research facilities were structured as a distributed network; the community was auto free; transit was by monorail; and the research component was based on public/private partnerships with Bell Laboratories.

This is where a review of the utopic precedent begins to get interesting. Although those visionary projects were never completed, some of their transportation ideas merit revisiting. Returning to Webber, the logical alternative to rigid, fixed-guideway transit (trains) is a mobility system that is flexible, responsive to demand, and many-to-many in its service coverage. Webber saw a future of shared vehicles on dedicated lanes, private jitneys that could be hailed when and where customers wanted (as in much of the developing world), and what might be called electronic hitchhiking. Webber's vision is uncannily similar to what is taking shape today: "We can now foresee metropolitan-wide transit systems, each focused on Transport Central's computer. A person wishing to go from here to there at a specified time phones the transport help line, say '711,' and places a request by punching the phone buttons. The computer then searches for a neighbor traveling at that time to that place and willing to share an empty seat for a fee. If none is found, it searches for the nearest publicly or privately owned bus, or van, or taxi, which it sends to the caller's front door."[62] That vision of merging information and mobilities, while in its nascent stage, is none other than intelligent infrastructure. Thus, a recovery of speculative proposals from the 1960s for new cities may offer practical solutions for today.

At the time, midcentury visions had difficulty surmounting their own conceptual framework, according to Guy Ortolano. They were simultaneously progressive and conservative: progressive because they imagined new ways of living; conservative because they sought to manage the future along familiar lines. In a future imagined in the midst of a rapidly changing present, men commuted to work, women stayed at home, and planners promised continuity with the past.[63] Visionary cities of the 1960s reimagined urban transport but not urban living. In retrospect, knowing what we do today about the social and environmental consequences of extended commutes, a truly futuristic

Fig. 6. Monorail trains, John Hench, 1959. Watercolor on paper. (© 1959 Disney)

city would rethink its inherited forms: rather than dispersing to the suburbs, it would densify the urban core. In the event, however, the cities of Milton Keynes and Los Angeles eventually built freeways for personal automobiles rather than train tracks. Instead of a monorail, they deployed fleets of buses. One could argue that point-to-point shuttles, jitneys, or buses offer more flexible service, but rail was, and remains, the most fuel-efficient and sustainable mode of transit available. What is important to take from this history is that the 1950s and 1960s previewed what ultimately happened in the next decades. Yet when midcentury planners decided to build more freeways, they did not foresee climate change.

By the early 1970s, the restructuring of the market economy and advances within the field of information technology had created a complex emerging society organized on a diverse cultural base through ready access to information (radio, television, and later the Internet). What Manuel Castells termed the "network society"[64] encompasses new forms of spatial and temporal organi-

Fig. 7. Transportation Center for Future World, EPCOT (Experimental Prototype Community of Tomorrow), delineating five layers of transit (project unbuilt), Herbert Ryan, 1966. Watercolor. (© 1966 Disney)

zation, a type of space allowing for distant, synchronous, and real-time inter-action.[65] Keller Easterling and Saskia Sassen describe this societal shift as global flows of information networks that link distant locales around shared functions and meanings, reconceptualizing spatial arrangements under trans-national, economic, and technological paradigms.[66]

By the 1990s, transportation and robotic engineers were beginning to explore the possibilities of merging information, communication, and mass transit as a means of both optimizing traffic flow and responding to the poly-centric city. One example is the Automated Highway System project (1997) developed by UC Berkeley's Partners for Advanced Transportation Technology (PATH): an intelligent transport technology designed to provide driverless cars on dedicated rights-of-way.[67] Later, William Mitchell's Smart Cities Group (2005) at MIT's Media Lab integrated wireless communications methodolo-gies with sharable, stackable electric cars. This was in tandem with rezoning urban centers, thereby freeing up traffic and reducing carbon emissions, as previously discussed. The Smart Cities Group was quickly followed in 2007 by the Defense Advanced Research Projects Agency's (DARPA's) Urban Challenge, a competition and test bed for autonomous ground vehicle (AGV) technology. This hugely successful robotic rally demonstrated that AGV technology had advanced so far that driverless cars could safely operate in urban areas populated by other vehicles and pedestrians.[68] In Silicon Valley and elsewhere, hackers and small start-ups were developing experimental mobility prototypes and applications, examples being projects at Saul Griffith's Otherlab and Shelby Clark's neighbor-to-neighbor ride-sharing app, Turo, formerly RelayRides.[69] Still others invented mashups such as Roadify, Local Motion, and Zimride; or novel applications such as Kogi BBQ, a mobile restaurant that went viral by transmitting its temporary location through Twitter to its patrons, a practice that was quickly adopted by many others.[70]

Academic research founded on participatory practices explored locative media interfaces—for example, the i-metro scalable prototype (2012), a free interactive public information access portal that synchronizes multimodal transit connections systems for ease of use.[71] As ideas continued to scale up, Silicon Valley became a magnet for connected car research. At Google X lab, Sebastian Thrun, formerly with Stanford University, developed a self-driving car that relies on a continuous machine-to-machine exchange of environmental information to navigate streets (2012). This interweaving of bits and matter, Mitchell argues, is fundamentally changing the way that we use space, distribute resources, and design our communities.[72]

Outline of the Book

What would an intelligent infrastructure look like, and how would we evaluate it? Those questions guided the formulation of this collection, with each essay opportunistically exploring the multiple knowledges interwoven in contemporary urban design. The invention and application of intelligent infrastructure are more than technical exercises: they have real-world implications. The essays herein, authored by scholars, researchers, and practitioners, offer a set of explorations describing how new protocols and adaptive systems are poised to instigate new metropolitan practices.

Intelligent Infrastructure: Zip Cars, Invisible Networks, and Urban Transformation is divided into three modalities of connective systems: Soft, Mashed (semisoft), and Hard. Soft Systems speak to the invisible networks, the sociohistorical systems that constitute—or at least contribute to—urbanity. Mashed Systems are the hybrid technical assemblages: the software, devices, and vehicles considered in combination. Hard Systems represent the urban context, generally termed the "built environment," or as architect Stan Allen defines it, "material practice and form making."[73] For clarity, each modal system is presented as a separate stream, although in actuality all are interrelated. At the conclusion, the three streams are brought together in a reflection on urban futures.

The theme that runs through the essays in this book is connection. Mobility systems connect people, practices, and places within everyday urban experience; the scholars, researchers, practitioners, and case studies featured here merge disciplines and methodologies. Essays on leading-edge research are interspersed with ones on experimental design prototypes, but all describe how intelligent infrastructural systems can contribute to a more equitable, accessible, and livable city.

For the purposes of the first section, Soft Systems are defined as invisible formative processes that include the social layer supported by ICTs. The objective of this section is to examine closely the circumstances in which the phenomena of networked urbanism arose. An examination of the background forces and political ideologies at work offers possible implications for urban form. In this section, we review a growing body of literature pointing to the dynamics common to the development of many infrastructures over many times and places. Effective infrastructures are accomplishments of scale, growing as locally constructed, centrally controlled systems are linked or assembled into networks and "internetworks" governed by distributed control and coordination processes.

First, in "The Conceptual Roots of Infrastructure," Mitchell Schwarzer discusses the etymology of the word *infrastructure*, revealing that it is relatively new. In the mid-twentieth century, the term was used to describe the coordinated military actions of multiple nations in the NATO Alliance. The concept was gradually extended to both building and transportation systems and later expanded further to encompass societal support systems (water and power, and waste management) as well as telecommunications and the Internet. The evolution of the word has paralleled the development of networks and globalization, furthering the notion of interconnectedness.

Next, in "Tinkering toward (A)utopia: Telecommunications and Transit in the Twentieth-First Century City," Anthony Townsend discusses the recent history of wireless activism in New York City from a policy perspective, initiating investigations into emerging areas of smart cities planning and management. He documents the rise of situated software—the wide adoption of smartphones, heavy use of online social networks, and GPS—connecting the Web to the physical world. Special emphasis is on open city data movement, DIY urbanism, and the contextuality of transit apps.

Concluding Soft Systems, Jordan Geiger considers what might become of outmoded analog transportation structures and imagines what new social opportunities they might afford. After establishing the historical background, in "Phantom Tollbooth Plaza," Geiger differentiates between the physical and digital formation of "Very Large Organizations" (VLOs) and what we typically call infrastructure. In light of the mass adoption of radio-frequency identification (RFID) technologies, increasing numbers of derelict toll plazas offer practical possibilities, suggesting how an infrastructure of the last century might be transformed into the site of a VLO, offering new opportunities for large-scale social, ecological, and spatial change. By opening up the discussion to include networked interrelationships, Geiger's essay prepares the reader for the next section.

In the second section, Mashed (semi-soft) Systems are defined as hybrid processes that effectively create new versions of personal and public relations. Mashed Systems bring together actants and devices; within the Internet of Things, smartphones coordinate the transit activities of the city and facilitate the sharing economy—in this case, Uber, Lyft, and Sidecar, among others. Mashed Systems are important for transportation because they coordinate options dynamically, in real time and on the fly—for example, with micro-leasable cars, as part of a mobility-on-demand system with one-way car sharing of light electric vehicles. Examples include car2go, Autolib' Paris, and GM's Electric Networked Vehicle or EN-V. In keeping with larger demographic and economic trends, the automobile industry's objective becomes not to sell cars in the traditional manner but to reserve, locate, and lease cars by the minute via mobile networked technologies.[74] Mashed Systems not only describe how the parts of the mobility ecosystem work together to form a whole but they also enumerate the new possibilities those parts offer.

Just as Soft Systems suggests that new technologies may predict new social practices, Mashed Systems provides viable examples. In "Mobile Networks as Tactical Transportation," I consider how distributed mobility systems can ameliorate commuting problems of the polycentric city through the application of intelligent ride-sharing systems synchronized with other forms of sustainable transport.[75] The essay describes a comprehensive, point-to-point mobility-on-demand system with an array of options so inexpensive, flexible, and well coordinated that it becomes competitive with private car ownership— not merely in terms of cost but also in convenience and ease of use.[76] Imagine the transit planner Citymapper fused with Paris's Vélib' and a taxi app such as Uber to create a single service with only one required payment. Frame it as a public utility, and the magnitude of possibilities quickly becomes apparent.

Moving on to "(Driver)less Is More," Bjarke Ingels and Kai-Uwe Bergmann of BIG Architecture present their provocative research proposals for Audi's Urban Future Initiative. These projects explore an evolving relation between people, transportation networks, and urban artifacts as cities seek new infrastructural solutions. It features the groundbreaking proposals BIG developed for the Audi Q3 Urban Future Award.

In "Ubiquitous Multimodality: A Vision for Urban Mobility in the (Near) Future," from the SENSEable City Lab at MIT, Carlo Ratti, Nashid Nabian, and Christine Outram illustrate the impact of emerging mobile technologies on public interaction through a discussion of sensor-embedded environments. Their examples show us platforms for exploring user-generated practices that are part of a sentient city.[77] Increasingly pervasive sensor networks generate enormous amounts of data, reflecting the ways in which people use urban space and infrastructure. Those digital traces, as large data sets, are not only transforming how planners study, design, and manage cities but also open up new possibilities for tools and applications that give people access to real-time information about urban dynamics. The essay focuses on ways urban designers can add new digitally mediated dimensions to physical space, with the ultimate goal of making mobility more efficient and less resource consuming.

Concluding the Mashed Systems section, Sven Beiker, former executive director of the Center for Automotive Research at Stanford University, argues in "The Future of Personal Urban Mobility: An Engineer's Perspective" that the personal automobile is not going to disappear and must be part of any future mobility solution.[78] More than a mode of transportation, the car signals a set of sociocultural expectations, offering freedom, independence, and flexibility. Any means of transportation replacing the personal automobile will have to respond to those desires. This chapter examines future directions for urban mobility that incorporate both personal vehicles and sustainable design. More importantly, Beiker discusses how autonomous driving is complicated not only by technological implementation, such as the development of robotic vehicles and sensors embedded in cars and infrastructure, but also by the resultant human and legal consequences.

The third and final section of the book discusses Hard Systems. This section synthesizes the findings from the previous two and considers the implications of new mobility strategies on urban form. Given that a city is a collection of different entities, what binds it together? The answer is, in a word, infrastructure. Technology—expressed as devices, hardware, and vehicles—effectively calibrates the form of a city. In such a way, intelligent infrastructure is generative or catalytic of other urban operations, some of which are unpredictable at the outset.[79] For example, the High Line formed a new, secondary space in Manhattan. The essays in Hard Systems explore similar catalytic effects of ICTs on urban form, extending the discussion to a global-metropolitan scale.

This final section includes essays by architects and urban theorists who share the position that classical planning imperatives have proven largely ineffective in metropolitan transportation. In "The Automobile, the City, and New Mobilities," Stanford's Frederic Stout offers an analysis of generational aspirations, supported by North American demographics, that reveals new patterns of consumption and habitation, such as resource sharing and transit-oriented development. He argues that urban mobility is not simply an engineering problem but rather an important component of the social sphere. This chapter enumerates the practical and ideological elements that influence how urban communities progress over time, and how such progress in turn contributes to ongoing personal, social, political, and cultural transformations.

Then Mitchell Joachim, of Terreform ONE (Open Network Ecology), presents his compelling ideas for a radical, sustainable future in "Rethinking Urban Utopias: A Manifesto for Self-Supported Infrastructure, Technology, and Territory." As a unique interdisciplinary laboratory for industrial design, biology, art, architecture, and planning, Terreform ONE explores the theoretical and practical frameworks of ecological design. The essay presents two case studies that integrate ecological and cultural possibilities for New York City. It concludes with a discussion of the implications for transportation and urban design today.

Turning to an international context, the next two essays contend that Western planning policies are no longer sufficient to solve mobility problems in the developing world. Alfredo Brillembourg and Hubert Klumpner of

Urban-Think Tank discuss emerging forms of urban mobility within informal cities of the global south, with the city of Caracas as an example. The dire lack of infrastructure in slums often leaves them unserviced by a rigid and over-burdened transport system, so steep steps and narrow alleyways substitute for roads and metros. In deference to a smart but static city, Brillembourg and Klumpner in "Urban Mobility in the Informal City" take a critical look at how informal systems based on wireless technologies could better meet the mobility needs of economically marginalized residents.

Lastly, "The Paradox of Urban Mobility and the Spatialization of Technological Utopia," by Chamee Yang, describes the smart ambitions of the Songdo International Business District in Incheon, South Korea. Within the context of East Asian developmental politics, Yang's essay foregrounds how policy makers' aspirations to realize a utopian ideal through the latest technological innovations have resulted in numerous strategies for "mobilizing" the city. Unfortunately, however, those policies, rather than creating an improved environment, have merely reinforced preexisting social exclusions.

Broader Implications

If the targets for reducing energy consumption outlined in the COP21: United Nations Convention on Climate Change are adhered to by countries around the world, visible changes in infrastructure and mobility strategies will likely result in changes in urban form, artifacts, and social practices. Many independent start-ups and university research departments are responding to the low-carbon priority by developing clean energy strategies such as solar, wind, and hydrogen-powered cars and zero-emission power stations. In Berkeley, Cambridge, Palo Alto, Singapore, Urbana-Champaign, Zurich, and many other areas, new models of community engagement are already taking shape. But as engineers and computer scientists have already discovered, society's inherited social and political structures are slower to change than technology. Dana Cuff, director of cityLAB at the University of California, Los Angeles, contends that many planning decisions could be made more effectively at the local level,[80] since intelligent infrastructure comprises not only technological artifacts but also social relations—the open-source movement, civic hacking, DIY urbanism, all of which are made possible by today's mobile Web 2.0.

By expanding the notion of personal infrastructure and merging it with public infrastructure, a ubiquitous wireless-networked interface activates urban inhabitants' combined role as critical agents for navigation, decision making, use operation, and play within the city.[81] This is where *Intelligent Infrastructure* enters into the discussion. As a detailed consideration of novel alternative ways of organizing intelligent infrastructure, this book offers insight into today's critical urban planning issues.

Given that technology is culturally and socially specific in terms of its use, deployment, sociability, and comprehension, the essays in this collection do not attempt to showcase universal usage of mobility technologies but rather to identify specific trends. Paying attention to these linkages allows us to better trace, imagine, and solve the sociospatial-political challenges affecting urban mobility and intelligent infrastructure, and thus prepares us to modify technologies to suit our diverse needs. This is a cyclical process involving the ways society in general is affected by what planners generate. Discussions such as those in this book visualize acute needs, raise public awareness, prompt public response, and eventually inform policy decisions.

During the last hundred years, humans have profoundly altered the biosphere. This is manifested by human-centered climate change and the increasing depletion of natural resources. However, serious reflection on a postcarbon landscape offers a real opportunity to reexamine the city as a site of invention. Through small-scale implementation, whether through transit-oriented developments, networked resource sharing, or mobility zoning, it is possible to reduce environmental impacts while creating a stronger sense of place and community. Although much more research is called for, the proposals in *Intelligent Infrastructure* offer design opportunities and prompt discussion of how cities can begin to think differently about sustainable mobility strategies.

The public aspect of intelligent infrastructure makes it inseparable from issues related to society. While most scholars agree that soft infrastructure—wireless technologies, the Internet, and social media—holds the potential to produce new kinds of space and enable new social practices, uneven accessibility remains a significant problem.[82] Graham and Marvin's *Splintering Urbanism* extensively documents uneven economic and technological development related to hard infrastructure—transportation systems, electrical grids, fiber optic networks—caused by a pattern of differential access to public services.[83]

While neither access nor policy making is a focus of this book, those topics intersect the public conversation in several important ways: sustainable environments, individual privacy issues related to data collection, and social equity. The adoption of ICTs within the urban public realm should not reinforce previously established inequities. Shin-pei Tsay, as a global adviser to the Energy and Climate Program of the Carnegie Endowment for International Peace, recommended that cities first initiate an expansive long-term vision and commitment for sustainable urban mobility. Second, she stated that economic support to local governments is needed if they are to implement projects that further the overarching sustainable transport vision. Third, governance will have to set concrete national standards for data collection and provide localities with the methodology to evaluate project outcomes according to various performance indicators, including equity, safety, and environmental impacts. Lastly, comprehensive cost-benefit analyses are needed at the local level to generate proposed projects.[84] Further, those analyses should address social, environmental, and economic issues relevant to the local citizens and context, including social equity.

Taken holistically, what we are proposing in this book is the establishment of sociotechnical infrastructures in the spheres of both ideas and mobility platforms by establishing the basic parameters of what is possible—behaviorally and ideologically. According to media theorist Terry Flew, *collective intelligence* refers to the capacity of networked information communication technologies to enhance the collective pool of social knowledge by expanding the extent of human interactions.[85] The notion of *civitas* encompasses particular sets of actions, relationships, and powers meant to ensure that all citizens can participate freely and fully in the life of their society. In this context, designers and engineers—both urban and software—have a shared responsibility. It is not enough simply to problem-solve: as IDEO consultant Barry Katz observes, we must also reflect on the social, political, and environmental implications of our design decisions.[86]

An approach that is humanistic—meaning one that emphasizes the value and agency of human beings, individually and collectively—places responsibility for the quality of city life on everyone—design professionals, engineers, policy makers, and average citizens alike. The future of urbanism depends on conceptualizing infrastructure not as a means of optimization, data collection, or control, but as a connective tissue of social relations binding a city together. Thus it becomes a collective venture, synthesizing public and private—one that must be inclusive and sustainable for the benefit of all urban dwellers.

Notes

1   Labels range from ubiquitous computing and urban informatics to the Internet of Things, from smart dust and ambient intelligence to sensor topologies. In 2012, the city of San Francisco commissioned Paradox Engineering to deploy a pilot industrial wireless network to manage urban infrastructure, effectively creating an Internet of Things (IoT) at the urban scale.

2   Transport systems have significant impacts on the environment, accounting for between 20 percent and 25 percent of world energy consumption and carbon dioxide emissions. Greenhouse gas emissions from transport are increasing at a faster rate than any other energy-using sector. See Ben Meyer and Brigid O'Kane, "Strategic Approaches to Developing Future Mobility Solutions by Applying Systems Integration and Thinking Methodologies" (paper presented at IDSA 2013 Education Symposium, August 21, 2013, Chicago).

3   Regarding the debate on how to measure urban growth, see Neil Brenner and Christian Schmid, "The 'Urban Age' in Question," *International Journal of Urban and Regional Research* 38, no. 3 (2013): 731–55.

4   Elliott Sclar. "Urban Professionals in the 21st Century: Challenges for Pedagogy and Professional Practice" (paper presented at Global Urban Summit, Columbia University, 2012), 7–8.

5   Edward Soja. *Postmetropolis: Critical Studies of Cities and Regions* (Hoboken, NJ: Wiley-Blackwell, 2000).

6   That approach is being advanced by Ryan Chin, managing director of the City Science Initiative at the MIT Media Lab. Chin conducts research on disruptive urban systems in the areas of urban mobility, live/work, building integrated agriculture, and big data analytics. He is creating Autonomous Mobility-on-Demand (MoD) Systems—a network of self-driving, shared-use, lightweight electric vehicles (EVs) for cities. He also developed MoD EVs including the GreenWheel, RoboScooter, Persuasive Electric Vehicle, and the CityCar—a foldable, electric, two-passenger vehicle.

7   Ash Amin and Nigel Thrift, *Cities: Reimagining the Urban* (Cambridge, UK: Polity Press, 2002); Stephen Graham, "Telecommunications and the Future of Cities: Debunking the Myths," *Cities* 14, no. 1 (1997): 21–29; Stephen Graham, "Constructing Premium Network Spaces: Reflections on Infrastructure Networks and Contemporary Urban Development," *International Journal of Urban and Regional Research* 24, no. 1 (2000): 183–200; Stephen Graham and Simon Marvin, *Splintering Urbanism: Networked Infrastructures, Technological Mobilities and the Urban Condition* (London: Routledge, 2001); Stephen

Graham and Simon Guy, "Internetting" Downtown San Francisco: Digital Space Meets Urban Place, in *Sustaining Urban Networks: The Social Diffusion of Large Technical Systems*, ed. Olivier Coutard, Richard E. Hanley, and Rae Zimmerman (London: Routledge, 2004), 32–47; Adam Greenfield, *Against the Smart City: The City Is Here for You to Use* (Helsinki: Do Projects, 2013); Rob Kitchin and Martin Dodge, *Code/Space: Software and Everyday Life* (Cambridge, MA: MIT Press, 2011); Mitchell L. Moss and Anthony M. Townsend, "How Telecommunications Systems Are Transforming Urban Spaces," in *Cities in the Telecommunications Age: The Fracturing of Geographies*, ed. James O. Wheeler, Yuko Aoyama, and Barney Warf (New York: Routledge, 2000), 31–42; Antoine Picon, *Smart Cities: A Spatialised Intelligence* (Chichester, UK: Wiley & Sons, 2015); Saskia Sassen, *Territory Authority Rights: From Medieval to Global Assemblages* (Princeton, NJ: Princeton University Press, 2006); Anthony Townsend, "Life in the Real-Time City: Mobile Telephones and Urban Metabolism," *Journal of Urban Technology* 7, no. 2 (2000): 85–104; Anthony Townsend, *Smart Cities: Big Data, Civic Hackers, and the Quest for a New Utopia* (New York: W. W. Norton, 2013).

8   Manuel Castells, *The Rise of the Network Society*, 2nd ed. (Malden: Blackwell, 2000); Ole B. Jensen, *Staging Mobilities* (London: Routledge, 2013); Robert Latham and Saskia Sassen, *Digital Formations: IT and New Architectures in the Global Realm* (Princeton, NJ: Princeton University Press, 2005); John Urry, "Social Networks, Mobile Lives and Social Inequalities," *Journal of Transport Geography* 21 (March 2012): 24–30; Mimi Sheller and John Urry, "The City and the Car," *International Journal of Urban and Regional Research* 24, no. 4 (2000): 737–57; Mimi Sheller and John Urry, *Mobile Technologies of the City* (London: Routledge, 2006).

9   Mark Shepard, *Sentient City: Ubiquitous Computing, Architecture, and the Future of Urban Space* (Cambridge, MA: MIT Press, 2011).

10   Robert Cervero, "Transport Infrastructure and the Environment: Sustainable Mobility and Urbanism," *Urban Development for the Twenty-First Century* (paper presented at Second PlanoCosmo International Conference: Infrastructure and Regional Growth for Inclusive Development, Bandung Institute of Technology, Bandung, Indonesia, 2013); Shin-Pei Tsay and Victoria Herrmann, *Rethinking Urban Mobility: Sustainable Policies for the Century of the City* (Washington, DC: Carnegie Endowment for International Peace, 2013).

11   Keller Easterling, *Extrastatecraft: The Power of Infrastructure Space* (London: Verso, 2014); Saskia Sassen, *The Global City: New York, London, Tokyo* (Princeton, NJ: Princeton University Press, 2001); Saskia Sassen, "Re-Assembling the Urban." *Urban Geography* 29, no. 2 (2008): 113–26.

12 Mimi Sheller and John Urry, *Mobile Technologies of the City* (London: Routledge, 2006).

13 Jayavardhana Gubbi, Rajkumar Buyya, Slaven Marusic, and Marimuthu Palaniswami, "Internet of Things (IoT): A Vision, Architectural Elements, and Future Directions," *Future Generation Computer Systems* 29, no. 7 (2013): 1645–60.

14 William J. Mitchell, Chris E. Borroni-Bird, and Lawrence D. Burns, *Reinventing the Automobile: Personal Urban Mobility for the 21st Century* (Cambridge, MA: MIT Press, 2010), 38.

15 Ibid.

16 Graham and Marvin, *Splintering Urbanism*.

17 Townsend, *Smart Cities*.

18 Ibid.

19 According to Patrick Meier, a dedicated interface was created to crowd-source disaster damage and geo-location, quickly mobilizing hundreds of dedicated volunteers. See Patrick Meier, *Digital Humanitarians: How Big Data Is Changing Humanitarian Response* (Boca Raton, FL: CRC Press, Taylor and Francis, 2015).

20 T. F. Tierney, "Crowdsourcing Disaster Response: Mobilizing Social Media for Urban Resilience," *European Business Review*, July 9, 2014, http://www.europeanbusinessreview.com/?p=4911 (accessed May 13, 2016).

21 Celeste B. Pagano, "DIY Urbanism: Property and Process in Grassroots City Building," *Marquette Law Review* 97, no. 2 (2013): 339.

22 Lee Anne Fennell, "Crowdsourcing Land Use," *Brooklyn Law Review* 78, no. 2 (2013): 385–415.

23 Fixed infrastructure represents a significant economic investment for countries—and what is constructed is often unevenly distributed, a topic explored in Graham and Marvin, *Splintering Urbanism*.

24 Pew Research Center, "Emerging Nations Embrace Internet, Mobile Technology: Cell Phones Nearly Ubiquitous in Many Countries" (survey report, February 13, 2014), http://www.pewglobal.org/2014/02/13/emerging-nations-embrace-internet-mobile-technology/ (accessed July 14, 2015).

25 There are two basic technologies used to operate mobile broadband (cell phone) networks: Global System for Mobile Communications (GSM) and Code Division Multiple Access (CDMA). GSM is more popular in Europe and Asia, and CDMA is more common in the United States. The major technical differences between the two systems have to do with the way each technology shares space on the radio spectrum. Without getting into details, both GSM and CDMA use different algorithms that allow multiple

cell phone users to share the same radio frequency without interfering with each other. Mobile broadband is also known as 3G, or third-generation cell phone technology. Both GSM and CDMA have developed their own 3G (and now 4G) technology solutions for delivering high-speed Internet access to mobile devices.

26 Hardware: A cell phone has a processor in it that converts the received digital information into an analog signal so that a voice can be heard. All this occurs in an average time of four to eight seconds. Each cell phone also contains its own transmitter to encode spoken information onto a radio wave.

27 Ultimately, these chips may even be able to "sip" energy harvested from their ambient environment, including stray electromagnetic radiation, thermal gradients, or even the rustle of a breeze. Saul Maulik, "Trends in Infrastructure: The Internet of Things," *Profit Magazine* 19, no. 1 (January 2014), http://www.oracle.com/us/corporate/profit/big-ideas/012314-smaulik -2112685.html (accessed August 14, 2014).

28 Ibid.

29 In 2012 San Francisco contracted Paradox Engineering to deploy such a prototype system. Embedded within municipal light standards, the intelligent unit houses an environmental sensor, a small computer, and a camera. Promoted as an energy-saving method to control traffic flow and other operating costs, the system could effectively double as an urban surveillance, invisibly monitoring the everyday activities of citizens by capturing their conversations and motions on cameras to be studied in some remote location.

30 Bruno Latour. "Where Are the Missing Masses? Sociology of a Few Mundane Artifacts," in *Shaping Technology / Building Society: Studies in Sociotechnical Change*, ed. Wiebe E. Bijker and John Law (Cambridge, MA: MIT Press, 1992), 225–58. In contrast, Graham Harman, among others, advances an object-oriented ontology where human existence is not privileged over nonhuman objects and objects exist independently of human perception. See Graham Harman, "Tool-Being: Elements in a Theory of Objects" (diss., DePaul University, 1999). Other OOO proponents include philosopher Levi Bryant and ecology scholar Timothy Morton, among others.

31 Harman, "Tool-Being." OOO is not without its critics. See Alexander Galloway, "A Response to Graham Harman's 'Marginalia on Radical Thinking,'" *An und für sich* (blog entry, June 3, 2012), https://itself.wordpress.com/2012 /06/03/a-response-to-graham-harmans-marginalia-on-radical-thinking/ (accessed July 28, 2014).

32   Stan Allen and Marc McQuade. *Landform Building: Architecture's New Terrain* (Munich: Schirmer/Mosel, 2011).

33   Moshen Mostafavi, *Ecological Urbanism* (Zurich: Lars Müller, 2010), 65.

34   Elizabeth Kolbert, "Rough Forecast: Comment on Climate Change," *New Yorker*, April 14, 2014.

35   Public works (or internal improvements) are a broad category of infrastructure projects, financed and constructed by the government for use in the greater community. They include public buildings (municipal buildings, schools, hospitals), transport infrastructure (roads, railroads, bridges, pipelines, canals, ports, airports), public spaces (public squares, parks, beaches), public services (water supply, sewage, electrical grid, dams and other, usually long-term, physical assets and facilities.

36   Townsend, *Smart Cities*.

37   Bruce Sterling, *The Epic Struggle of the Internet of Things* (London: Strelka Press, 2014): 30, 40–43.

38   Thérèse F. Tierney, *Public Space of Social Media: Connected Cultures of the Network Society* (London: Routledge 2013), 13–18.

39   Information gleaned from mobile wireless networks includes with whom we come into contact and for how long, what value we, as individuals, offer as a node in the network, and broad mobility dynamics concerning our movement as a group; all are important data for determining the reconfigurable topology and routing protocols implemented by the network, its efficiency, and overall performance.

40   Tierney, *Public Space of Social Media*.

41   Rachel O'Dwyer, "Network Media: Exploring the Sociotechnical Relations between Mobile Networks & Media Publics" (paper presented at ISEA Conference, Istanbul, 2011).

42   An extensive prehistoric water and sewage system was discovered in Mohenjo-daro in Pakistan, part of the Indus Valley Civilization.

43   "As a science of human settlements, Ekistics offered a vehicle for analyzing and understanding urban landscapes as complex matrices of mutable and evolving networks of information." Nataly Gattegno, "Building in the Inevitable City of the Future" (paper presented at the conference on Constantinos A. Doxiadis and His Work, Athens Greece, January 2007).

44   Mark Wigley, "The Architectural Brain," *Network Practices: New Strategies for Architecture and Design*, ed. Anthony Burke and Therese Tierney (New York: Princeton Architectural Press, 2007), 36–40, 43.

45   Mark Wigley, "Network Fever," *Grey Room* 4 (Summer 2001): 82–122,

46   Melvin Webber, "Order in Diversity: Community without Propinquity,"

in *Cities and Space: The Future of Urban Land*, ed. Lowdon Wingo (Baltimore: Johns Hopkins Press, 1963), 23–54.

47 Reynar Banham, *Los Angeles: The Four Ecologies* (New York: Harper & Row, 1971).

48 Melvin Webber, "The Urban Place and the Non-place Urban Realm," in *Explorations into Urban Structure*, ed. Webber (London: Oxford University Press, 1964), 116.

49 See Webber, "Order in Diversity," 29.

50 "Never before in human history has it been so easy to communicate across long distances. Never before have men [sic] been able to maintain intimate and continuing contact with others across thousands of miles; never has intimacy been so independent of spatial propinquity" and to have the capability to unite all places within an almost equal time distance. Webber also viewed the automobile as "an important instrument of personal freedom." See Webber, "Urban Place," 40–43.

51 See "Driverless Pods to Ease Parking and Travel Woes in MK," *Milton Keynes Citizen*, October 31, 2013, http://www.miltonkeynes.co.uk/news/local/driverless-pods-to-ease-parking-and-travel-woes-in-mk-1-5636619 (accessed March 31, 2016).

52 After Britain passed the New Towns Act after World War II, the government quickly chose land for new developments to accommodate the increasing population, and several new towns were founded. Following the 1950s baby boom, a renewed interest grew for new towns during the 1960s; new propositions turned the subject into an opportunity to develop more avant-garde research.

53 Guy Ortolano, "Planning the Urban Future in 1960s Britain," *Historical Journal* 54, no. 2 (2011): 477–507, http://journals.cambridge.org/action/displayAbstract?fromPage=online&aid=8273300 (accessed August 14, 2014).

54 Some people believe that the abandonment of the Los Angeles streetcar was accelerated by an alleged nationwide monopolization scheme—the "General Motors streetcar conspiracy." When streetcars were still the primary transport mode, cars were to the urban systems the new transport alternative. One of the main challenges facing this new means of transport was the need to gain more street space. In 1936, General Motors, in partnership with several oil and tire companies, established the National City Lines, a holding company that bought tram lines across America. They converted many streetcar lines to bus routes and replaced the streetcars with buses built by General Motors. With that being said, however, the question

remains, why are freeways, which privilege private automobile ownership, publically funded?

55 This led to the Southeastern Wisconsin Regional Planning Commission (SEWRPC) reducing the freeways in its plan. The most controversial segment was when citizens took the issue to the courts. The battle raged for a few more years, until a nonbinding referendum on November 5, 1974. Freeway opponents gained the upper hand and eventually forced the abandonment of nearly all the proposed freeways in the region in 1977.

56 Midcentury utopian ideas were important catalysts for change. According to Hilde Heynen the most challenging aspects of architecture have to do with the necessity to resuscitate a utopian mode of thinking. See Hilde Heynen, "The Need for Utopian Thinking in Architecture," https://lirias.kuleuven.be /bitstream/123456789/75940/1/berlage-Heynen.js.doc, n.d. (accessed May 16, 2016). David Harvey remarks in *Spaces of Hope* that it is only by revitalizing the utopian tradition that we will be able to fuel a critical reflection and act as conscious architects of our fates. In the face of social inequity and environmental degradation if architects are not willing to support the status quo, we should recognize the need for a revitalization of utopianism, if only as a means to explore other possibilities. David Harvey, *Spaces of Hope* (Berkeley: University of California Press, 2000), 159.

57 In 1959, English architect, urban planner, and landscape designer Sir Geoffrey Jellicoe (1900–1996) argued, "Motopia is not only possible, but it is practical because it is economical." He further told the Associated Press, "The dwellings would be no more expensive than housing for a similar population in tall buildings, such as those used by the London City Council in some of its developments." The residents would have driven to the roundabout closest to their home, taken an inclined driveway leading to their parking space, and then an elevator to their home. See Geoffrey Jellicoe, *Motopia: A Study in the Evolution of Urban Landscape* (New York: Praeger, 1961).

58 See Yona Friedman, "Mobile Architecture, http://www.yonafriedman.nl/ ?page_id=225, n.d. (accessed September 4, 2015).

59 See Sam Gennawey, *Walt Disney and the Promise of Progress City* (New York: Theme Park Press, 2014).

60 Ibid., 336.

61 According to biographer Neal Gabler, Disney allied with a group called the Motion Picture Alliance for the Preservation of American Ideals, which was an anti-Communist and anti-Semitic organization. Neal Gabler, *Walt Disney: The Triumph of the American Imagination* (New York: Alfred A. Knopf, 2006).

62 Melvin M. Webber, "The Marriage of Transit and Autos: How to Make Transit Popular Once Again," 1998, https://faculty.washington.edu/jbs/itrans/webber.htm, (accessed March 31, 2016).

63 Ortolano, *Planning the Urban Future*.

64 Manuel Castells, *The Rise of the Network Society*, 2nd ed. (Malden, MA: Blackwell, 2000), 12.

65 Manuel Castells, *The Informational City: Information Technology, Economic Restructuring, and the Urban Regional Process* (Oxford, UK: Blackwell, 1989), 146.

66 Keller Easterling, *Extrastatecraft: The Power of Infrastructure Space* (London: Verso, 2014). See also Robert Latham and Saskia Sassen, *Digital Formations: IT and New Architectures in the Global Realm* (Princeton, NJ: Princeton University Press, 2005); also Saskia Sassen, *Territory Authority Rights: From Medieval to Global Assemblages* (Princeton, NJ: Princeton University Press, 2006).

67 The roadways are embedded with digital data with the cars controlled by onboard computers receiving input from external and internal sources. Typically cars can travel in "platoons" or groups of eight to twenty-five "cars." Through the NAHSC/PATH I-15 demonstration project, AHS technology verified that the concept is feasible with vehicles per hour flow rates doubled or tripled even in adverse weather. Alexandra Kahn, "MIT Group Presents Research on City Car of the Future," *MIT News*, September 1, 2004, http://web.mit.edu/newsoffice/2004/smartcars.html (accessed August 14, 2014).

68 This technology would be appropriate for the autonomous guiding of vehicles over conventional city streets. The demonstration project required that fully autonomous cars be capable of driving in traffic, merging, passing, parking, and negotiating intersections. The vehicles were also required to interact with both manned and unmanned vehicles in an urban environment.

69 Gerald Tierney, moderator, "E-Mobility as a Service" (Agrion conference, San Francisco, June 26, 2012).

70 In Los Angeles, food and alcohol are highly regulated. Kogi leveraged existing codes to create one of the first mobile restaurants and fan culture. Kogi fan culture includes designing T-shirts, social media updates, blogs, naming the vehicles, and YouTube videos. "Kogi Korean BBQ Taco Truck," *Los Angeles Times*, uploaded February 16, 2009, http://www.youtube.com/watch?v=n_MtLrjwOaA (accessed August 14, 2014).

71 Thérèse F. Tierney, director of URL: Urban Research Lab at the University of Illinois at Urbana-Champaign, investigates urban systems, both physical and virtual, as they pertain to infrastructure, software, ecologies, and environments. URL: Urban Research Lab, http://www.arch.illinois.edu/URLab/.

72 William J. Mitchell, *Me++: The Cyborg Self and the Networked City* (Cambridge, MA: MIT Press, 2004), 55.

73 Allen and McQuade. *Landform Building.*

74 Chris Borroni-Bird, "Advance Technology Vehicle Concepts" (paper presented at Mobility & the City Colloquium, San Francisco, September 25, 2010). Carsharing has the potential to increase vehicle utilization rates, which are currently below 10 percent for private automobiles, and to promote sustainable urban land use because fewer cars require less parking space.

75 Taking a practical approach to the intractable "last mile problem," Ryan Chin, director of City Science Initiative at MIT media lab, envisions MoD as a network of lightweight electric vehicles distributed throughout cities, whereby users can simply pick up and drop off vehicles at any station, thus creating an intermodal mobility ecosystem. As an example of the new sharing economy, MoD systems solve the first and last mile problem by shifting users to lower energy modes and, more importantly, transform the urban landscape by reducing parking requirements and by creating new social mobility hubs that integrate charging infrastructure at distributed points within the city. See Ryan Chin, "Solving Transport Headaches in the Cities of 2050," BBC, June 18, 2013, http://www.bbc.com/future/story /20130617-moving-around-in-the-megacity (accessed January 12, 2014).

76 Helsinki has announced plans to transform its existing public transport network into a mobility-on-demand (MoD) system by 2025. The hope is to furnish riders with an array of options so cheap, flexible, and well-coordinated that it becomes competitive with private car ownership not merely on cost but on convenience and ease of use. Subscribers would specify an origin and a destination, and perhaps a few preferences. The app would then function as both journey planner and universal payment platform, knitting everything from driverless cars and nimble little buses to shared bikes and ferries into a single, adaptable mesh of mobility.

77 MIT SENSEable Cities Lab is directed by Carlo Ratti. The increasing deployment of sensors and hand-held electronics in recent years is allowing a new approach to the study of the built environment. Studying these changes from a critical point of view and anticipating them is the SENSEable City Lab's goal.

78 The autonomous car (AV) was first developed by the Defense Advanced Research Projects Agency (DARPA) for combat purposes. More recently, GoogleX, an experimental research and development division of Google Corporation, has made significant advances with a self-driving Google Car.

Audi, Ford, GM and Apple also have AVs under development. Under current legislation, autonomous cars are permitted under certain conditions in the states of Nevada, California, and Florida with other states pending legislation.

79   Reinhold Martin, "Multi-National City: Inside Outsourcing," in Burke and Tierney, *Network Practices*, 198–205.

80   Dana Cuff, director, "cityLAB" (paper presented at Future of Urbanism conference, University of Michigan, March 20, 2010).

81   Many cities in Europe, and to a lesser extent in the United States, have implemented free Municipal Wireless Networks throughout their cities. Municipal Wi-Fi (or Muni Wi-Fi) effectively creates a Wireless Access Zone at the urban scale, making access to the Internet a universal service. This is usually done by providing a municipal broadband via Wi-Fi by deploying a wireless mesh network block by block. The typical deployment design uses hundreds of routers deployed outdoors, often on poles. The network operator acts as a wireless Internet service provider.

82   The CFC Media Lab in Toronto developed Murmur as a documentary oral history experiment using the cellular telephone as an ubiquitous computing device. The interactive installation enabled people in the city to record personal stories about specific places, buildings, neighborhoods, and experiences for other visitors to access. Each account added additional layers of meaning, thereby enriching the conception of the city beyond that of the officially endorsed versions perpetuated by tourism boards and commercial enterprises. See Murmur, http://murmurtoronto.ca/about.php.

83   Graham and Marvin, *Splintering Urbanism*, 43–45.

84   Shin-pei Tsay was the former director of cities and transportation in the Energy and Climate Program at the Carnegie Endowment for International Peace.

85   Terry Flew, *New Media: An Introduction* (Oxford: Oxford University Press, 2007), 21.

86   Barry Katz, "Design and the Human Condition: An Untimely Meditation" (lecture, Hewlett Foundation, Menlo Park, CA, February 14, 2008).

Part I

Soft Systems

Today, the study of infrastructure has become the focus of much scholarly investigation, and it continues to raise new questions in the wake of technological advances. Soft systems consider the sociohistorical, philosophical, and material context of infrastructure to understand the broader shifts of the discipline, how it affects society, and how society impacts infrastructure over time. This section offers a close examination of the background forces that are contributing to new versions of personal and public relations, as well as a theoretical discussion of culture and urbanity.

The Conceptual Roots of Infrastructure

Mitchell Schwarzer

Cities and architecture cannot be divorced from their infrastructure. If villages arose around water sources and strongholds, their expansion into towns happened through channels that distributed water for agriculture and human needs and walls that secured their perimeters. Larger human settlements owe their existence to pivots in routes through the landscape, a crossroads, ferry, or bridge that acted as node for a transportation and trading network. Layovers, transfers, and inspections generated space needs for buildings. Forts, one of the earliest types of enhanced building, or architecture, exerted militarily a city's power over a hinterland. Shrines and palaces owe their existence to infrastructure, too. Like forts, palaces were a means of empowering a ruler's control over territory, this time through tribute and loyalty obligations amid displays of scale, wealth, and aesthetics. Temples, cathedrals, and mosques were elaborated places of gathering and pilgrimage, where sacred stories, laws, and rituals were enacted and then disseminated further afield. Throughout history, infrastructure enabled the densities and certainties that made cities possible and the intensities that brought about architecture.

While we can trace rudimentary aqueous, military, transportation, and communications infrastructures from antiquity, the word *infrastructure* did not exist until modern times. It was first used by the French around the turn of the nineteenth century and furthered by them through the mid-twentieth century. It was not popularized in English until the "infrastructure crisis" of the 1980s, when American society abruptly became concerned with deteriorating roads, bridges, and public works. Since then, infrastructure has epitomized our networked economy and society, interconnected via steadily higher volumes of ground, air, and shipping traffic as well as cable, fiber, and satellite telecommunications.

In order to gain a sense of the word's conceptual evolution, it is important to distinguish how infrastructure has been projected in time: as it describes a set of concurrent objects or events, and as it is retroactively applied to objects and events from the past that were not understood in their own time as "infrastructure." Thus history books regale us with tales of the magnificent road infrastructure of the Inca Empire or the remarkable canal infrastructure of the Sui dynasty in China, extensions of the word to places and periods where the concept was not in use. Or as urban historian Frank J. Costa tells us: "the Roman model of city building was the first instruction in the science of creating a viable infrastructure."[1] Roman roads and its postal system were infrastructures of communication and law.[2] Roman baths and aqueducts were water supply infrastructures. While there is no doubt that ancient societies possessed aspects of what we now regard as infrastructure, as far as we know, the Incas, Chinese, and Romans had not conceptualized such developments. In using the word *infrastructure* to describe their transport and water systems, historians associate the modern concept and premodern practices, and imbue those practices at times with certain significances unknown at the time.

Vitruvius Marcus Pollio's *De Architectura*, written in the first century BCE, contains a discussion on street layout with respect to the winds but shows no awareness of the interrelationship of regional road networks and urban development. It includes a chapter on aqueducts, wells, and cisterns, but here again Vitruvius writes on construction and material details, and not of ideas that link such devices into systems that enable urbanization beyond prior bounds. This is not to say that the Romans were averse to intellectualizing concepts when it suited their aims. Although infrastructure eluded their grasp, at least philosophically, *De Architectura* opens with copious definitions of architectural education and the principles of architecture. The Roman appropriation and handling of the Greek word *architecture* purposefully differentiated it from building, setting the basis for architecture's later evolution in early modern and modern times as a profession, art, and arena of knowledge.

Today, a taking stock of modern infrastructure is called for. This article begins that effort, analyzing categorizations and conceptualizations from the nineteenth century to the present, with particular emphasis on the period after the Second World War and with added attention to its relationship to architecture. In the words of scientists, social scientists, military strategists, historians, architects, and landscape architects, infrastructure has been used to describe extended built constructions composed of nodes of command and control and networks of elaborate configuration. It has been imported into scientific, arts, and humanistic discussions to explain the dependence of individual works upon larger and often unseen systemic backgrounds. In both concrete instances and abstract speculations, infrastructure has brought about new ways of shaping society: a scaling of interbuilding systems to the region, nation, and globe; a partial or full mechanization/automation of those systems; the creation of a sociopolitical dimension alongside technical matters; and an advance over time from the movement of batches of material to flows of chemical substances (like oil or gas) and electrons (for both power and information).[3] Any inquiry into the concept of infrastructure must also attend to its peculiarities: static devices facilitating movement; aging systems promoting progress; global networks producing localized autonomy; and, finally, a simultaneous invisibility, necessity, and disruptiveness, machines humming beneath our feet while we walk about barely recognizing their extent.

Early Uses

Infrastructure is made up of the Latin words *infra* (below/under) and *structura* (construction/organization). Its linguistic development occurred principally within French (and other Romance languages), an outgrowth of the new discipline of engineering that got underway after the establishment of the École nationale des pont et chaussées (School of Bridges and Highways) in 1747. Nineteenth-century French engineering texts mention works of infrastructure alongside those of superstructure, mainly with reference to railways and roads; infrastructure was the right-of-way of rockwork or masonry work that supported iron rails and wooden ties; superstructure was the structure built atop, sometimes also comprising the rails, and other times the trains and other equipment. Toward the end of the nineteenth century, *infrastructure* was translated from French into English as "groundwork," "foundation," or "roadbed."[4]

The French concept of infrastructure has come to mean both transportation networks and underlying building elements: roads, rail lines, and airports that underlie urbanization; the supportive aspects of a building such as plumbing and sanitation or foundation—what in English are meant by internal systems and substructure. Yet the French concept of infrastructure also takes in a broader range of meanings, including those installations and equipment necessary for life in the modern world; the makeup of the earth's crust or lithosphere; and a borrowing from Karl Marx's idea, expressed in *A Contribution to the Critique of Political Economy* (1859), that cultural institutions and political ideology (the Superstructure) are determined by economic factors including the division of labor and distribution of income and the control and valuation of land and property (the Base, or Infrastructure).[5] In 1978, anthropologist Maurice Godelier's article "Infrastructures, Societies, and History" succinctly ordered these various meanings into three tiers that ascend from nature to technology to industry. Infrastructure describes the process by which human society develops from rudimentary circumstances to civilization: first, ecological and geographical parameters; second, the material and intellectual means by which nature is transformed into society; and, third, the relations of production by which modern industrial society proceeds.[6]

During the first half of the twentieth century, *infrastructure* crept into English in two principal ways. Engineering texts began to employ the French meaning of railbeds or roadbeds. Less frequently, French scholars writing in (or translated into) English grappled with the word's elemental implications— that which lies beneath something else and enables it—in philosophical or historical speculations. In 1921, in one of the earliest of such appearances of the word in an English text, the French philosopher of mathematics Maximilien Winter wielded infrastructure to conclude an article on the ensemble of theories that constitute the functional calculus. For the penultimate sentence, Winter wrote that "we cannot deny that mathematical physics retains an essentially theoretical and philosophical character: its main purpose is not to further the progress of industry but rather to make known the infrastructure of the universe."[7] Here infrastructure refers generally to our concepts of understanding the entirety of things and specifically to those mathematical equations that decipher the universe's structural details, grappling with the continuous infinity of unknowns comprised in any and all of its intervals. Infrastructure constitutes lineaments through the unknown, the routes or structure that lies beneath or between familiar things and whose delineation may explain or establish them.

This speculative framework recalls old metaphysical questions. The ancient Greeks were preoccupied with the difference between appearance and reality, the manifold particulars we apprehend immediately with our senses and the deeper truth that can only be approached through an engagement with eternals or ideals. Following Plato's discourse on ideal solids, Democritus proposed a theory of matter in which everything visible and divisible is made up of invisible atoms, themselves indivisible and constituting the fundamental building blocks of the universe. It took over twenty-five hundred years for modern science to prove the existence of atoms through observation and, concurrently, to recalibrate the divide between appearance and reality into one of layers of traceable reality. J. J. Thompson's discovery of the negatively charged electron in 1897 was followed by Ernest Rutherford's evidence that atoms have positively charged nuclei in 1911; two years later, Niels Bohr proposed the planetary model of atomic structure. The ensuing development of quantum mechanics gave proof to the idea that an unpredictable microscopic landscape girds the macroscopic universe, an infrastructure of exotic particles, forces, and fields whose identities as fluctuations are responsible for the universe's non-uniform structure of galaxies, stars, planets, nonlife and life forms.

Nor was physics the only science that sought its bearings by investigating underlying realms. In 1936, the seismologist Inge Lehmann discovered that the center of the earth was made up of a two-part (solid and liquid) inner core, launching a line of geological inquiry that would lead to the delineation of the earth's layers and eventually, in the 1960s, the theory of plate tectonics that describes the lithosphere (or crust) upon which we reside as a terrain of interlocking plates set in perpetual, dynamic formation. While the first biological cell was discovered by the natural philosopher Robert Hooke in 1665, it took until the 1950s for the biologist James Watson and the physicist Francis Crick to discover DNA, the microscopic molecule containing genetic instructions that guide evolution and produce the macroscopic forms of life. In modern times, the fields of physics, geology, and biology have all undergone paradigm shifts by delineating previously unknown, underlying realms.

Sigmund Freud's theory of psychology rests, likewise, upon a layering of appearances and realities: in this case, the strata of the unconscious and preconscious mind that exist beneath conscious awareness and have great bearing upon it. In 1949, French psychologist René Zazzo's English-language article "Sociometry and Psychology" expanded the psychic development of an individual within history and culture and employed the concept of infrastructure as an external layer of consciousness. A person's cultural milieu, made up of the "material infrastructure of civilization," was the background for their individuality.[8] Infrastructure consists, then, of a set of foundational influences both internal, or beneath awareness, and external, or via the sensations of consciousness. This example of the use of infrastructure in psychology, akin to Winter's usage in philosophical mathematics, demonstrates how the term, originally associated as structure beneath structure was becoming flexible in its geometries and ability to pinpoint causal relationships.

Shortly after the First World War, infrastructure acquired a military application when it was used to describe the then-modern fortifications of Verdun, the labyrinth of corridors, chambers, and gun embrasures that made up the French bastion.[9] Those military connotations grew after the Second World War, as Cold War alliances depended upon precise coordination of people and material among multiple nations. I. Willis Russell's article "Among the New Words" (1953) introduced the word into the English language via a snippet from a 1950 speech by Winston Churchill that had appeared a year later in *Newsweek Magazine:* "the infrastructure of supranational authority."[10] Churchill meant infrastructure to explain the coordination of communications and services necessary for the establishment of new military bases. Installations of the recently formed North American Treaty Organization (NATO) might be located in single countries but depended upon the alliance's common infrastructure to distribute and pinpoint resources. Churchill's treatment pointed out infrastructure's potential to explain the channels, loops, and circuitry of extra-large, indeed region-sized machines. Subsequently, infrastructure became associated with military operations involving the unseen movement of equipment and equally secretive nature of communications. During the Vietnam War, the phrase "communist insurgent infrastructure," referring to trails, tunnels, and safe houses, was used to describe Vietcong and North Vietnamese Army incursions, a means to explain the pinpoint coordination of a largely unseen set of actions along linear networks through landscape.[11]

Through the City and Architecture

In French discussions of ancient buildings, infrastructure often referred to building foundations and somewhat extended to courtyards, columnar screens, and other spatial organizing devices.[12] After midcentury, the term was used to explore certain supporting systems for cities. Arthur Karasz's 1950 article

Mitchell Schwarzer

"Resistance in the Iron Curtain Countries" wielded infrastructure as a way to conceive a previously whole urban ensemble now missing many of its parts. Describing the reconstruction of damaged prewar buildings, the Romanian legal economist wrote: "there is a great difference between the erection of a new bridge, for instance, and the mending of an old one for which the plans, surrounding roads, and infrastructure, already existed."[13] Infrastructure called to mind the total idea of a building or bridge, its present elements measured against its absent pieces, its visible physicality understood in light of the varied past elements that went into it. In such ways, infrastructure was well on its way to becoming a system that coordinated immediate perceptions and unseen or unearthed evidence into an idea of the city as existing not only in space but also in time.

Toward the end of the 1950s, in an article on programs of economic assistance to war-damaged countries, Commander Robert Jackson, an Australian naval officer and one of the guiding spirits behind the United Nations Relief and Rehabilitation Administration (UNRAA), enlarged infrastructure to the most comprehensive terms up until that point. Recommending "investment in what the French call 'infrastructure,'" he continued: "This covers basic needs as ports, transportation, urban housing, and power development which are the preconditions of more varied economic advance."[14] Jackson went on to mention the importance of the human infrastructure—education, technical training, health and social services—that are vital for enabling an expanding, well-managed community. Infrastructure made up the industrial equivalent of agriculture, a set of material, technological, and social factors that form the basis of societal functions and improvements.

Similar aggrandizement was quick to come, and from quarters distinct from military matters, proof of the striking interdisciplinary character that the development of the concept of infrastructure was engendering. In the preamble to his 1962 book *The Shape of Time*, the art historian George Kubler argued for the importance of understanding art as a system of formal relations that can be sensed independently of verbal meanings; this meant solids and voids for architecture and sculpture as well as tones and areas for painting. Kubler went on to write: "Similar regularities govern the formal infrastructure of every art."[15] That same year, 1962, the architectural historian Reyner Banham mentioned the international nature of the "mental infrastructure of modern architecture."[16] In these statements from military science and art history, infrastructure was treated as an enabling system of material or mental relations, be they the transport and communications networks tying the military bases of different alliance members together, the combined elements of paint, surface, and frame that go to make up the painterly world, or the ideological discourse that contributes transnational meanings to a building.

By this point, development of the concept was proceeding along two paths: the explication of regionally extended technological machines that facilitate efficiency and comfort; and the underlying structure of natural and cultural systems. The first line of inquiry associated infrastructure with works making up the built environment: building types and transport facilities such as roads, railways, airports, and seaports. Immobile, this physical infrastructure would soon be contrasted with moving things such as goods, people, and vehicles.[17]

In a startling outgrowth from this idea, Hungarian-French architect Yona Friedman's manifesto *Architecture Mobile* (1958), developed later through the projects in his *Ville Spatiale* (1958–62), cast infrastructure as the fixed stage for a mobile, modern lifestyle. Here building types bifurcate into static and dynamic actors. Individuals live in elevated superstructures above the ground supported by a collective infrastructure. "The essential for the spatial town is what I call 'spatial infrastructure': a multi-level space-frame grid supported by pillars separated by large spans," Friedman surmised. "This infrastructure represents the fixed part of the city; the mobile part consists of the walls, floorslabs, partitions, which make possible individually decided space arrangements: the 'filling in' within the infrastructure."[18] While individuality was associated with mobility and choice, infrastructure became the collective and technological backbone supporting such freedoms of choice. In 1968, the magazine *Progressive Architecture* presented an extended essay entitled "Omnibuilding," describing the new phenomenon of expansive building systems with common structural armatures. Somewhat differently, infrastructure was cast in the role of the dynamic network along which movement (of energy, water, people) takes place, in contrast to "fillings," the enclosed spaces used for habitation or localized movement. Despite reversing Friedman's distinction in regard to fixity and mobility, PA's editors went on to link Friedman's work with Archigram and the Japanese Metabolist works (like Kenzo Tange's extension of Tokyo into Tokyo Bay), which contributed to "the creation of an `infrastructure' supported by an overall structural system that permits individual dwelling or business units, standardized or otherwise, to adhere to its walls or platforms in whatever configuration and for whatever length of time seems expedient."[19]

Despite these advances, the word *infrastructure* remained scarce within historical discourse on architecture and cities, as preeminent historians struggled to describe the coordinated impact of machines and systems upon building and urbanization. In *Mechanization Takes Command* (1948), Siegfried Giedion wrote on the transition from hand to mechanical production, the integration of machines into assembly lines, and efficient work processes in the workplace and home. Lewis Mumford's The *City in History* (1961) recognized the importance of water supply, transportation, power, and communications systems and lamented the weakness of social and political processes to ameliorate their relentless extension and excessive centralization. Neither author took the next step to describe such mechanized, metropolitan systems as constituting a new conceptual phenomenon—infrastructure. Even Banham, in his 1965 essay "A Home Is Not a House," wrote insightfully of those systems' increasingly dominant role within building culture without using the term: "When your house contains such a complex of piping, flues, ducts, wires, lights, inlets, outlets, ovens, sinks, refuse disposers, hi-fi reverberators, antennae, conduits, freezers, heaters—when it contains so many services that the hardware could stand up by itself without any assistance form the house, why have a house to hold it up?"[20]

It would take some time for architectural historians to accept that such emerging delivery networks represented a new foundational organizing principle of domestic, urban, and regional development—akin to architecture itself. Indeed, as Banham intuited, infrastructure could be regarded as an invader of architecture, its technological challenger or successor. Might the slow adoption of the concept, then, have been delayed by its revolutionary implications?

Architecture means the commanding construction. Infrastructure signifies the underlying construction. Architecture stands for control from above, a visible building system whose effects are consciously determined. Infrastructure, whose effects are exerted from below or around, is far less visible or noticed, and oftentimes the instigator of manifold and far-reaching impacts, only some of which are planned. Architecture epitomizes creation by talented designers. Infrastructure is a means of making that results from the collective contributions of inventors, engineers, industrial scientists, systems builders, businesspeople, and politicians. Architecture invites closure, the building emerging triumphantly as a finished object. Infrastructure remains open ended, forever in service of other machines, buildings, and people. Far more than architecture, infrastructure responds to the transitory imperatives of economics, society, and technology.

New York as Exemplar

By the 1970s, more architects became more fascinated with infrastructure's potent metaphors for large systems of technological, organizational, or social complexity. Emilio Ambasz, in an attempt to encapsulate the manifold attributes of the borough of Manhattan in New York City, expanded the list of infrastructural aspects to encompass subterranean subway and train passages, postal tubes, sewage chambers, water and gas pipes, power wires, telephone, television, and computer lines. "Manhattan is, in essence," Ambasz observed, "a network . . . an infrastructure for the processing and exchange of matter, energy and information."[21] The Argentine architect clung to the idea that any infrastructure needs a superstructure, something assembled atop it or from it. Infrastructure becomes less of a physical support for a given site and more of systemic enabler of dispersed urban events. Even more dramatically, Ambasz pointed out the temporal nature of such events. Infrastructure, in effect, stages the stories of the city, its tales of memory and of imagination. Contrary to architecture's stabilizing presence, infrastructure reflects the ephemerality of the present, its constant slippage into the technologically obsolete and oncoming.

In the time and place of Ambasz's essay, 1970s New York City, it would be accurate to state that urban past, present, and future were largely a matter of infrastructure. To a greater extent than older world cities like London and Paris, New York developed its characteristic physical form after the Industrial Revolution, a period of astounding invention and expansion of transportation webs, public works projects, and eventually telecommunications. The city's growth over the nineteenth and twentieth centuries stands in as an outsized history of modern infrastructural developments and a case study of their formal attributes: dendritic or rectilinear directionality; straightness or curviness; converging or diverging corridors; channel width and materiality; hierarchies of levels; complexity of circuitry; linkages per node, reach of networks.[22]

The Commissioners Plan of 1811 established a rectangular street grid of

11 avenues and 155 streets, within which the city developed and redeveloped. The grid was framework for blocks, lots, and buildings. It was corridor for power and transportation routes: the 1820s lanes for gas street lighting followed half a century later by rows of arc lamps powered by electricity; the 1820s horse-pulled omnibuses succeeded, in 1883, by steam-powered cable cars; the electric streetcars following soon afterward; in 1903, the electric, elevated trains running on tracks three stories above the streets; and a year later, the rapid subway trains snaking beneath the streets that eventually became a 722-mile long system. Public works were prominent as well. In 1812, a stream become sewage ditch was covered, and Canal Street built above it. By 1842, the Croton Aqueduct began carrying water to all parts of the city in underground tunnels from the Croton River and Reservoir in Westchester County. As the city grew, the catchment basins became larger and more distant, and lengthy water mains—over 5,700 miles in length—brought water to city customers. Over time, subterranean Manhattan turned into a marvel of stairways, elevator shafts, viaducts, conduits, tunnels, vents, pipes, pneumatic tubes, and encased wires, transporting people, trains, automobiles and trucks, fresh water, storm runoff, underground water, sewage, steam, electric power, gas, and telephone, cable and Internet signals.

Aboveground, New York's bridges, highways, and airports count among the city's most celebrated landmarks. The principal waterways, the East River, Hudson River, and the opening from the harbor to the ocean are crowned, respectively, by the Brooklyn Bridge (1883), George Washington Bridge (1931), and Verrazano Narrows Bridge (1964). Many of the earliest limited-access highways in the world were built in New York City, including the Bronx River Parkway, where construction began in 1907 and sections opened as early as 1922. Robert Moses, working through various city and regional authorities at midcentury, was one of history's greatest builders of infrastructure, engineering the building of myriad bridges, tunnels, highways, parks and playgrounds, housing projects, and sports complexes. Finally, John F. Kennedy International Airport hosts one of the most renowned terminals in the world, Eero Saarinen's plastic rendition of a bird in flight, the TWA Flight Center, completed in 1962.[23]

"Sleek bridges spanning the rivers or steam rising from the stacks of the electric-power plants conveyed as unequivocally as an image of the Woolworth Building that New York was quintessentially a 20th-century city," rhapsodized then art critic for the *New York Times* Michael Kimmelman.[24] But it is also a fact that skyscrapers themselves hosted infrastructural systems reaching far beyond the building's bounds. In 1932, radio broadcasting began from the Empire State Building, via small antennae attached to the spire; and in 1952, transmission of FM radio and signals from the city's seven television stations were launched from a new antenna structure. In 2015, the 408-foot spire/antenna of One World Trade Center resumed broadcasts of FM and TV signals from the site of the 9/11 terrorist attacks.

Public Works and Large Technical Systems

Until the 1970s, most historians writing on technology focused on inventors and illustrious machines. Subsequently, as part of a methodological turn within the discipline of history from great men and political events to material culture and everyday life, studies began to emphasize the involvement of individual machines within larger technical and social systems. This reorientation is exemplified by the publication of *History of Public Works in the United States, 1776–1976*, commissioned for the Bicentennial. The editor, Ellis Armstrong, defined public works as "the physical structures and facilities developed or acquired by public agencies to house government functions and provide water, waste disposal, power, transportation, and similar services to facilitate the achievement of common social and economic objectives."[25] Chapters told the history of the engineering profession and covered a long list of publicly assisted technical systems, including waterways, roads/streets/highways, traffic controls, railroads, urban mass transportation, airways and airports, water supply, flood control and drainage, irrigation, light and power, sewers and wastewater treatment, solid waste, public buildings, educational facilities, parks and recreation, military installations, and aerospace. Though not yet called out by name, infrastructure was on its way to becoming a recurrent descriptor of technology and urbanity.[26]

In 1988, a similarly focused volume, *Technology and the Rise of the Networked City in Europe and America*, defined public works through the categories of transportation, water and waste systems, energy, heat, and power, and added the largely privatized telephone, television, and communications systems. Chapters, on topics ranging from railroads to sewage, emphasized how modern America grew through a dependence on interconnected technological systems.[27] "Technological infrastructure," as editors Joel Tarr and Gabriel Dupuy announced, "makes possible the existence of the modern city and provides the means for its continuing operation, but also increases the city's vulnerability to catastrophic events such as war or natural disaster."[28] The editors went on to stress the uneven insertion of infrastructure into existing urban environments and the effects, both productive and damaging, it caused to them.

At the time, historians of public works and infrastructure could not ignore the looming "infrastructure crisis." The 1981 publication of economist Pat Choate and Susan Walters's *America in Ruins: Beyond the Public Works Pork Barrel* alerted the nation to serious problems with its industrial infrastructure. Governmental funding for public works was declining, not keeping up with a growing economy and population.[29] Public works were aging and, in some cases, failing or falling apart. Once in the public eye, the concept of public works merged with that of infrastructure.[30] Prior to this time, as we have seen, the concept of infrastructure had been disseminated within the realm of specialists, from civil engineers to military planners to philosophers and architects. In the media glare cast by *America in Ruins*, infrastructure emerged from being an invisible societal necessity to a visible societal and legal liability. In 1984, the Public Works Improvement Act created the National Council on Public Works Improvement to assess the condition of American infrastructure, coming to the dire conclusion that it will not sustain a stable and growing economy. A subsequent study by the National Council, *Fragile Foundations: A Report on America's Public Works* (1988), agreed that while water supply and resources were in good shape, solid waste and hazardous waste disposal had serious problems. Declining public investment here and in other arenas, like highways and mass transit, were to blame, and new mechanisms for planning, building, operating, maintaining, and financing infrastructural systems were explored.[31]

By 1997, the U.S. President's Commission on Critical Infrastructure Protection defined infrastructure as "a network of independent, mostly privately-owned, man-made systems and processes that function collaboratively and synergistically to produce and distribute a continuous flow of essential goods and services."[32] Infrastructure could neither be limited to public works nor to physical systems. A totalizing approach, crossing private and public boundaries and melding technical, political, and social considerations,[33] was called for.

Yet another concept debuted—large technical systems, inspired by Thomas Parke Hughes's 1983 book *Networks of Power: Electrification in Western Society, 1820–1930*. In one of the first comprehensive histories of a large technical system, Hughes traced the development from small intercity lighting companies during the nineteenth century into the gigantic regional power systems that had emerged by the Great Depression. In studies ranging across the United States, Great Britain, and Germany, Hughes shifted attention from inventors/ devices to systems and their formation amid political interests, national competition, economic cycles, and technological advances. Despite the universal physics of electricity, systems of power generation, transformation, control, and utilization, or power transmission and distribution networks, differed, depending upon their cultural context. Hughes asked key organizing questions: how does a large technical system evolve and acquire momentum, based on its capital investments in machines, devices, and other physical artifacts as well as persons and organizations; how are systems transferred from one region and society to another?[34]

In texts such as *The Development of Large Technical Systems* (1988), edited by Hughes and Renate Mayntz, a sequenced methodology unfolded for contending with the massive spatial dimensions and vertical integration of large technological systems (or LTSs): 1) the phase of initial invention, of economic and political adjustment, and of innovation for functional efficiencies; 2) transfer, or how a technology changes under different geographical, political, legal, and historical circumstances; 3) growth, competition, and consolidation, where goals of rationalization, efficiency, and capital intensification come to the fore. Likewise, in *The Governance of Large Technical Systems* (1992), contributors zeroed in on extra-technical questions, the immaterial standards, and institutional practices of regulation and deregulation; hierarchical versus decentralized organization; mass production versus client-oriented processes; the rise of public distrust of public utilities and governmental authorities; the conundrum that people want increased services yet oppose system expansion.[35]

The Lives of Systems

From the 1990s through to the 2010s, infrastructure has been understood as the networked manifestation of our technological age. Building on the preceding discourse on public works and large technical systems, architects, landscape architects, and historians have delved into the dynamics of infrastructural transformation and their implications for the substances and services rendered. Like buildings, infrastructures have lifespans: periods of gestation, onset, maturation, aging, and demolition. And like building functions, infra-structures are regularly replaced with more efficient or less costly technological conveyances to achieve similar, if often altered objectives. But whereas build-ings house people and their goods, infrastructures are vessels for energetic flows and are thus inherently more transitory. Depending on the society, newer buildings coexist with others of vastly different ages. Infrastructure rarely per-mits such indulgences to past ways of doing things. Its systems mandate con-nections between buildings and devices, and extensions to regions previously not served. Because of its geographic scale, an infrastructural system cannot persist for long as an outmoded, isolated, or bypassed artifact. Infrastructure must evolve. In the nineteenth century, as architectural historian Robert Brueg-mann tells us, "canals competed with railroads, cable cars vied with trolleys, and gas lighting contended with electric illumination in a kind of Darwinian economic struggle."[36] This economic struggle is unpredictable and often out-side the bounds of technological logic. As infrastructures spread from place to place, they sometimes adopt incompatible measures, such as different widths for rail carriages and different voltages for electric lines. As infrastructures grow and consolidate, some systems are replaced altogether. Often, gateways are created to allow previously incompatible systems to interoperate, gateways structured by social conventions.[37] New infrastructures grow alongside the bureaucratic frameworks of older systems.

Landscape architect Kelly Shannon and urbanist Marcel Smets understand infrastructure as subject to such conditions of flux. Infrastructure, they write, "stimulates movement to the limits of its own capacity or the endurance of the settlement it has helped to create. A static object that frames flows, it inces-santly needs to renew itself and search for alternatives."[38] During the 1830s, the electric telegraph superseded optical semaphores, facilitating communication beyond earshot and the visual limits set by the reach of human vision and the earth's curvature. Transmitted by wires encased in cables, telegraph messages traversed the continents and oceans, creating the first great instance of instan-taneous global community. Some fifty years later, however, the invention of the telephone assumed many of the communicative functions of the telegraph, and long-distance telegraph routes, such as the 1858 trans-Atlantic cables, the first to cross an ocean, were replaced by transatlantic telecommunications cables. In 2006, a little over a decade into the Internet era, Western Union sent its last telegram. Person-to-person telegraph communication reached the end of its lifespan in societies that now conversed via mobile phones, emails, and text messages.

A similar saga of technological evolution occurred to the infrastructure of breakbulk freight shipping, the mode of loading cargo goods in small batches, which was in common use around the globe since antiquity. In a remarkably short period of time, between the late 1950s and 1970s, container shipping swamped breakbulk freight shipping, eventually restricting it to small seaports bypassed by the great shipping routes. The cost efficiencies of containerization ushered in the epoch of intermodal transit (factory to rail/truck to container ship to rail/truck to distribution center to store), a chain of enormous ships plowing the world's sea routes, capable of carrying close to ten thousand TEUs (twenty-foot equivalent units), and seamlessly connecting to land transportation systems and other infrastructures.[39]

It has often been the case that an infrastructural system intended for one purpose, say for communication, impacted the development of other systems, say facilitating transportation. "In the nineteenth century," historian Philip Steadman remarks, "the telegraph wires followed the railways. After the Second World War, the international cables followed shipping routes and connected the same cities as airlines. In the late twentieth century, the optical-fiber cables were being laid along existing railways and motorways, which provided convenient, established rights of way."[40] As they proliferated across the globe, such systems altered the perception of space and time. Space compressed as the speed of train and then airplane travel brought places closer together. Railways and similarly air routes instituted a notion of universal time, coordinating actions across the globe.[41] Indeed, the state of a nation's infrastructure is a key measure of its state of modernization, and the lack of adequate infrastructures in much of the developing world, epitomized by dismal roads and transit and the lack of potable water and toilets, accounts for much of its ongoing misery and stagnation.

Architect Stan Allen characterizes infrastructure as: "open and anticipatory. It has nothing to do with a specific message; rather it is the design of the system that makes it possible to send any number of messages."[42] This condition applies to many aspects of the National System of Interstate and Defense Highways, launched in 1956 after many delays to augment/replace the U.S. Highway System of the 1920s.[43] The forty thousand miles of the Interstate Highway System are made up of a technical layout of right-of-ways, roadbeds, bridges, rest stops, and intersections, aimed at facilitating freedom of movement. Among large technological systems, the highways allow for a considerable level of personal decision making. Drivers choose their routes, enter and exit the system at will, and, up to now, are not regulated (at least computationally) as to their driving methods. Nonetheless, the system imposes societal standards and uniformities concerning signage, lane widths, and driving regulations and speed limits. Safety considerations of vehicle loads at given speeds influenced both the physical width of roads and the intended spacing of vehicles.

The freedoms allowed for the flows of infrastructure depend upon the type of system and its contents.[44] Airways are more regulated than highways, even though flight paths possess an immaterial infrastructure as compared with the latter's macadam, concrete, and metal structure. Pilots and their routes are tightly regulated by institutional arrangements, like the U.S. Air Traffic Control System, which encompasses thousands of airports, hundreds of thousands of aircraft, and an even larger number of airway miles. Planes are further guided by visual and radio frequency navigational aids, including nondirectional beacons (NDBs), used to chart position, or VHF omnidirectional range finders (VORs), supplying directional information.[45] Of late, a Global Information Infrastructure (GII) contained within the Internet, linking governmental and commercial communications systems (like the U.S. Department of Defense's Global Positioning System, or GPS), is assuming increasing aspects of air traffic management.

At the same time, if aircraft movements are more tightly regulated than automotive movements, they enjoy more autonomy than trains, telephone transmissions, or electric power grids, whose connective networks are structured by physical objects—rails, wires, power grids.[46] And such physical devices do not always constrain the freedoms of the contents sent through them. Whereas power grids or water and sewage lines precisely regulate the nature, scale, and force of the contents transmitted, telecommunications lines facilitate the movement of messages without regard to their precise content. Their latest iteration, the Internet, has grown into the most consequential infrastructural system in history.[47] It has advanced from the streaming of text to that of sound, photograph, and moving image, reshaping the industries of publishing, music, photography, and motion pictures. Combined with digitization and algorithmic computation of big data, information technologies of the Internet have a habit of detaching contents from their origins, opening them to new configurations of sensation, thought, and communication.

Node and Network

In 1964, French philosopher Jacques Ellul, in *The Technological Society*, critiqued the ways proliferating technical systems were impoverishing culture and nature by narrowly charting the course of progress. To Ellul and subsequent critics, postwar systems were beholden to standards and minimum efficiency requirements determined by engineers and their related corporate and governmental bureaucracies. They were conceived and built in isolation from each other and other aspects of urban or regional life.[48] These practices reduced the role of aesthetic and holistic considerations and the involvement of architects and everyday users. Nor were most infrastructural developments coordinated with an ecological perspective that takes into account their demands on natural resources as well as the impacts that systems exert on the land, water, and airways they traverse. Even though the constructed world is nested in the natural world, the ultimate infrastructure, the workings of the former incorporated few correspondences with those of the latter.[49] This line of critique raises the question of what and whom infrastructure serves. How might infrastructural systems achieve better overall social equity? How might infrastructural projects complement cultural/natural places they serve and through which they pass?[50] How could the movement of goods, services, material, flows, and ideas from their sources to their destinations take into account the surfaces and spaces of the networks on which they travel?[51]

That infrastructure has been disconnected from the environs through which it travels and even the places it engenders should not be surprising. Infrastructure evolved with respect to lines and junctions, and not the areas around, below, or above them. Interestingly, for a term that began as the substrate beneath structure and philosophically grew to become the systemic backdrop behind individual forms, the technical implementation of infrastructure has only rarely expanded on those dependencies and formulated an all-around rapport with the landscapes through which networks pass and of which nodes control. The Interstate Highway System was first and foremost a linear network aimed at regional and national mobility. Scant regard was given to the cities, towns, farmland, and wilderness it blasted through and divided. Like the railroad before it, the Interstate Highway System rewired the nation's transportation net, favoring urbanization along its corridors and intersections, bringing untold rural locales into rapport with metropolitan regions, and diverting investment and population from countless small towns and inner city neighborhoods. Similarly, oil pipelines and oil tankers have taken even less notice of the environs along their linear networks. Their focus has been on beginning and end points, the oilfields and, hundreds or thousands of miles away, the refineries and gasoline stations near customers. The middle land or sea path in-between, aside from concerns to manage its technical efficiencies, has been neglected, with dire consequences for natural ecosystems. The Internet has disrupted older infrastructures it has remediated. Building from earlier infrastructures of central heating, air-conditioning, lighting, and the telephone, it has oriented societal life inward and yet, at the same time, publicized private life online.

In our evolving Anthropocene, infrastructures have facilitated tremendous control over the variability of temperature, light, power, water and food, material goods, and other services and ideas. They deliver a platform of predictability that allows technological civilization to develop in hitherto impossible ways. As historian Paul Edwards notes: "infrastructures constitute an artificial environment, channeling and/or reproducing those properties of the natural environment that we find most useful and comfortable; and eliminating features we find dangerous, uncomfortable, or merely inconvenient."[52] They amplify, reduce, or mimic natural energies like sunlight. They provide access to places and things when we want them. They remove things when we don't want them. But as Edwards also muses, while infrastructures harness enormous energies within the most global, technological systems ever invented, they are experienced often, and usually intentionally, as practically invisible, a smooth functioning background.[53] In part, it is the invisibility of the systems that sustain our splendid artificial environments that leads to the neglect of ambient nature, urbanity, and infrastructure itself.

If infrastructural design and construction is to expand its purview to its social and natural effects, it must be recalibrated from unnoticed background to conscious foreground, from linear networks to encompassing landscapes. For too long it has been our proclivity to be served by systems and yet be largely disconnected from their residual consequences. But is an outward-looking gaze upon the full infrastructural landscape likely? For as new infrastructures are called upon to support superstructures ever more profoundly serviced with functions and connected with applications, won't those functions and applications align our sensations ever more tightly to the pulses of the network?

Up to a certain point in history, long before the word was coined, manual infrastructural networks favored the creation of nodes of density and activity that, in turn, generated the public spaces of cities and the works of monumental architecture. During the tumultuous evolution and expansion of infrastructural systems in the modern era, the scale and mechanization of nodes exploded beyond the purview of architecture and urbanity. Certain nodes—airports, container ports, oil refineries, dams, power plants, electrical substations/grids, sewage treatment plants/piping—grew so sizeable and imperious with respect to space that they constitute sprawling terrains of their own right. Infrastructure is the most expansive and dynamically changing aspect of the built landscape. As significantly, infrastructural networks have broadened to a servicing of hundreds of millions of nodes, masterfully interconnected yet also, because of the potency of their artificially enhanced environments, more disengaged from their non-networked surroundings. These are the places we live, work, and recreate. Each new linkage, each improved connection, brings about new comforts and opportunities, yet also new circumventions and bygone relationships. As mobile networking demonstrates, individuals are increasingly sustained, infrastructure-wise, on the go. Half a century ago, Yona Friedman and other architects envisioned the city dominated by a gigantic, fixed infrastructure that would enable a superstructure where individuals benefited from maximal mobility and opportunity. Yet today individuals enjoy many of those freedoms in practically any location. And like other built infrastructures discussed in this essay, the Internet's multifiber cables and data centers (hosting servers, storage devices, heating and cooling units) are largely out of sight. Wireless transmissions (using radio waves) allow us to function as mobile nodes within a world rapidly becoming an interconnected informational organism.[54]

Notes

1   Frank Costa, "The Evolution of Planning Styles and Planned Change: The Example of Rome," *Journal of Urban History* 3.3 (May 1977): 271.

2   The Roman Code of the Twelve Tables, dating to the middle of the fifth cen-
    tury BCE, was the basis for European law and one of the earliest examples of
    a state directive concerning infrastructure. It required that straight roads be
    eight feet wide and curved stretches sixteen feet wide, and it also specified
    that landowners maintain roads bordering on their property.

3   On the characteristics of modern systems, see Thomas P. Hughes, *American
    Genesis: A Century of Invention and Technological Enthusiasm* (New York: Viking,
    1989), 184–87.

4   Karl Karmarsch, Ernst Otto Röhrig, and Karl Dill, *Technologisches Wörterbuch,
    deutsch-englisch-französisch* (Wiesbaden: Verlag von J. F. Bergmann, 1887),
    395. It is worth noting that the English word *microstructure* often substituted
    for instances referring to internal elements or components.

5   For an early Marxist application, see Jean Bourdeau, *L'Évolution du Socialisme*
    (Paris: Félix Alcan, 1901), 93.

6   Maurice Godelier, "Infrastructure, Societies, and History," *Current Anthropol-
    ogy* 19.4 (December 1978): 763.

7   Maximilien Winter, "The Principles of the Functional Calculus," *Monist* 31.4
    (October 1921): 634.

8   René Zazzo, "Sociometry and Psychology," *Sociometry* 12 (February–August
    1949): 43.

9   See *La bataille de Verdun: 1914–1918* (Clermont-Ferrand: Michelin & Cle,
    1921), 84.

10 I. Willis Russell, "Among the New Words," *American Speech* 28.4 (December
    1953): 295.

11 See Michael Charles Conley, *The Communist Insurgent Infrastructure in South
    Vietnam: A Study of Organization and Strategy* (Washington, D.C.: American
    University Center for Research in Social Systems, 1967).

12 Georges Perrot, *Histoire de l'art dans l'antiquité* (Paris: Librarie Hachette,
    1898), 414.

13 Arthur Karasz, "Resistance in the Iron Curtain Countries," *Annals of the
    American Academy of Political and Social Science* 271 (September 1950): 153.

14 Commander Sir Robert Jackson, "An International Development Authority,"
    Foreign Affairs 37.1 (October 1958): 55.

15 George Kubler, *The Shape of Time: Remarks on the History of Things* (New
    Haven: Yale University Press, 1962), viii.

16 Reyner Banham, *Guide to Modern Architecture* (New York: Van Nostrand, 1962),
    124.

17 A. G. Wilson, "Models in Urban Planning: A Synoptic Review of Recent
    Literature," *Urban Studies* 5 (November 1968): 255–56.

18 Yona Friedman, *Architecture Mobile* [1958] (Tournai: Casterman, 1970), quoted in Ruth Eaton, *Ideal Cities: Utopianism and the (Un)built Environment* (New York: Thames & Hudson: 2002), 221.

19 "Omnibuilding," *Progressive Architecture* 49 (July 1968), 101.

20 Reyner Banham, "A Home Is Not a House," *Art in America* 2 (1965): 109.

21 Emilio Ambasz, "I: The University of Design and Development; II: Manhattan: Capital of the Twentieth Century; III: The Designs of Freedom," *Perspecta* 13/14 (1971): 362.

22 Spiro Pollalis, Andreas Georgoulias, Stephen Ramos, and Daniel Schodek, eds., *Infrastructure Sustainability and Design* (London: Routledge, 2012), 40.

23 The architectural masterstroke was likely made possible by architect Wallace Harrison's master plan of 1955, which mandated the construction of separate terminals for individual airlines.

24 Michael Kimmelman, "What Really Makes New York Work: The Infrastructure; the Body and Soul of the City Machine," *New York Times*, April 8, 1990.

25 Ellis Armstrong, ed., *History of Public Works in the United States, 1776–1976* (Chicago: American Public Works Association, 1976), 1.

26 Howard Rosen, "The Saga of American Infrastructure," *Wilson Quarterly* 17.1 (Winter, 1993): 48–49.

27 Joel Tarr, "Sewage and the Development of the Networked City in the United States, 1850–1930," in *Technology and the Rise of the Networked City in Europe and America*, ed. Joel A. Tarr and Gabriel Dupuy (Philadelphia: Temple University Press, 1988), 159.

28 Tarr and Dupuy, *Technology and the Rise of the Networked City*, xiii.

29 See Pat Choate and Susan Walters, *America in Ruins: Beyond the Public Works Pork Barrel* (Washington, D.C.: Council of State Planning Agencies, 1981).

30 Carl Patton, "Infrastructural Decay in the United States," *Built Environment* 10.4 (1984): 231–44.

31 National Council on Public Works Improvement, "The State of U.S. Infrastructure," *Urban Land* 47.5 (May 1988): 20–21.

32 U.S. President's Commission on Critical Infrastructure Protection, *Critical Foundations: Protecting America's Infrastructures* (Washington, D.C.: U.S. Government Printing Office, 1997), 3.

33 John Eberhard and Abram Bernstein, "A Conceptual Framework for Thinking about Urban Infrastructure," *Built Environment* 10.4 (1984): 255–60.

34 Thomas Parke Hughes, *Networks of Power: Electrification in Western Society, 1880–1930* (Baltimore: Johns Hopkins University Press, 1983), 1–17.

35 Olivier Coutard, introduction to *The Governance of Large Technical Systems*, ed. Olivier Coutard (London: Routledge, 1999), 5–6.

36   Robert Bruegmann, "Infrastructure Reconstructed," *Design Quarterly* 158 (Winter 1993): 9.

37   "Understanding Infrastructure: Dynamics, Tensions & Design" (report of a workshop on History and Theory of Infrastructure: Lessons for New Scientific Cyberinfrastructures, University of Michigan, Ann Arbor, January 2007), n.p.

38   Kelly Shannon and Marcel Smets, *The Landscape of Contemporary Infrastructure* (Rotterdam: NAI, 2010), 14.

39   Brian Cudahy, *Box Boats: How Container Ships Changed the World* (New York: Fordham University Press, 2006), 239–41.

40   Philip Steadman, "Telecommunications and Cities since 1840," in *American Cities and Technology: Wilderness to Wired City*, ed. Gerrylynn Roberts and Philip Steadman (London: Routledge, 1999), 257.

41   John Urry, *Mobilities* (Cambridge, UK: Polity Press, 2007), 150–51.

42   Stan Allen, "Landscape Infrastructure," in *Infrastructure as Architecture*, ed. Katrina Stoll and Scott Lloyd (Berlin: Jovis Verlage, 2010), 43.

43   The system was launched in 1944, under President Franklin Roosevelt, but did not get off the ground until 1956, midway through Dwight Eisenhower's presidency. Owen Gutfreund, *Twentieth-Century Sprawl: Highways and the Reshaping of the American Landscape* (Oxford: Oxford University Press, 2004), 37–58.

44   Wolf Mangelsdorf, "Metasystems of Urban Flow," AD: *Architectural Design* 83.4 (July 2013): 95.

45   Brian Hayes, *Infrastructure: A Field Guide to the Industrial Landscape* (New York: W. W. Norton, 2005), 440–51. Airways further stack one atop the other, separating larger and smaller craft and accommodating space spacing for planes flying in the same direction or those crossing paths.

46   Todd La Porte, "The U.S. Air Traffic System: Increasing Reliability in the Midst of Rapid Growth," in *The Development of Large Technical Systems*, ed. Renate Mayntz and Thomas P. Hughes (Frankfurt am Main: Campus Verlag, 1988), 223.

47   Edward Malecki, "The Economic Geography of the Internet's Infrastructure," *Economic Geography* 78.4 (October 2002): 401–4.

48   Ying-Yu Hung, "Landscape Infrastucture: Systems of Contingency, Flexibility and Adaptability," in *Landscape Infrastructure: Case Studies by SWA*, ed. Gerdo Aquino (Basel: Birkhaeuser, 2013): 16.

49   Hilary Brown, *Next Generation Infrastructure: Principles for Post-Industrial Public Works* (Washington, D.C.: Island Press, 2014), 7.

50   Annalisa Meyboom, "Infrastructure as Practice," *Journal of Architectural Education* 62.4 (May 2009): 72.

51   Elizabeth Mossop, "Landscapes of Infrastructure," in *The Landscape Urbanism Reader*, ed. Charles Waldheim (New York: Princeton Architectural Press, 2006), 171.

52   Paul Edwards, "Infrastructure and Modernity: Force, Time and Social Organization in the History of Sociotechnical Systems," in *Modernity and Technology*, ed. Thomas Misa, Philip Brey, and Andrew Feenberg (Cambridge, MA: MIT Press, 2003), 189.

53   Ibid., 191.

54   On this concept, see the discussion in Luciano Floridi, *Information: A Very Short Introduction* (Oxford: Oxford University Press, 2010), 9–12.

Tinkering toward (A)utopia
Telecommunications and Transit in the Twentieth-First-Century City

Anthony Townsend

On October 28, 2008, John Geraci launched the DIYcity.org website to convene and challenge the growing band of geeks who wanted to hack their own smart cities. "Our cities today are relics from a time before the Internet," he wrote. "What is needed right now is a new type of city," he continued, perhaps unwittingly echoing the call to arms of the People's Computer Company some four decades earlier, "a city that is like the Internet in its openness, participation, distributed nature and rapid, organic evolution—a city that is not centrally operated, but that is created, operated and improved upon by all—a DIY City."[1] He outlined his vision of an online community where "people from all over the world think about, talk about, and ultimately build tools for making their cities work better with web technologies."[2]

But DIYcity wasn't only about talking. Geraci wanted the movement to build "a suite of tools that residents of any city, anywhere, can plug into and use to make their area better." He had his eye on Washington, DC, where Apps for Democracy, the first city-sponsored apps contest, had run during the preceding autumn. Geraci had concluded that apps contests were an inspired idea but too open-ended and too driven by government data and the programmers' own desires instead of the problems of citizens. So he devised a series of DIYcity Challenges that started with problems—ride sharing, bus tracking, tracking the spread of communicable diseases. To accelerate the process, and keep the focus on users, not tools, he even dictated key parts of the design solution—for instance, a Twitter bot to crowd-source traffic reports. And rather than inviting competition, Geraci's approach was for the entire community to collaborate on a single solution.

The first challenge produced DIYtraffic, a service for creating personalized text-message alerts based on a feed of traffic-speed data Yahoo provided at the time, culled from roadway sensors and anonymous tracking of mobile phones by wireless carriers. Presaging the popularity of crowd-sourced traffic apps like Waze that would arrive a few years later, DIYtraffic also allowed users to add their own reports to the official feed.

And then, just as fast as it had blown up, DIYcity was gone. But DIYcity did live long enough to become an inspiration, catalyst, and blueprint for organizing civic hacking groups for years to come. It was a People's Computer Company for a generation weaned not on PCs but on social media, mobile computers, and open data. It's no coincidence that present in the crowd at that sole DIYcity meet-up in Manhattan was a cadre of civic hackers who would go on to shape the grassroots smart-city movement: Dennis Crowley and Naveen Selvadurai launched Foursquare a few months later; Nick Grossman and Philip Ashlock of Open Plans would write open-source software for online 311 systems as well as start Civic Commons, a repository for open-source cityware; Nate Gilbertson, a policy adviser to the director of the Metropolitan Transit Agency, would push an open-data initiative through a creaking bureaucracy; and his colleague Sarah Kaufman would see it through.

Alongside the DIYcity challenge, in 2004, social-media guru Clay Shirky gave a name to the kind of technology created by place-based communities: "situated software."[3] Years before Apple launched its App Store, Shirky noticed that his students at New York University's Interactive Telecommunications Program (ITP) were building social software for themselves using nothing but open-source code and microcontrollers. Their approach was antithetical to the "Web School" that had prevailed up to that point, "where scalability, generality, and completeness were the key virtues." Instead, situated software was "designed for use by a specific social group, rather than for a generic set of 'users.'"[4]

Shirky's essay was a powerful premonition of how the smartphone software ecosystem would enfold. Situated software also connected the Web to the physical world. In fact, those connections were critical to making the designs successful. As the same conditions that had existed inside ITP were duplicated in entire cities—wide adoption of smartphones, heavy use of online social networks, and a sensory infrastructure that phones could use to orient themselves to the physical world—demand for situated software exploded.

Now that it's on the street, computing will never be the same. You can find situated software on any smartphone, for almost any life situation one might encounter. Some apps are only for use on the go. Others are for certain kinds of places, or specific social settings. For instance, iTrans will give you the schedule for the subway into Manhattan, and Exit Strategy will tell you which car to ride so you're closest to the correct egress when you disembark. It also cleverly caches a street map of Manhattan that you can browse offline underground, because New York is alone among world cities in its lack of underground mobile coverage. In San Francisco, Uber can summon a taxi with one click. In Manhattan, most of us still hail our cabs by hand. But in a pinch you might reach for CabSense, an app that analyzes millions of location-tagged taxicab pickup records collected by the city to identify the best corner to catch one. And Apple's Siri, which hails from Silicon Valley, might be the most suburban technology ever created: its voice recognition is perfect for connected cars but completely useless on noisy city sidewalks.

Fishing for Apps

Chastened by the struggles to build municipal wireless networks and hampered by chronic budget shortfalls, many cities today are seeking risky ways to experiment with smart technologies. In recent years a growing number have tapped software firms and freelance hackers in their own backyard, fishing for useful apps with government data and cash prizes as bait.

It all began in Washington, DC. In just thirty days, local citizen-programmers created forty-seven different web and smartphone apps that tapped the DC Data Catalog. Apps contests and open city data spread quickly after DC's initial success. The low-cost combination was an irresistible tool for mayors facing growing demand for interactive services from smartphone-toting citizens and an economic recession that decimated their budgets. As stimulus funding ran out and fiscal austerity took hold, it was a model that could deliver innovation with nearly zero funding. The needed data was already mostly online in many cities, but scattered across a constellation of government websites. All a city had to do was assemble it in one place. Within a year, New York, San Francisco, and Portland, Oregon, all launched similar efforts, and DC held a second round of Apps for Democracy in 2009. Over the next several years the idea spread abroad as Edmonton, Canada (2010), Amsterdam (2011), and Dublin (2012) followed suit. Meanwhile, the World Bank was exporting the model to the developing world through its own Apps for Development contest held in 2010.

As good as they were for brainstorming and stretching the notion of the possible, apps contests have produced few scalable, sustainable successes over the long run. Of the hundreds of apps submitted in the first two BigApps contests in New York, just one received any significant venture-capital financing to continue its work—a clunky city guide called MyCityWay that was basically just a browser for many of the city's newly public data sets. And it was financed by so-called dumb money, $5 million from BMW's i Ventures arm, a newly launched strategic fund whose management lacks the deep industry knowledge and connections that entrepreneurs value highly in investors. The winner from 2010, a crowdsourcing transit app called Roadify, has received some angel funding.

The real problem with apps contests driven by new government data, as we have seen, is that they rely on programmers to define problems, instead of citizens or even government itself. It wasn't just the focus on smartphones that left regular people out, however. Without a formal process to connect programmers to a representative group of citizens, unsurprisingly the contests tended to produce apps that solved the problems of a connected elite.

The one clear sweet spot for city apps has been public transit. All transit operators face the thorny problem of communicating schedules, delays, and arrival information to millions of riders. Apps provide a quick, cheap, flexible, intuitive, and convenient way to push both schedules and real-time updates to anyone with a smartphone. As of early 2012, over two hundred transit agencies in North America were publishing some form of schedule information using a machine-readable format called General Transit Feed Specification, developed in 2005 by Google engineer Chris Harleson and Bibiana McHugh, a technology manager at the Tri-Met transit authority in Portland, Oregon.[5]

Unlike most contest-generated apps, transit apps have a huge preexisting market, making it possible to build viable businesses that leverage open government data. Francisca Rojas, a researcher at Harvard University's Kennedy School of Government, has studied the impacts of open transit data. As she explained to me, "The difference with transit data is that developers are maintaining and improving the apps rather than abandoning them. Users are willing to pay for transit apps and continually suggest new features to developers to make them better, and transit agencies keep releasing new and improved data sets."[6]

Investing in transit apps is also good public policy. They're highly inclusive, and the benefits accrue to the working poor, who depend on public transportation the most. For a working mom struggling to balance childcare and a long commute, knowing the arrival time of the next bus is a huge help. And as apps make transit easier to use (and also enable the carsharing economy), they might help tempt drivers out of their cars and onto buses and trains, where they can be distracted by their online lives more safely and productively even as they cut their carbon emissions.

As cities grow, they create social problems too. They typically have higher rates of crime and more disease. But social technology also enhances our ability to address the problems of urbanism. Nowhere is this clearer than the ways these technologies are created. Whether it is Foursquare's API workshops or DIYcity's all-night hackathons, grassroots smart-city hackers all share a vital bit of DNA—the desire to connect, collaborate, and share. They fully leverage the sociability of big cities—the ease of face-to-face meeting, the diverse range of talents and interests—in order to create tools to amplify urban sociability even further. This approach gives them a distinct advantage over big technology companies, where openness is often an impossible cultural and mind shift.

Sociability will also provide new tools to address global warming, the greatest threat of all to cities' future. Because cities tend to cluster along coasts, they are especially at risk from rising sea levels caused by the melting of polar ice caps. And so, through organizations like the Large Cities Climate Leadership Group (also known as C40), in the absence of a global compact on climate change, cities from Amsterdam to New York have launched their own coordinated efforts to reduce greenhouse gas emissions. The smart-city visions of the smart infrastructure are an important part of these cities' efforts. But efficiency is not enough. Even in Amsterdam, one of the world's leaders, emissions are still climbing.

One promising approach to reducing greenhouse gas emissions that exploits sociability is what design geeks call "product-service systems"—most people just call it "sharing." The basic idea is to use energy-intensive manufactured goods more intensively, so we don't have to make as many in the first place. Take the carsharing service Zipcar, for instance. By transforming cars from something you own into a service you subscribe to, Zipcar claims that each of its shared vehicles replaces some twenty private ones.[7] Smart technology plays a huge role in making Zipcar practical, by automating many of the traditional tasks involved in renting a car. GPS telemetry tracks vehicle location and use, web and mobile services eliminate centralized rental depots so cars can be placed close by, and an RFID card allows the renter to unlock one.

But as smart as Zipcar is, it's not very social. But take the same business model and weave in social software to connect people to others with idle vehicles, and suddenly you don't even need Zipcar. San Francisco–based Relay-Rides helps its members rent their cars to each other, using a social-reputation system to instill trust and good behavior. While insurance companies have recoiled, three states have passed laws to protect carsharers from losing coverage.[8] The model is spreading, and now there are social technologies powering peer-to-peer systems for sharing all kinds of expensive private assets. Airbnb does the same for renting out homes for short-term stays and logged five million bookings worldwide in 2011. While they do compete on price with traditional businesses, these services also bait us into more efficient behaviors by turning faceless commercial transactions into human social encounters. It's infinitely more rewarding to rent the poet's flat in San Francisco on Airbnb than to book a soulless hotel room on Expedia. Sharing systems can be deployed rapidly—often the only additional infrastructure that's needed is the Web. And there are tangible environmental benefits.

San Francisco is just one of thousands of civic laboratories, innovative communities where people are eagerly adapting smart technology to unique local needs. This is a strange development for a world where multinational corporations have become adept at standardizing and spreading new innovations. As discussed in other essays, companies like IBM and Cisco would love to do the same with smart technologies for cities. An IBM advertisement issued a terse rebuttal: "A smart solution in one city can work in any other city." It sounded like a proposal to mass-produce urban intelligence.

The beauty of cities is that no two are precisely the same. Each has a unique history, architecture, politics, and culture. Even the smallest town is a collection of households who have over the years built up a shared identity and arrangements for working, living, and playing together. New communities differentiate in this way astonishingly fast, typically in a generation or less.

Nonetheless, this can sometimes create problems, and as I speak with Sascha Haselmayer by Skype from his office in Barcelona, he paints a convincing picture of situated software gone wrong. "Look at Germany. You have twenty-four cities which each have their own mobile app for parking. Every city backs its own local service provider thinking that they're helping the next Google to emerge. They reinvent the wheel and dress it up as a big local innovation program." Across Europe, he has discovered fifty-six cities that have built their own bad variations of the same service. And not only are citizens stuck with subpar apps, but they need to use a different one every time they drive to the next town.

Haselmayer set out to design a fix. In 2010 he drafted a handful of cities to issue challenges, and he invented his network of start-ups to show how their technology could address them. The Living Labs Global Awards, which entered its fourth year in 2013, are selected by a jury convened by each city. The award was designed to "give these companies visibility, help them to get an opening internationally." When we spoke in late 2011, there were signs that the model was working—he reported that pilots based on winning projects in 2011 were up and running in Chicago, Taipei, and Lagos.

I'd thought often about Germany's parking app fiasco. As much as I believed that the organic approach to smart-city innovation was better in the long run, Haselmayer's story had raised serious concerns about the wisdom of building smart-city technology locally. I'd embraced the notion of civic laboratories as factories for situated software, of quirky local apps, and infrastructures that put a unique local spin on technology. Twenty years of studying cities told me that building small, local, and human-scale was always better. But his research showed that most cities didn't actually have the capacity to create good apps. Perhaps I hadn't appreciated how hard it is for good technology to spread and take root where it was needed.

A common new starting point for building smart cities will speed the diffusion of good ideas and technology. But in the rush to set standards, we should heed the lessons of those early struggles over the Internet's DNA. For if the lessons of these civic laboratories and the situated software they generate tell us anything, it is to be careful how much structure we impose from the top down. The Internet's development shows how the combinatorial approach to innovation, though by nature incremental, can add up to big breakthroughs that quickly scale planet-wide. The endless variety of pilots, prototypes, and experiments popping up across the globe demonstrates that this style of combinatorial innovation is alive and well in the realm of smart cities. Every day, tinkerers around the world are showing that smart technologies are a very different beast than mere urban utilities. They are complex assemblages crafted to solve the everyday needs of small groups of people. With luck, just like the Web, over time these small, localized advances will add up to big positive changes in how we all live and work. Perhaps we should hold our options open a bit longer and resist the urge to standardize too much.

In 2010, Geoffrey West, the physicist who studies cities, remarked at a gathering of urban scholars in New York that if we don't have a science of cities, "then the cities need to be dealt with individually."[9] But for designers, dealing with cities individually is the only proper approach. This growing tension between expedient deployment and careful design in smart cities isn't going away. Every city is its own sticky knot of people, places, and policies. Even if every smart city was crafted from a common template, it will need to be customized to get the right fit with the existing city. Every city will have to strike a balance based on its patience, its financial resources, and its capacity to innovate locally. Clearly this is going to take time. We should settle for the long hack.

Notes

From *Smart Cities: Big Data, Civic Hacking, and the Quest for a New Utopia*, Anthony M. Townsend. © 2013 by Anthony M. Townsend. Used by permission of W. W. Norton Co., Inc.

1 DIYcity, "DIYCity: How Do You Want to Reinvent Your City?" July 25, 2010, http://www.icyte.com/system/snapshots/fs1/0/5/6/2/056225d480d27604332 6229910d11701abae39965/index.html.

2 "About," DIYcity, n.d., http://diycity.org/about.

3 Clay Shirky, "Situated Software," first published March 30, 2004 on "Networks, Economics, and Culture" mailing list, http://www.shirky.com /writings/situated_software.html.

4 Shirky, "Situated Software."

5 Matthew Roth, "How Google and Portland's TriMet Set the Standard for Open Transit Data, San Francisco Streets," *Streetsblog*, January 5, 2010, http://sf.streetsblog.org/2010/01/05/how-google-and-portlands-trimet-set -the-standard-for-open-transit-data/.

6 Francisca Rojas, telephone interview by author, November 15, 2011.

7 April Kilcrease, "A Conversation with Zipcar's CEO Scott Griffith," *GigaOM*, December 5, 2011, http://gigaom.com/cleantech/a-conversation-with -zipcars-ceo-scott-griffith/.

8 Ron Lieber, "Share a Car, Risk Your Insurance," *New York Times*, March 16, 2012, http://www.nytimes.com/2012/03/17/your-money/auto-insurance /enthusiastic-about-car-sharing-your-insurer-isnt.html.

9 "City Protocol Framework," n.d., http://cityprotocol.org/framework.html.

Phantom Tollbooth Plaza

Jordan Geiger

Consider the lowly, increasingly unstaffed tollbooth, the "phantom tollbooth" and more, its entire peri-urban landscape—what we might just coin a "phantom tollbooth plaza." In 1961, author Norton Juster and illustrator Jules Feiffer published the novel *The Phantom Tollbooth*, a children's book in which the eponymous roadside shed and architectural work of mini-infrastructure was recast as a gateway to another world. Something like a latter-day rabbit hole for the America that had been borne of midcentury automotive development, or a black hole on the asphalt, the humble tollbooth was suddenly imbued with magical powers to transport the book's protagonist to a parallel universe. This book reached enduring popularity with youth of its time and in the decades thereafter, likely embedding itself in the cultural consciousness of a generation now long since grown: people such as myself. In hindsight, it seems to have been an ingenious vehicle for the story, not in its timelessness but rather in its fleeting *timeliness*; these sheds had their roots in the Middle Ages, but their particular formation with highways, cars, not to mention the growing coordination of interstate law enforcement, was an utterly fresh and foreign appearance. The tollbooth seemed otherworldly even before the story imagined it as a portal to another world, and the ubiquitous toll collectors—often experienced as a disembodied outstretched hand—already ghostly in their impersonality.

Toll crossings and pass control stations are last century's familiar polyps in road development, the ubiquitous spots where two lanes expand to ten. Inverse diagrams of automotive speed on the ground, these add up to surprisingly vast tracts of sacrificial lands at the gateways of cities and, indeed, of nations. The entire conurbation that goes without sarcasm under the rubric "plaza," has nonetheless performed as a vacuum on social interactions and relations between urban center and periphery. As such, they are also something like social inversions of plazas yore.

Today, our real-world tollbooths, and in fact entire toll plazas, have an immediate and emergent chance to transport us to new netherworlds: not merely into the city but to transitional zones at the hazy boundaries of cities and even nations, where the ecological and social fallout of last century's infrastructure can be rethought and remade with new digitally inflected public space interactions. Thanks to the gradual introduction of radio-frequency identification (RFID) tags, Nexus Cards, and other electronics for toll payment and border services, tollbooths grow derelict, and these lands are now open to being rethought. These amount to a mammoth public zone where the toll plaza once served: a Phantom Tollbooth Plaza.

Such spaces and interactions already exist in mundane and generally "calm" computing routines of our daily lives, but these routines are now ripe, too, to be made more engaged, deliberate, and known. Computer scientist Mark Weiser initially framed what he termed ubiquitous computing in 1991 as "calm technology."[1] In Weiser's conception, and later in his collaborative writing with John Seely Brown, computers were charged with being "quiet, invisible," such that "technology . . . create[s] calm."[2] But as we see today, an insidiousness attends such calm: there always exists the chance for invisibility to be rather stealthy, to enable issues to remain unseen and unengaged. Instead, we can now look for a "new calm" at the border, one based on real engagement.

As it grows increasingly devoid of humans, a redevelopment of the phantom tollbooth plaza can open potential for new peri-urban and binational zones and new forms of land use for new kinds of public interaction. These sites— each a hybrid architectural/landscape object enabled by a sensory and database infrastructure—are suggestive of new forms of shared space, urban boundary, and mobility to enter the city. These are the subject of a series of ongoing case studies: at entries to Manhattan, at the U.S.-Canadian border, and elsewhere.[3]

Infrastructure versus Very Large Organization

In order to grasp the opportunities for mobility at the Phantom Tollbooth Plaza, it must be understood as an emergent form, no longer a mere infrastructural object but now the space of a Very Large Organization. Today, human-computer interactions in the built environment are marked by the rapid development of Very Large Organizations (VLOs), a term that I have elsewhere proposed to describe a phenomenon of our day, as the built environments of work, public assembly, agriculture, incarceration, trade, travel, education, even death join global financial and communications networks.[4] The planning and implementation for these VLOs command logistics, capital, and an order of population magnitude that must all accommodate volatile shifts with spatial and computational stability. Adaptability is at the crux of dealing with diverse users or publics and unprecedented technical, cultural, social, and ecological challenges; and it is where control can give way to engagement and participation.

It is important that we also recognize what these are not. VLOs are distinct from both the built realms of globalization and of infrastructure, although they may include both. Instead, they reflect the intersection of numerous physical and nonphysical orders—at minimum, spatial and administrative, but frequently also legal and technological. To elaborate, one might look at typical aspects of infrastructure and how they are augmented in the spaces of VLOs. Entry to a city or nation might have historically been monitored and regulated from the citadel, with functions of law, control, and governance; or through an arch or portal within city gates that served to protect and control passage. These, along with familiar associated constructions like the roads and bridges that lead to them, would historically fall under the rubric of infrastructure. Less visibly, but equally essential, is that they would all be constructed and maintained by the single authority that was served by them. By contrast, many stakeholders come together with sometimes competing interests in the formation of a VLO. The built environment of that VLO carries an associated burden to service all those demands. For example, a passenger bridge that crosses national borders today is financed, maintained, and managed by two neighboring countries, regulated by their import and immigration policies, their regional traffic regulations, and any private partners that are contracted to local port authorities or transit agencies on both sides. Passage might be invisibly controlled by a digital infrastructure to verify identity for regular commuters, all under purview of a private vendor. Tolls might be collected both ways via electronic transponder and routed from banks worldwide; a third party could hold databases for automotive registration that is cross-referenced as a vehicle crosses and possibly alerts law enforcement agencies. Hence the bridge, an old infrastructure, might serve as substrate to the administrative, technological, legal, and material amalgam that comprises a border crossing as a VLO. Further, unlike the relatively limited burden on and top-down concerns of an arc de triomphe past, the border VLO, as we shall see, hosts cultural and environmental events generated by any person who crosses it.[5]

Very Large Organizations—and their spaces—take such diverse forms as to defy easy recognition: space programs, big agriculture, border controls, electromagnetic field regulations—all these are Very Large Organizations, as they each manifest novel intersections of built environments and computing technologies. VLOs also bridge tiny material and extra-planetary scales, since they so often conjoin the designs of things like a human-computer interaction with the planning of a satellite network, placing architecture and landscape literally in the middle. Yet for the same reason, they defy easy typological or scalar recognition and need to be defined inductively, case by case. Border controls have long existed, for example, but Nexus cards and RFID-enabled passage have not. The transformation of borders and toll crossings is nearly invisible, but it is architectural, if not greater, in the scale and nature of its design implications.

For many reasons, work on VLOs is uniquely suited to the generalist professional skills of architects, even as they demand the assistance of numerous other fields of knowledge like organization theory (sociology), game theory (economics), and diverse areas of computer science.

Un-tolled Plazas

At places around the U.S.-Canadian border, as a sample set, the Phantom Tollbooth Plaza's ongoing mutation as a VLO is marked by recent political and technological ripples at the Peace Bridge. Located where the city of Buffalo, New York, meets Fort Erie, Ontario, across the Niagara River, this site has many salient characteristics of U.S.-Canadian land crossings today. It handles heavy but fluctuating traffic across a land and water border, sometimes concentrating plumes of air pollution from idling engines right above the airspace of one of the Great Lakes. In contrast with the U.S.-Mexican border, these stations are many and are growing increasingly streamlined in their handling of automotive traffic, because economic and political relations encourage the easy passage of regular commuters and therefore a highly porous national border. Until 2009, crossing was permitted with an ordinary driver's license check.

Fig. 1. Land area of the Phantom Toll Plaza as compared to North America's largest parks. Land areas at the largest twenty-four sites around the Great Lakes alone total 2,904 acres, or over 4.5 square miles. By comparison, this is over one-tenth the land area of Buffalo, New York (40.6 square miles). It also dwarfs some of North America's largest urban parks: Toronto's High Park is 398 acres, Central Park is 843 acres, Boston's Emerald Necklace is 1,100 acres, and San Francisco's Golden Gate Park is 1,017 acres, to name a few. Viewed together as a dispersed asset, these amount in scale to the land area equivalent to a vast park or a small border town. (Jordan Geiger)

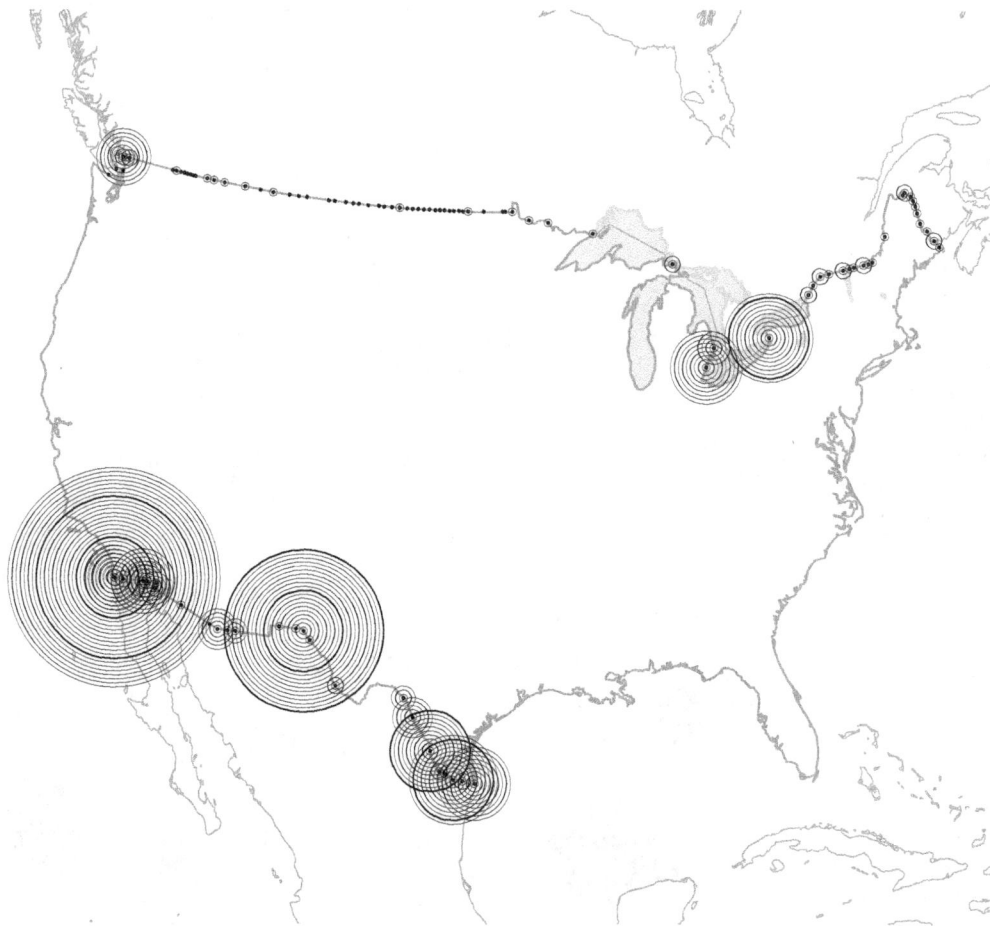

Fig. 2. Unequal mobility and control at the borders. As one zooms out to the view of the entire nation's map, it becomes clear that a grand social disparity is to be resolved between borders to the north and south. Where the U.S.-Canadian border is a porous edge, a chain of many tiny crossing points that reflects a relative trust and openness between the two countries, the U.S.-Mexican border is just the opposite: a few points at which traffic is funneled and clogs. Both of these edges have an architectural and landscape counterpart, an environmental impact and a social condition that visualizations like these identify—but also call to remediate. Here are the sites of their remediation. (Jordan Geiger)

Today, that same crossing requires a passport control, but its cumbersome and time-consuming process has in turn given way to the advent and increasing subscribership of NEXUS Cards: electronically read, biometrically referenced IDs for prescreened regular commuters in both countries.[6] Between RFID toll collection and facial recognition used with NEXUS cards for border control, the plaza grows "un-tolled"—unprogrammed and left to tell or host new stories.

Shown here are recent studies of highway toll plazas that tie together ubiquitous computing (here, RFID and its successors) and ecological impact (enabling automotive commutes) to a large set of toll crossings around the Great Lakes, all landscape-architectural objects similar to the Peace Bridge. These cases have global implications and represent perceptual shifts in spatial practices, all predicated on understanding the broader implications in the changing makeup and protocols of automotive border crossings. RFID-enabled toll crossings are not only the familiar convergence of diverse personal data such as banking records, automotive registration, and law enforcement info. A driver crossing a border also identifies mentally as a visitor or commuter and carries a personal role in the area's air quality. Hence the toll plaza is more than just the locus of physical entry and data transfer, but of cultural and environmental events too. Clearly, since the growth of RFID use, tollbooths are growing unstaffed and obsolete. But thinking further, it isn't enough to conclude that systems such as the NEXUS card represent a mere streamlining of pass control to satisfy demands for security yet speed passage for regular border commuters. This is because the protocols and technologies remain in transition. Just as RFID transponders obviate tollbooths, RFIDs themselves may soon vanish too; in Germany, for example, truckers are already charged perpetually by GPS.

The Phantom Tollbooth Plaza is therefore a new peri-urban and binational zone for new forms of public interaction. Its sites must be taken as suggestive of new forms of shared space, urban boundary, and mobility to enter the city for anyone in transit in the thickened leftover spaces between borders.

Mobility across Scales and between Nations

This brings us to grapple with understanding roles of technology across scales: from RFID transponder to car to city to the potentials for a new binational zone, one that redresses the same tangle of personal, urban, and supranational interactions that are already rife with potential at such fringe conditions today. Recent battles over the Peace Bridge hold a great resolution in the potential to create something previously unimaginable: a binational "gray zone."[7] The grayness of the zone is constituted in its liminal status, as it exists in transit, straddling borders, both architecture and landscape, and often across land and water. In this proposal, the zone is a salvaged remnant and made grayer, capturing a permanently transitory character in its physical and legal makeup, but also serving fleeting social encounters where visitors are also gray, not defined by their passport.

As recently as spring–summer 2013, disputes over land use and land values around this area sparked between New York State and Ontarian officials.[8] These reflect not so much the economics of the moment per se as the surfacing of increasing tensions over land use redevelopment, symptoms that the two ends of the bridge are becoming destinations at the edges, new nodes of mobility at the borders.[9]

They also identify the supranationality of these places that straddle borders and their relation to mobility today, as their protocols in both technological and legal respects are dictated by networked databases to international banking and to numerous enforcement authorities. The very representation of such conditions is growing subject, even in architectural practice, to more and more reliance on satellite technologies.[10]

Yet the changes at the toll plaza gesture toward the promise of new interactions that can occur at the same spaces that they have liberated. If recognition and identity are now conditioned by biometrics, then the architecture and landscape of the Phantom Tollbooth Plaza should likewise become a social space at the interstitial zone between countries, one that lets visitors meet directly and in play with the assistance of biometric indicators.[11] These need not answer to the same end goals as homeland security, though. Rather, play and interpersonal engagement should govern interactions in the zone. Can the ground itself grow responsive to one's weight, to gait? Could it warm or light passages to others, or to views and rest areas? Could the touch of a palm on a handrail initiate a soundscape?[12] How might an engagement with nature, with data, and with other people mark the zone between borders? These are some questions that are implicit in the redevelopment of the zone.

With redevelopment, the Phantom Tollbooth Plaza can become both a site of ecological remediation and a field of slow pedestrians rather than idling engines. Ground surfaces for ecological remediation can host plantings that consume carbon oxides and that sequester particulate matter. Drivers can have a space between lands where they can stop, leave their car, and meet one another in a walkable zone that was previously most forbidding, yet most tempting to explore for its diverse conditions. And a new form of sociality can be prototyped here within the zone, marked by and engaged with the digital controls that enabled its very creation.

These sorts of changes carry enormous spatial and experiential implications. They promise that boundaries will no longer be about toll plazas as gateways (points) but rather about perpetual sensing on the roads (lines). With a switch from RFID to GPS tracking, the very spatial and temporal performances of mobility are poised to shift further. Borders will no longer appear as lines, but rather as zones and meshes—as durations of space and time to be occupied by diverse publics. This perpetuity, this duration, touches all issues at play here: movement, banking records, ecological fallout, and place-based identity. "Duration" is at the heart of this momentous opportunity; and it is an aspect to a new notion of the calm at hand. If Weiser's calmness was predicated on invisibility and nonintrusiveness, this one is rather about a regular and conscious engagement—or disengagement—with technology's place in urban mobility. Old practices like wardriving used to chalk wireless hotspots and associated information right onto the streets, and many other practices have proceeded from similar impulses to make networks and also their liabilities for privacy visible. These include activist and artistic practices that foreground placement of CCTV (closed-circuit TV) cameras, detourned use of bluejacking, and more. But in all these, the space and time of the digital encounter is punctual or linear; it can be chalked as a spot, or traced as a line. Duration-based experiences of sensing and tracking, on the other hand, prompt us to confront, get aware of, and also grow used to how mobility, freedom, and privacy now correlate—at the borders.

Mobility and a New Calm

Finally, this work relies on a full engagement with information and its representation. Information sources for the project are all publicly accessible yet come from a wide range of sources. Land readings are a combination of satellite photographs read from Google Earth and GIS data that is available on some international border-crossing parcel lines. These can, in turn, generate calculations of accumulated lands that can be made visible by comparison to familiar sites. Other information is a product of inference and calculation: where statistics are provided for average wait times and volume of traffic, a relative graphic measure has been established to represent tonnage of CO_2 emissions. This is an arbitrary spatial measure that is easily contested, but its relative disparity across the map is not.

Such discoveries can only emerge from cross-referencing, from interpretation, from debate. Even within the conceptualization of sites of mobility, information wants to be visible and the medium for social discourse, rather than a servile and ostensibly objective background hum. Similarly, our engagement with one another now through digital media must continually rethink where we've come with ubiquitous computing, and whether we can indeed put forth a new calm. With visible and social engagement at our borders, in short, come new ecologies and new mobilities for tomorrow.

Notes

1   Mark Weiser, "The Computer for the 21st Century," *Scientific American*, September 1991.

2   This was originally framed around a discussion of the work "Dangling String," by artist Natalie Jeremijenko. Mark Weiser and John Seely Brown, "Designing Calm Technology," *Xerox PARC*, December 21, 1995, http://www.ubiq.com/hypertext/weiser/calmtech/calmtech.htm (retrieved July 18, 2013).

3   Toll plazas are neither particularly contemporary nor uniquely American objects in the landscape; by some accounts, toll roads and collection areas date back as far as the Susa-Babylon highway under Ashurbanipal, seventh century BC. Today, toll roads are active in Asia (Bangladesh, China, India, Pakistan, Taiwan, and more); Africa (South Africa and Morocco); Europe (seventeen different countries), North and South America, and Oceania. This suggests that toll roads and plazas are rather a ubiquitous and global phenomenon, although many of these are now transitioning to open road tolling, which renders toll plazas obsolete.

4   See, for instance, Jordan Geiger, "Maximal Surface Tension: Very Large Organizations and Their Apotheosis in Songdo," *Scapegoat: Architecture, Landscape, Political Economy*, ed. Adrian Blackwell and Chris Lee, (Toronto: Scapegoat, 2013).

5   Here, we revisit Paul Virilio's prophetic 1983 writings, which crucially
     identified a "new perspective devoid of horizon (within which) the city
     was entered not through a gate nor through an arc de triomphe but rather
     through an electronic audience system." "Thanks to satellites," he wrote,
     "the cathode-ray window brings to each viewer the light of another day
     and the presence of antipodal space." That text looked at effects of airports
     and CNN on cities and time-space relations globally. Thirty years later,
     perhaps paradoxically, we now ask what became of those older gateways.
     Paul Virilio, "The Overexposed City," in Paul Virilio, The Lost Dimension
     (Los Angeles: Semiotext[e], 1991), 12–14; the essay is also available at
     http://www.gla.ac.uk/ot4/crcees/files/summerschool/readings/Virilio_2002
     _TheOverexposed/City.pdf.

6   The NEXUS program has been administered by U.S. Customs and Border
     Protection with the Canadian Border Services Agency since 2009, when
     a valid driver's license was no longer sufficient for passage, and drivers
     would otherwise be required a passport check. The program permits "pre-
     approved, low-risk travelers" to cross land borders more quickly by use of
     reserved lanes that are equipped with card readers and cameras. Surpris-
     ingly, a brief interaction with a border agent is then required, but this
     appears to be slated for phaseout as the system is debugged and enrollment
     grows. Pre-approval involves an online or printed application, an in-per-
     son interview, portrait photograph, and fingerprint scans. Applicants are
     approved based on passing checks for criminal history, FBI searches, and
     immigration status. A companion to NEXUS, SENTRI (Secure Electronic
     Network for Travelers Rapid Inspection), is a similar program for border
     crossings between the United States and Mexico. "Welcome to GOES—The
     Official U.S. Government Web Site," https://goes-app.cbp.dhs.gov/.

     The emergence of these programs owes to a number of factors that typify
     the emergence of border controls as a VLO. These seem best explained by
     Bush administration policies set in place to meet the real and perceived
     needs for antiterrorist security measures since 9/11. But economic and other
     factors vitally coalesce here too. These are seen in rancor over undocu-
     mented immigrants and their roles in local employment; the increasing pri-
     vatization of federal programs in the prison and postal systems is present
     here as well, as lucrative contracts to collect biometrics and build databases
     of traveler profiles that can be shared across agencies.

7   For over a hundred years, U.S.-Canada border relations have been marked
     by this mix of sensitivities (environmental, territorial, cultural, and so on),
     in which air and water pose thorny challenges to protocols for customs on

the ground. This history can be traced back at least to the Boundary Waters Treaty of 1909, which provided a tool for resolving disputes around Great Lakes waters as an economic and ecological asset; it was less concerned with defining borders as with conceptualizing its fluid shifts. In our era, the U.S.-Canada Air Quality Agreement of 1991 resulted from pressure applied by Prime Minister Brian Mulroney on President Ronald Reagan to take accountability for the considerable acid rain resulting from U.S. industry in the Midwest, particularly coal production. In this case, air as a medium was conceptualized as both asset and liability in border relations on the ground.

8   Danny Hakim, "The Peace Bridge (What Else?) Sets Off a Cuomo-Canada War," *New York Times*, May 27, 2013.

9   Danny Hakim, "Cuomo and Canada Have Peace Bridge Deal," *New York Times*, June 26, 2013.

10 See notes on the "Stack" and "Cloud Megastructures" as they are described by Benjamin H. Bratton in his book *The Stack: On Software and Sovereignty* (Cambridge, MA: MIT Press, 2013). Also of central importance is the ongoing work of Keller Easterling with regard to spatial products of international capitalism and technology. Notably, see Keller Easterling, *Enduring Innocence* (Cambridge, MA: MIT Press, 2007) and *Extrastatecraft: The Power of Infrastructure Space* (London: Verso, 2014). Parts of this have appeared, for example, in Keller Easterling, "Zone: The Spatial Softwares of Extrastatecraft," Places Blog (2012), https://placesjournal.org/article/zone-the-spatial-softwares-of-extrastatecraft/, June 2012 (accessed April 14, 2016).

11 Such ideas have appeared before in a different form, in the brilliant "brain-coat" that was developed by EAR studio for Diller-Scofidio's Blur building. Sadly, this clever insertion in the pavilion's mists was never implemented. But the logic was both timely and surprising: visitors were to carry luminous devices in the pockets of their clear rain jackets, loaded with personal profiles of their wearers. They would glow green or red based on proximity to others they might be compatible or incompatible with, respectively, a sort of digital analog to "blushing."

12 Again here, we can look to a precedent project for inspiration in artist Teri Rueb's "Core Sample" project of 2007 for Spectacle Island in Boston Harbor and the Boston Institute for Contemporary Art's Founders Gallery. Rueb writes: "Core Sample is a GPS-based interactive sound walk and corresponding sound sculpture that evokes the material and cultural histories contained in and suggested by the landscape of Spectacle Island. . . . The installation has a corollary presence in the Founders Gallery at the Boston

Institute of Contemporary Art where a ninety-nine foot sound sculpture appears as an architectural element installed along the length of the gallery which offers panoramic views of Boston Harbor." Teri Rueb, "Core Sample," 2007, http://www.terirueb.net/core_sample/index.html (accessed May 16, 2016).

Part II

Mashed Systems

In this section, hybrid systems are discussed as processes that reconfigure relationships between agents and things. These "mashed systems" are socio-technical assemblages: the actants, software, and devices considered in combination. In parallel with the widespread adoption of wireless mobile networks and ubiquitous computing, mashed systems initiate a set of relations for the sharing economy and mobility-on-demand, from acquiring transit information to summoning an autonomous car. This section describes how the parts of the mobility ecosystem work together to form a whole, while also enumerating their future possibilities.

Mobile Networks as Tactical Transportation

*T. F. Tierney with Ben Feldman, Katherine Handy,
Tyron Marshall, Dinesh Perera, and Gerald Tierney*

What if mobility evolved into a service as ubiquitous as water or electricity, always available as a flow or current responding to diverse requirements? That kind of responsive system relates to intelligent infrastructure, defined as infrastructure imbued with self-awareness through sensors and computing, a notion that becomes increasingly important when considering future scenarios for metropolitan areas.[1] Intelligent infrastructure comprises not only technological artifacts but also social relations, such as the open source movement, the sharing economy, crowdsourcing, and other networked participatory practices—all of which have their own generative potential, for example, when social media begins to initiate new political practices and becomes a platform for redistributing resources. Herewithin intelligent infrastructure denotes adaptive systems, such as wireless mobile communication devices, used as a means to organize people and vehicles in real time. This essay indicates the possibilities of such a conceptual shift, by outlining how advanced protocols and adaptive systems are poised to instigate new metropolitan forms, programs, and fictions.

Theory and Background

Although many advances in communication and transportation technologies occurred during the last decade, the theoretical foundations originated much earlier during the late 1950s and 1960s when a discourse on *spatial practice* emerged. That discussion included many avant-garde architects, artists, writers, and critics, known as *spatial urbanists*, who envisioned a set of possibilities for future human settlement and transportation. An international network of

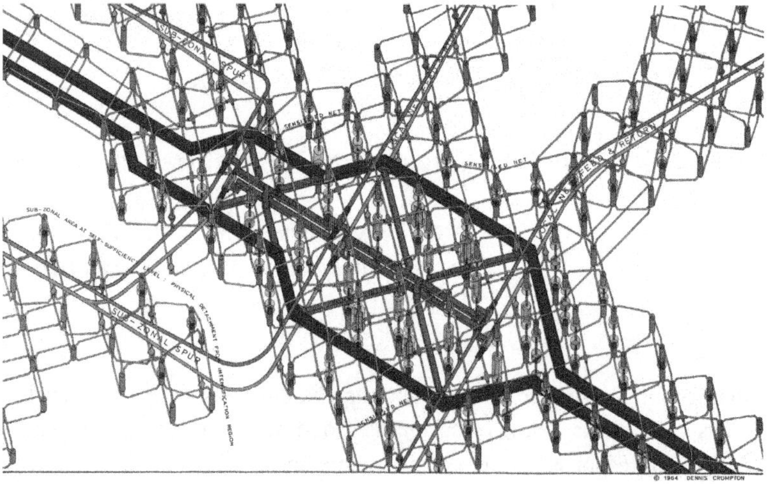

Fig. 1. Computer City, Dennis Crompton of Archigram, 1964. Ink line drawing on tracing paper with color film overlay. (© Dennis Crompton)

experimental practice included the Situationist International, Archigram, the Metabolists, Superstudio, and others. Most of the speculative projects were a response to the government's planning policies and its Kafka-esque bureaucracy, which many architects considered the first obstacles to the implementation of their radical urban designs.[2] Drawing upon the political and cultural ferment of the time, Melvin Webber, an urban planner at UC Berkeley, argued that the quality of the "urbane" might not be defined by buildings but instead by a rich exchange of information.[3] Other spatial theorists envisioned relational structures as conceptual models that could be projected onto physical social space. In particular, Webber, with his "city as a communication system" from "Order in Diversity," and Reynar Banham, with his "autopia" from *Los Angeles: The Four Ecologies*, contributed to an increased understanding of the urban condition as a dynamic social space.

Some designers of that time envisioned utopian cities taking the form of massive grids or meshes suspended above the ground, with all parts (and inhabitants) circulating in a smooth, synchronous rhythm. For example, the Dutch artist Constant Nieuwenhuys conceptualized streets and structures constituting a gigantic work of plastic art or interactive machine.[4] In this new urban world, technology and automation were expected to be positive forces, providing for material needs as well as time and space for leisure. With the

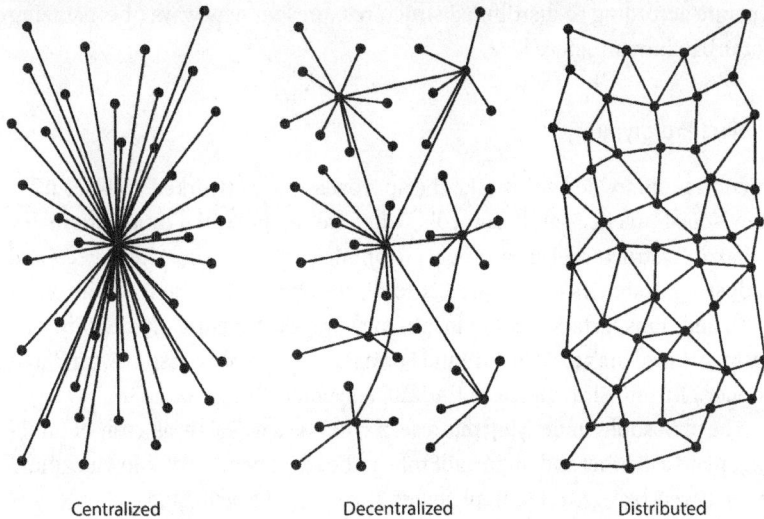

Fig. 2. Network organization, Paul Baran, 1962. (From Paul Baran, "On Distributed Communications Networks," © RAND Corporation)

Centralized   Decentralized   Distributed

advancement of a computational paradigm within design theory and methods, the architect and mathematician Christopher Alexander analyzed urban organizational structures and made an even simpler distinction between trees and semilattices to describe the social organization of the contemporary city. He argued that the unnatural tree structure, as a diagram of discreet and non-overlapping sets, formed the basis of virtually all modernist urban plans. In lieu of an exclusionary tree model, architects and planners should be designing urban space in a semilattice organization to create a better fit between physical spaces and social practices that energize them.[5]

By 1996, Manuel Castells's seminal notion of "spaces of flows" expanded on Alexander's ideas—describing cities that are conditioned by cultural networks that fall across a spectrum, from centralized to distributed; in other words, from trees to semilattices. The distributed semilattice network offers a very different model of social organization than centralized or tree models, which still tend to dominate the hierarchical structure of the city.[6] A distributed network is dispersed and nonhierarchical; it is not self-organizing in the sense of functioning automatically but in the sense that its organization is not determined by a centralized, dominant power within or above the network. As Peter Mörtenböck likewise suggests, contemporary networked cultures, which

Mobile Networks as Tactical Transportation   89

operate according to distributed structures, present new ways of organizing for urban infrastructure.[7]

Project Prototype

If contemporary designers take the approach that networked cultures offer new social practices and protocols, what are the potential implications for urban infrastructure? During 2009, an interdisciplinary team of architects and industrial designers came together to discuss how fundamental changes in ICTs and transportation could inspire new ways of organizing mobility. The team included the 510 Collective and Format Design in consultation with Christopher Borroni-Bird, director of Advanced Vehicle Concepts at GM.[8]

The philosophy underlying this research holds that design, as a way of thinking, plays a distinct and important role in the advancement of knowledge and human well-being, a role complementary to those of science and technology as designers are concerned with the application of technologies to specific human needs in particular contexts.[9] The projects that the team has been engaged with concern the public realm and, in particular, leveraging existing technologies and infrastructure and repurposing toward a distributed transportation system. The background research employed a mixed methodology to better understand the relationship between information access and transit riders: commuters, students, tourists, and others. It was structured in three parts comprised of a literature review, ethnographic studies, and data analysis—all of which contributed to the concept design of Los Angeles_REDCAR (LA_Redcar). This prototype system utilizes existing street and freeway infrastructure, along with emerging P2P (peer-to-peer) communications networks to create a new public-realm transportation overlay by reversing the current top-down fit-the-user-to-the-technology approach of traditional public transit.

City as a Test Bed: Los Angeles

One of the current challenges for expanding cities is the design of a flexible transportation infrastructure that can respond to an ever-increasing demand— and one that can also carry forward the vision of a socially equitable and sustainable society. Many metropolitan areas continue to experience rapid growth, and some cities such as Los Angeles are receiving up to five hundred new residents every day. This model of infrastructural response necessitates a rethinking of traditional personal mobility strategies. Networked systems, in particular, can solve some of the problems that the modern city has inherited, including a fixed infrastructural system that is expensive and slow to respond to changes in the activity of a city.

This research project confronts four principal urban issues:

1. *The Polycentric City.* Most mass transit systems are designed around an assumed centralized urban core, which does not address the polycentric organization of Los Angeles and many other rapidly growing cities in the developing world.[10]
2. *Low Density.* Suburban population dispersion over a wide geographic area, with resulting reduced densities, does not make optimal use of a centralized transportation system.
3. *User Preference.* Traditional mass transit systems are predicated on a top-down methodology, which ignores user preferences (i.e., autonomy) and usage patterns (prework versus postwork social practices).[11]
4. *Ride Sharing.* Current ride-sharing scenarios have limitations: (a) They can only accommodate one or two additional riders per one-car unit. (b) In our current cultural climate, sharing rides with strangers raises perceived safety issues among segments of the population.

As a design response, LA_Redcar is an example of a networked system—one that combines technology with social, economic, and cultural exchange. In this respect, LA_Redcar is a tactical intervention that builds upon the region's existing autopia ecology by leveraging social software with ubiquitous mobile technology as a means to promote connectivity. If adopted as designed, flexible networked systems have important implications for the future of transportation and urban development. Along with increased zoning densities and new models of transit-oriented development (TOD), networked systems can create a better transit experience for many urban residents.

Tactical System Components

The positive effects of sustainable transportation practices are already well documented. It has also been established that the personal automobile is inefficient in its manufacture, marketing, and utilization. In *Reinventing the Automobile*, William J. Mitchell, Christopher E. Borroni-Bird, and Lawrence D. Burns set out four ways in which personal transportation will likely adapt to fuel

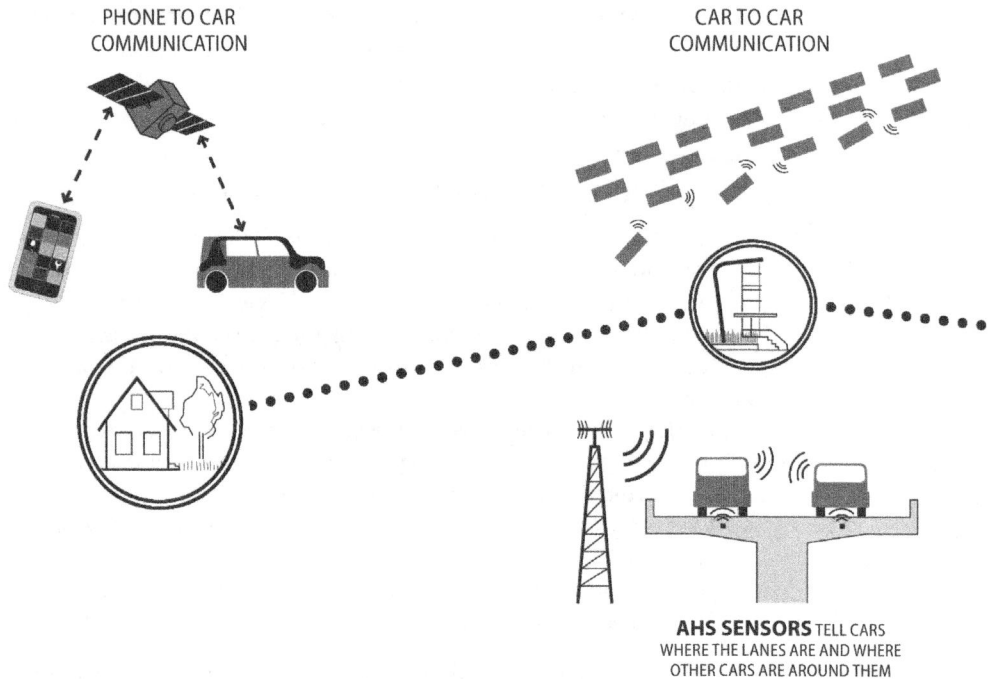

PHONE TO CAR COMMUNICATION

CAR TO CAR COMMUNICATION

AHS SENSORS TELL CARS WHERE THE LANES ARE AND WHERE OTHER CARS ARE AROUND THEM

Fig. 3. Mobile system layout. (Katherine Handy and Dinesh Perera, © Format Design)

scarcity: (1) an underlying design system based on electric-drive and wireless communications; (2) a mobility Internet for sharing traffic and travel data; (3) smart electric grids based on renewable energy; and (4) dynamically priced markets for electricity, road space, parking space, and shared-use vehicles.[12] These four future systems describe some of the ways in which intelligent infrastructure will impact the urban experience. All could be considered *adaptive systems*; for example, wireless mobile communication devices as a means to organize people and vehicles through sensors. As part of an ongoing reconfiguring of urban transportation systems, LA_Redcar prototype integrates three components: (*a*) a mobile communication device that is (*b*) overlaid with a social software application operating in real time, and (*c*) an autonomous vehicle. The layer of social software in addition to the autonomous vehicle is what sets the LA_Redcar prototype apart from other later informal mobility platforms, such as Uber or Lyft.[13]

T. F. Tierney et al.

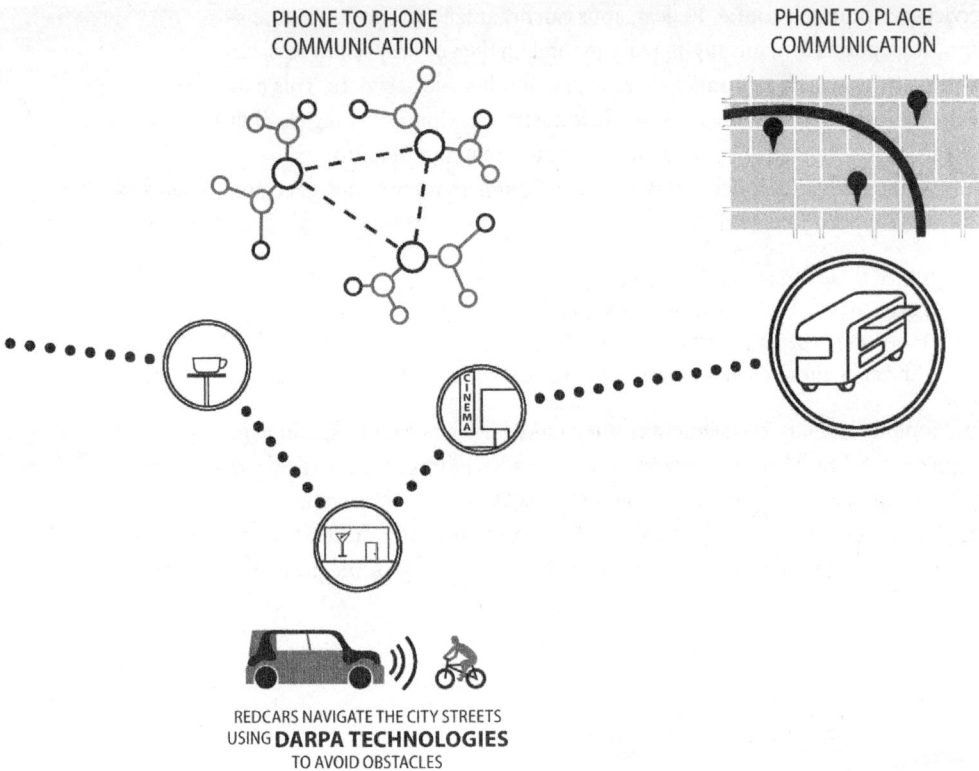

PHONE TO PHONE
COMMUNICATION

PHONE TO PLACE
COMMUNICATION

REDCARS NAVIGATE THE CITY STREETS
USING **DARPA TECHNOLOGIES**
TO AVOID OBSTACLES

(a) *Mobile Communication Device (smartphones or other).* While the cell phone started out as a mobile communication device, it has evolved into a portable computational device enabling any number of social practices: image sharing, banking, purchases, and so forth, which will only become more extensive in the future. The wider acceptance and distribution of wireless and episodic networks enable what could be termed "personal infrastructure" characterized by the ad hoc dynamic sharing of physical and virtual resources among heterogeneous devices. Information, entertainment, and financial services on demand effectively replace fixed shared services. Thus what is being proposed is an autonomous mobility-on-demand system, since wireless networks connect robotic vehicles to riders in real time.

(b) *Application.* The social software application organizes people, goods, and services. Importantly for LA_Redcar, apps can organize and coordinate transportation options dynamically, in real time and on the go—especially leasable (timeshare) cars such as from Zipcar, car2go, or other such services. This may be the future direction of the automobile industry—no longer selling cars but instead leasing vehicle usage in units of time to urban dwellers.[14]

Angelinos will be able access LA_Redcar through a variety of designed and developed applications such as:

- "I need to get somewhere fast" (solo-speed priority)
- "I need to do errands" (vehicle timed-transfer ok)
- "I need you to be my designated driver" (help!)
- "I'm new to the city and want to see the sights" (timing less important)

Autonomous mobility-on-demand as a networked transit system is intelligent, bespoken, and responsive; it reacts and evolves to address the social/work/recreational tasks and preferences of the user. Those rider preferences and profiles access and reorganize a cache of real-time data to fit riders' actual needs. A distributed transit system such as this solves many of the problems

REDCAR APPS

ADD FRIEND_Add friends to network.

TOUR GUIDE_takes rider along scenic route passing by places of interest. User feedback loop defines interest locations.

RIDE SHARE_Share rides w/ friends in network. Algorithm calculates which friends to pick up based on user preferences, activity, and path of travel.

DESIGNATED DRIVER_Takes rider to home location and pairs riders w/ other riders who have activated DD, while avoiding riders in professional network.

TRANSIT ASSIST_Assists user in arriving and transferring various modes of transit.

TASK SHARE_Share errands w/ network riders. Calculates shortest trip route, riders to share errands with, and meeting locations for item exchange.

Fig. 4. Mobility applications. (Katherine Handy and Dinesh Perera, © Format Design)

inherent with fixed transportation infrastructure including the first and last mile problem.

(c) *Autonomous Vehicle.* Also known as driverless car, self-driving car, or robotic car, the term describes an autonomous vehicle capable of sensing its environment with such techniques as GPS, radar, lidar (a laser surveying technology), computer vision, and navigating without human input. Advanced control systems interpret environmental information to identify navigation paths as well as obstacles and relevant signage. One of Google's principal engineers was Sebastian Thrum, former director of the Stanford Artificial Intelligence Laboratory, whose team at Stanford created the robotic vehicle that won the 2005 DARPA Grand Challenge. The system combines information gathered from Google Street View (which Thrum invented) with artificial intelligence that combines input from video cameras inside the car, a sensor on top of the vehicle, radar sensors on the front of the vehicle, and a position sensor attached to one of the rear wheels that helps locate the car's position on the map. Google anticipates that the increased accuracy of its automated driving system could help reduce the number of traffic-related injuries and deaths, while allowing for more efficient use of energy and space on roadways.[15] There are still many legal issues to resolve; however, self-driving cars are now allowed in Nevada, Florida, Michigan, California, and the District of Columbia, at least for testing purposes. Other states are considering their legalization. Uber and Lyft, among others, introduced a taxicab version of MoD (mobility-on-demand), yet the recent acquisition of Uber by Google has given rise to speculation that in the future, Google's self-driving car will be orchestrated by Uber's mobile platform. Other important research in this area is being conducted by Ryan Chin, director of the City Science Initiative at the MIT Media Lab, whose autonomous MoD system is organized as a network of self-driving, shared-use, lightweight electric vehicles (EVs). He also developed the CityCar—a foldable, electric, two-passenger vehicle.

As with EVs, environmental considerations figure prominently in the development of alternative transportation systems. It is projected that by 2030, gasoline-fueled vehicles will be limited for strategic use only.[16] The zero-carbon-emission-producing LA_Redcar can be configured to carry more passengers than conventional private automobiles. The intent is that through higher utilization rates the LA_Redcar prototype will allow for the replacement of conventional automobiles at a 1:3 ratio. Other future scenarios include ve-

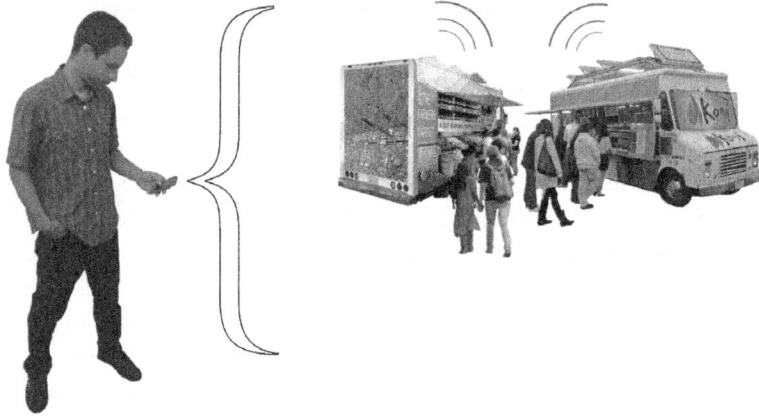

Fig. 5. Network technologies are organizing new spatial practices by connecting audiences with mobile events, thus creating dynamic social "hot spots." (Katherine Handy and Dinesh Perera, © Format Design)

hicle configuration. Building upon the National Automated Highway System Consortium NAHSC/PATH I-15 demonstration project, "platoons" of up to twenty-five cars can be ganged together to share part of a route, or they can "mate" to create a shared mobile social interest platform.[17]

As a flexible socially responsive transit system, autonomous MoD could spark the development of emergent nodes. If past studies on urban growth hold, commercial development will naturally emerge from the urban fabric in response to social hotspots triggered by both physical space, which is to say, locations of transfer from vehicle to transit, and social swings. The overlay of efficient route-processing software upon the physical realm will create serendipitous social and transit "hot spots" to emerge, thus creating an organic evolution of actual transit-oriented developments (TOD).[18]

New Social Practices

While the previous section focused on functional aspects of transportation systems, such as everyday commuting, mobile technologies are also rapidly modifying other urban spaces and practices. It follows that new forms of urban space might emerge attendant upon new media. One of the more interesting is the upswing in mobile restaurants connected via Twitter. In Los Angeles, one of the best known is Kogi (Asian fusion), whose late-night itinerary is disseminated to Twitter followers. In San Francisco where high real estate

T. F. Tierney et al.

values deter small neighborhood restaurants, hungry hipsters flock to Seoul on Wheels or Chairman Bao after receiving a pre-lunchtime text announcement via their cell phones. Today Manuel Castells would define this as a "material organization of time-sharing social practices that work through flows."[19] Alternative ways of organizing existing resources, both transportation and otherwise, demonstrate that design ideas can be leveraged into strategies that are environmentally responsible and socially equitable by enabling new forms of public interaction.

Conclusion

While it is clear today that we are deeply embedded in cultures formed in part by new information technologies, we still move within existing urban systems: streets, rails, and subways are not disappearing. In the example of LA_Redcar, both the hardware and software are components of extensive mobile social networks supported and distributed through fixed roadways, guideways, and transportation.

William Mitchell suggested that the digital revolution will alter patterns of human settlement and land use to the same degree as the industrial and agricultural revolutions did in earlier times. For cities of the future, Mitchell proposed our intelligent interaction with information and communication technologies. That interweaving of information and matter will fundamentally change the way we use space, distribute resources, and interact within our communities.[20] As designers and engineers continue to work across a variety of disciplines to solve seemingly intractable urban problems, there is still much potential and cause for future research.

Notes

1   Intelligent infrastructure is responsive to its environment through wireless network systems (WNS), sensors, and computational technologies. Richard Cook, "Ecotopia" (lecture, Intelligent Infrastructure, New York, February 16, 2011).

2   Melvin Webber, "The Urban Place and the Non-Place Urban Realm," in *Explorations into Urban Structure*, ed. Webber (Philadelphia: University of Pennsylvania Press, 1964).

3   Ibid.

4   Mark Wigley, "The Architectural Brain," in *Network Practices: New Strategies for Architecture and Design*, ed. Anthony Burke and Therese Tierney (New York: Princeton Architectural Press), 30–53.

5   See Christopher Alexander, "A City Is Not a Tree" http://www.bp.ntu.edu .tw/wp-content/uploads/2011/12/06-Alexander-A-city-is-not-a-tree.pdf (accessed May 15, 2016).

6   Manuel Castells, *The Rise of the Network Society*, 2nd ed. (Malden, MA: Blackwell Publishers 2000), 1–76.

7   Peter Mörtenböck, "Placemaking Dialogues," *Gateways: Art and Networked Culture*, http://blog.goethe.de/gateways/archives/10-Peter-Moertenboeck -about-Placemaking-Dialogues.html (accessed August 16, 2011).

8   The 510 Collective includes the author, Ben Feldman, Tyron Marshall, and Gerald Tierney; Format Design includes Katherine Handy and Dinesh Perera. LA_Redcar was first exhibited at "New Infrastructure: Transit Solutions for Los Angeles," curated by Peter Zellner at Southern California Institute for Architecture (SciArc), Los Angeles, March 21–28 2009.

9   Projects at the URL: Urban Research Lab of the University of Illinois at Urbana-Champaign have investigated systems, both physical and virtual, as they pertain to infrastructure, software, ecologies, and environments.

10   These issues are especially important in the United States where land-use patterns have moved more jobs and people to lower-density suburbs that are often not within walking distance to existing public transportation, making public transit use less practical. Critics claim this promotes a reliance on cars, which results in more traffic congestion, pollution, and urban sprawl. See "In Focus: The Last Mile and Transit Ridership," Institute for Local Government, January 2011.

11   According to Ryan Chin, PhD, managing director of MIT's City Science Initiative, low-energy per capita systems—for example, mass transit systems like subways, bus rapid transit (BRT), buses, and trams—suffer from inflexible routing and schedules as well as the "first and last mile problem," where distances are too far to walk to a transit hub. This problem is compounded by poor coordination during intermodal switches as well as environmental conditions (e.g., excess humidity, rain, or snow).

12   William J. Mitchell, Chris E. Borroni-Bird, and Lawrence D. Burns, *Reinventing the Automobile: Personal Urban Mobility for the 21st Century* (Cambridge, MA: MIT Press, 2010).

13   Daimler-Benz's program, "car2go," is currently operating across North America including Vancouver, Austin, San Diego, and all other major cities. See www.car2go.com (retrieved November 25, 2014).

14 Christopher Borroni-Bird, "Advance Technology Vehicle Concepts" (paper presented at Mobility & the City Colloquium, San Francisco, September 25, 2010).

15 John Markoff, "Smarter Than You Think: Google Cars Drive Themselves in Traffic," *New York Times*, October 9, 2010.

16 There is an ongoing debate whether "peak oil" has been reached, or if it will be reached in 2020. See Kenneth S. Deffeyes, "Current Events—Join Us As We Watch the Crisis Unfolding," When Oil Peaked, January 19, 2007, https://www.princeton.edu/hubbert/current-events-07–01.html (retrieved April 5, 2016); Deffeyes, *Beyond Oil: The View from Hubbert's Peak* (New York: Hill and Wang, 2005).

17 This platoon control demonstration was held in San Diego by the National Automated Highway System Consortium (NAHSC) on August 7–10, 1997. PATH showed an eight-car Buick LaSabre platoon in combined longitudinal and lateral control on the I-15 HOV lanes. The vehicles were driving themselves at 6.5 meters spacing and 60 mph. The scenario involved vehicle #2 splitting, doing a lane change, falling back, and doing another lane change to join back with the platoon as vehicle #8. PATH also showed a single Buick minidemo at Miramar College, in which Senator Barbara Boxer rode. The vehicle was fully automated, going forward and in reverse, on a tight course set up with cones. Steven Shladover, "AHS Demo '97 'Complete Success,'" *Intellimotion* 6, no. 3 (1997), http://www.path.berkeley.edu/sites/default/files/documents/intel63.pdf (accessed May 15, 2016).

18 Conversation with Ben Feldman, Los Angeles architect and urban planner, June 23, 2009.

19 Manuel Castells, "Grassrooting the Space of Flows," in *Cities in the Telecommunications Age: The Fracturing of Cities*, ed. James O. Wheeler, Yuko Aoyama and Barney Warf, (London: Routledge, 2000), 147.

20 William J. Mitchell, *City of Bits: Space, Place, and the Infobahn* (Cambridge, MA: MIT Press, 1996).

(Driver)less Is More
A Tale of Two Cities

Bjarke Ingels and Kai-Uwe Bergmann

Thinking big has nothing to do with the scale of projects, but with the power of an idea.

Demographic shifts assure that the future will be urban. At the same time, the cities of the future will probably be much like the cities we live in now, because the majority of the buildings in those cities-to-come are already built. However, over time, cities may become radically different in many other ways—in terms of use, mobility, and social practices.

One of architects' objectives is to try to shape the urban environment so that it more closely aligns with the ways we would want to live—with our cultural imaginings. Our cities don't look the way they do because they have to, or because it is their "natural" state. They look that way because that's how we created them. If later on those cities don't fit new needs or demands that have evolved—or our dreams—we have the means and the power to re-imagine them.

Looking at the present-day built environment, the field of architecture seems to be dominated by two extremes. One is wild and expressive, but very expensive and unrealistic. The other, more dominant extreme is practical and rational, but often unambitious and uninspiring. What Bjarke Ingels Group (BIG) endeavors to do is occupy the middle ground between these two extremes, through what we like to call "pragmatic utopianism."

Urban Future

The art of reinterpretation, adaptation, and appropriation happens much faster than policy or physical construction can. With that in mind, developers and policy makers need to better understand how a design emerges out of different social demands and concerns—how it emerges from society. What makes the process interesting is that, as designers, we have the means and the skills to look at how life in the city evolves and what new patterns emerge, and then we try to create a physical framework around it.

When life changes, so should the architecture. When people inhabit a city in new ways, the city can evolve and adapt to these new ways of living. Transportation provides a case in point. When we examine the mobility infrastructure, public transportation is not the problem. Bicycles are not the problem. Pedestrians are not the problem. The problem is cars—particularly the car in the centralized core area.

In 2010, for the Audi Urban Future Award competition, BIG focused on finding an urban planning strategy that combined the desire for individual freedom and mobility with the need for collective coordination of all this free movement. At the center of the strategy is the self-driving, super-compact Audi A2 concept car. In our vision, the A2 and cars like it are a prerequisite for a networked, mobile future. A driverless car communicates with its environment through sophisticated sensory and computational technology that constantly observes and calculates the dynamic space that the living city constitutes.

Our Urban Future design initiative has two parts: a multimodal planning framework that activates the public realm with different mobility experiences, and a method for the coordination of mobility options. For the first part, rather than focusing on designing an iconic urban master plan, we wanted to create an interconnected urban mobility network that did not privilege the personal automobile. Our alternative was a planning framework resembling a Scottish tartan: three separate but interrelated networks: (1) interlinked canals, (2) a linear but connected park system, and (3) a set of sidewalks and streets.

The three networks allow for different experiential spaces that facilitate both movement and social interactions throughout the city. The canals extend the harbor into the city core, allowing people to walk along the waterways, while the canals themselves can be traveled by different types of boats such as waterbuses and taxis. The layer of parks provides an informal infrastructure for sports and

CURRENT TRAFFIC

DRIVERLESS TRAFFIC

DRIVERLESS CARS COULD USE
OUR EXISTING INFRA STRUCTURE
BY MOVING IN SUPER-EFFICIENT
PATTERNS, ELIMINATING THE
BOTTLENECKS!

AND WITH NO POLUTION OR NOISE,
COULD WE IMAGINE LIBERATING
ALL SPACES AND BLURRING THE
LINE BETWEEN ARCHITECTURE
AND INFRASTRUCTURE?

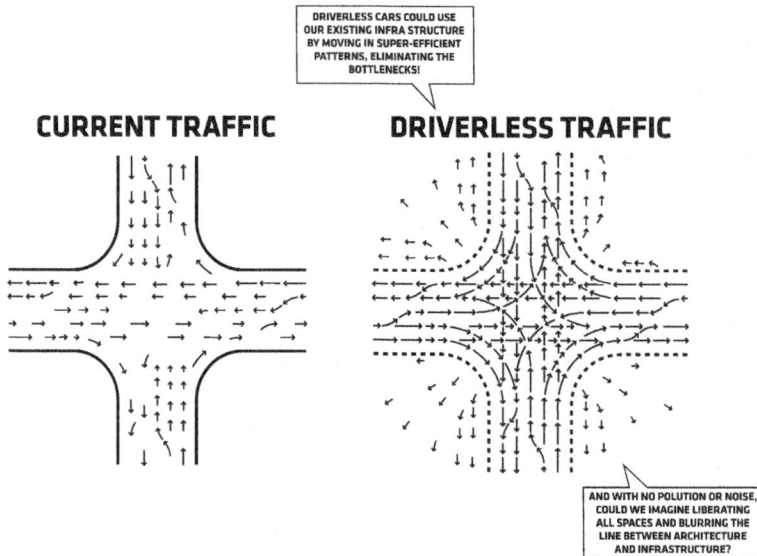

Fig. 1. Diagram, BIG Audi Urban Future Initiative 2010. (© BIG: Bjarke Ingels Group)

other leisure activities, as well as bicycle paths. And finally, there is the network of streets. However, rather than proposing a traditional static layout for these networks, we proposed a planning framework that would ensure urban dwellers access to various kinds of public space *within the same physical space*, as needed.

At the micro scale, our future city would be paved with a digital programmable surface that liberates the streets from existing boundaries and allows for a new flexibility of public use.[1] This enables an architecture of movement whose forms are not predetermined by the architect but are constantly being recomposed by the people populating the space. So, if we imagine an existing city in twenty-five years' time, while the vertical facades appear unchanged, elements such as streets, sidewalks, and city squares no longer exist in their present fixed form. Instead, the street has become a responsive surface, adapting to diverse uses over the span of a day, week, or season. We reimagine urban space and urban movement as alive, with a form that coevolves in a continuous feedback loop, each part constantly adjusting to the other.[2] Urban space, in this scenario, is ideally flexible.

The second part of our proposal envisioned the collective coordination of mobility options. In ten to twenty years, cars will be virtually noiseless. They're

Bjarke Ingels and Kai-Uwe Bergmann

Fig. 2. Reprogrammable surface, BIG Audi Urban Future Initiative 2010. (© BIG: Bjarke Ingels Group)

going to be pollutionless. And they will be driverless. The last is what makes all the other parts of the plan possible. As soon as cars can operate independently of humans, we have the possibility of collective coordination of transit in the central urban core. Cars can operate much closer together and move together seamlessly. Traffic jams will be a thing of the past.

This method of coordination is already being applied, for example, in elevators. One of the best ways of increasing the capacity of elevator banks is a system in which, instead of pressing a button to call an elevator and then pressing another button once you get inside the car, you enter your destination floor on a keypad in the elevator lobby, and it tells you which elevator to take. The result is the same: you still have the individual freedom to decide which floor you go to when, but the system coordinates which elevator cars go where and how often. It collectively coordinates individual mobility.

In this future vision, inner cities that currently must restrict cars through taxation or tolls to relieve congestion will simply become driverless, rather than car-less. Driverless cars will combine individual mobility outside city limits with collective mobility within, because self-driven cars will be able to move in coordinated concert with their fellows while occupying a quarter of the space human-driven cars require.

Further, because the new generation of cars will be quiet and nonpolluting,

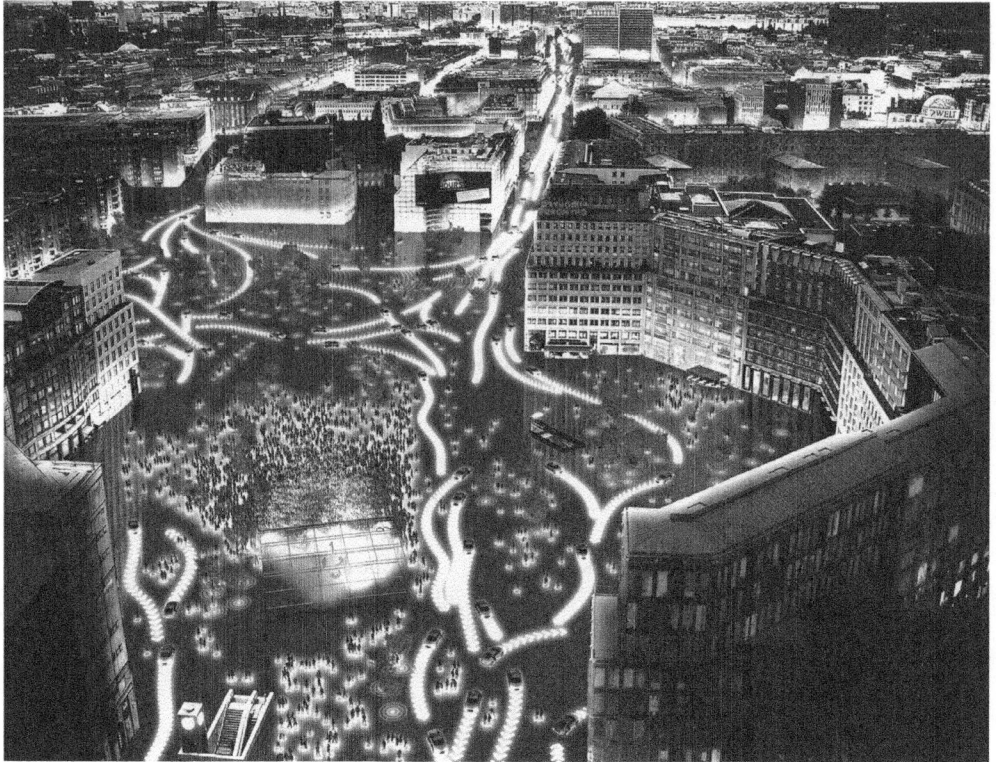

Fig. 3. AUDI bird's-eye view of traffic flow with programmable urban space, BIG Audi Urban Future Initiative 2010. (© BIG: Bjarke Ingels Group)

there will no longer be the need to separate cars from pedestrians and bicyclists to ensure comfort, health, and safety. And, again, because the digital road surface will adapt to all users and control traffic, what we think of now as roads could become an elastic urban space that expands and contracts throughout the day, accommodating traffic at peak hours and then allowing a playground, plaza, or sidewalk café to emerge to fit the demands and desires of its citizens at other times.[3]

Loop City

Let's turn to now to the super-macro metropolitan scale. BIG takes unconventional approaches to infrastructure that require equal amounts of intelligence

Fig. 4. Loop City, Albertslund Hersted Industrial Park. (© BIG: Bjarke Ingels Group)

to be invested in each form of movement: walking, bicycles, cars, trains, and buses. Planning carefully for each mode of movement requires a balancing act, in that no form of mobility can be privileged over another.

One example of this line of thinking is the Loop City project. The project was commissioned by the ten municipalities that make up greater Copenhagen to investigate potential urban development along a proposed light-rail line around the Øresund strait area of Denmark and neighboring Sweden. The concept of Loop City is to find as many ways as possible of efficiently integrating all the various forms of movement.

Since 1947, Copenhagen has had what is called the Five-Fingered Plan, because it looks roughly like a hand. Each finger is a corridor of dense urban fabric, with the palm, or middle, being downtown Copenhagen. As the individual outlying cities evolved, the fingers grew longer and longer, making the

Fig. 5. Bjarke Ingels Group, Denmark Pavilion, Shanghai XPO, China, 2010. (Photograph © Iwan Baan, courtesy of Bjarke Ingels Group)

connection to downtown longer and longer, and leading to more and more congestion.

Loop City, in contrast, will be essentially a circle of mobility surrounding the palm and eventually connecting to Sweden on the opposite side of the strait. By plugging into the existing infrastructure of trains and highways (and building a necessary four-kilometer-long bridge), we can create a single metropolitan loop in which no destination is more than forty minutes away from any other by public transportation.[4]

The loop connecting the two countries will be roughly the same size as the San Francisco Bay's circumference and will essentially become one of the first truly cross-border metropolitan regions. As we imagine this loop, it consists of not only a traditional transportation infrastructure but also a utilities infrastructure for handling waste, carrying drinking water, and transmitting energy—with room for leisure activities.[5] We call this strategy "coupling" because it joins multiple functionalities. One idea is to use the existing electric lines to provide power to the light-rail train and then extend its function to powering electric automobiles. Another possibility is that during the late-night hours when the light-rail doesn't run, the same track line could be used to transport waste to nearby waste-energy plants. Finally, a smart power grid could combine Sweden's hydroelectricity with Denmark's wind power to provide an intelligent, sustainable infrastructure for all aspects of human life.[6]

Projects such as Loop City could potentially change the suburbs from being bedroom communities on the outskirts of the city into novel urban centers with increased public life in the streets. Urban-ness is all about density. If we assume that transit stations can serve as social attractors, then over time, businesses, cafés, and thriving commercial areas will emerge around them, and then around the entire loop. As a social condenser, Loop City will bring together both people and multiple functions.

Instead of continuing to allow cities to sprawl across the surrounding landscape, eating up more and more resources and dispersing people over a greater area, we need to find a way to let cities grow within their current footprints by breathing new programmatic features into existing areas.[7] By densifying our existing suburban areas, we would not only create a much more resource-efficient city but also one that's far more culturally engaging and, simply, livable.

Notes

1   Bjarke Ingels and Andreas Klok Pederson of BIG teamed up with IG, Kollision, and Schmidhuber & Partner for AUDI at Design Miami (November 30–December 4, 2011) Miami, FL.

2   Interview with Bjarke Ingels in conjunction with Audi Urban Future Award, "Building a Vision for 2030," http://audi-urban-future-initiative.com/blog/bjarke-ingels-and-big (accessed May 13, 2016).

3   See Audi Urban Future Initiative, http://audi-urban-future-initiative.com/api/fallback/blog/bjarke-ingels-group (accessed December 10, 2014).

4   Dominick Blackwell Cooper, Design Build Source, "Urban Mobility 2011: Loop City" video, uploaded August 2, 2011, https://www.youtube.com/watch?v=m6ENC3_D9eI (accessed December 10, 2014).

5   Andreas Klok Pederson, BIG partner in charge of Loop City, interviewed by Cooper in ibid.

6   Soren Martinussen, BIG project leader of Loop City, interviewed by Cooper in ibid.

7   Karen Cilento, "LOOP City / BIG," September 3, 2010, *ArchDaily*, http://www.archdaily.com/76482/loop-city-big/ (accessed December 15, 2014).

Ubiquitous Multimodality
A Vision for Urban Mobility in the (Near) Future

Carlo Ratti, Nashid Nabian, and Christine Outram

In this essay we present a vision. A vision where using shared or public transportation is not difficult; it doesn't involve long wait times (or if it does, you can plan other local activities accordingly); you have access to vehicles on demand, and you can seamlessly switch between a bus, a train, a bicycle, a car, or any other transport device. In this vision, public transportation services the entire city; it doesn't just drop you somewhere that is "close enough" to your final destination but, if you need it to, it can cover the last mile and take you to your door, doing so in a sustainable manner that saves you money and reduces your and your city's energy consumption.

Pipe dream? We don't think so. Through examining emerging trends in urban informatics and providing concrete research and real-world examples, this essay aims to show that the future of transportation in cities is likely to include real-time information systems and an on-demand network of vehicles that are customized by "riders on the run" and that have every possibility of being just as reliable and flexible as private transport. In other words, the (near) future holds ubiquitous multimodal transportation systems—transit where and when you want it—a scenario that not only affects our mobility habits but also changes the way we *consume* existing transportation networks and the form that our future cities will take. To introduce readers to this concept, we begin with a scenario of the (near) future as told through the eyes of Marcus, our protagonist, who demonstrates the affects that real-time transportation networks can have on the daily mobility routines of urbanites. We then discuss how transportation networks can be more efficiently consumed, before closing with examples that show how the traditional fixed-hub models of transportation networks are likely to change with the onset of real-time information and on-demand vehicles.

The Multimodal Commute

As Marcus walks towards his favorite local café, he hears a familiar "ding-ding" chime coming from his pocket. The preprogrammed sound alerts him to the fact that the no. 9 express bus will be in his vicinity in around ten minutes. "Time to check the line," he thinks as he reaches into his pocket to get more information. A few quick key presses let him know that the wait at his local café is short, and that he still has time to grab a coffee before he heads toward the nearest bus pickup point.

Coffee in hand, he leaves the café and looks toward the pickup point where three other passengers are waiting. "Right on time," he thinks to himself as he sees the bus coming from the other direction.

Stepping onto the bus, his phone buzzes again, this time indicating that he has paid his fare and anonymously "checked in" to the transport system's real-time optimization and routing network. The transportation authority uses Marcus's anonymized information (such as his personal updates about what days and times he wants to use public transportation; the time he actually catches the bus; and the other transportation modes he uses) to make public mobility more efficient. Marcus knows this and is happy to contribute his data for a more seamless commute.

Sipping at his coffee, he quickly checks the availability and options for vehicles that are around the stop where he will get off. As it turns out, there are four bikes and three cars within a seven-minute walk of his stop. Being in a suit and with a big meeting that morning, he books one of the cars. The app then warns him that through using a car, he may not reach his personal exercise goals for the day, and he makes a mental note to take a bike on the way home.

Marcus's phone "checks out" as he steps off the bus and walks toward his waiting car. A single thumb press to the door unlocks the car for him and checks him back into the transportation app. He gets into the driver's seat and programs his destination, after which a projected note appears on the dashboard asking him if he has time to refuel the car. After checking his watch, he selects that he has an extra ten minutes to spare, and the car automatically reroutes his path to include the cheapest local gas station that will get him to his destination on time.

Approaching his office, the car remotely books Marcus into the closest parking spot. Marcus parks; his phone checks him out of the transportation app and, as requested by Marcus, sends a summary of his journey (environmental impact, distance, time, etc.) to his personal transportation account and via email so that he can optimize his journey himself and is reminded to set his transportation goals for the following week.

Carlo Ratti, Nashid Nabian, and Christine Outram

Fig. 1. Networked dashboard. (Carlo Ratti, © SENSEable City Lab, Massachusetts Institute of Technology)

Reliability and Flexibility: Problems of the Past?

Despite the ease of Marcus's multimodal and digitally augmented commute, convincing an increasingly mobile population of urbanites to make use of public transport is not without challenges. Two traditional concerns in this area have been reliability and flexibility, both of which make urban commuters somewhat hesitant to plan their daily trips around services offered by a public transport system. In this section, we discuss these two limiting factors and further explore how a network of real-time information and the existence of on-demand vehicles and services can alleviate these issues and encourage greater use of public and shared transportation.

In terms of reliability, public transport is perceived by urban users as uncertain due to both the actual wait-time and the burden of waiting for transit.[1] However, when real-time information regarding current location and the projected route of a vehicle (including the time gap between arrival of two consecutive public transport vehicles, transport-time variance, and possible delays) are offered to the traveler in situ and on the run, travelers are provided with three things: the ability to plan their trip according to their needs; the ability to minimize actual wait time; and a changed perception of the wait time, thereby reducing the burden of the wait and building a greater receptiveness to public transportation. A smartphone application like Next Bus—now available in over ninety cities in the United States—already utilizes Global Positioning System (GPS) tracking satellites and combines this data with predictive software on buses to provide accurate vehicle arrival/departure information and real-time maps to passengers on public transit, shuttles, and trains. However, we envision an extended network of information that includes all types of transportation: buses, taxis, trains, shared bikes and cars, and even private vehicles that are heading in the same approximate destination as you are.

When real-time information is combined with on-demand vehicles (cars, buses, trains, bikes, etc. that are available when and where you need them), it also positively affects the flexibility of a transportation system—not only for travelers, but in the system's structure as well.

For example, when travelers have access to real-time information, they can be informed that the next bus is not coming soon, therefore allowing them to make an alternative decision—perhaps walking, taking a train, or hailing a cab. While smart apps like Next Bus already provide this, in the near future additional information, such as whether or not the bus is full, can also smooth demand spikes: as passengers learn which buses are full, they adjust their schedules accordingly, and peak demand is distributed without the need for increasing the number of vehicles.

Lastly, while conventional multimodal transportation systems need a network of fixed hubs in space where commuters change modes of transportation, with new advancements in digital and telecommunication technologies and where smart dust (networked microsensors) saturates the space of urbanity, the possibility of ubiquitous sensing emerges as an eminent condition. Through this condition is born the idea of ubiquitous multimodality, where an urban dweller jumps out of the bus onto a city bike and from the bike into a taxi—seamlessly and with ease. With real-time location and route information on public transport and the location and origin/destination information of the commuters integrated into one-information architecture, there would be informal ad hoc transportation hubs forming and dissolving as required—a truly flexible system.

This vision of flexible transportation interactions made possible through real-time information and a ubiquitous multimodal system adds a virtual depth or cybernetically mediated dimension to the city that moves us away from the constant need to intensify physical transportation infrastructures (our railway lines, bus lanes, or subway systems) or the need to purchase more vehicles in order to cope with peak transportation loads. Instead, through creating a real-time feedback loop of information about available vehicles, arrivals and departures, or associated data that could help us match our needs with available services, we are moving toward more efficient ways of consuming existing transportation options.

Two contrasting visions about mobility from 1925 help explain this idea. The first is a postcard that imagines future New York City as a utopian "City of Skyscrapers." The scene depicted includes multiple levels of infrastructure, juxtaposed on the urban fabric, including a system of elevated train tracks and flying machines as means of transport. Although the future proved this particular vision wrong, the subtext of such an imaginative response quite aptly reflects the reality of today's urban condition: our cities have been physically densified each time peak transit demand has grown. In other words, we have responded to demand by increasing (with associated environmental and monetary costs) our physical transportation infrastructures—the highways, overpasses, passenger terminals, central rail systems, and their associated vehicles, and so forth—that support these increased flows.

In contrast, Hugo Gernsback's syndicated piece in a 1925 edition of the *San Antonio Light* presents a different subtext about the future of urban mobility. Gernsback speculates on an alternative mode of transport where everybody will be their own taxicab—riding electronic skates that are powered through wireless electricity. In the cartoon that accompanied the text, the urbanites are not depicted as "users" of transportation, but as instruments of mobility in their own right.[2] While we haven't achieved wireless electricity yet, the idea that individuals can impact the efficiency of transportation is a theme that is resurfacing in the digital age and that, we believe, leads directly to a more efficient consumption of existing transportation infrastructures and vehicles.

What follows are examples of how real-time information can help us more efficiently consume existing transportation networks, without the need for deploying more vehicles, additional services, or physical infrastructures. Our first two examples are FriendFreight,[3] a theoretical delivery service, and UShip,[4] an existing delivery service.

Both FriendFreight and UShip use the real-time location information of people and goods and the ability for members of a community to deliver items for others while moving through and between cities themselves. While FriendFreight (which alerts people in your community who are nearby about an object you want delivered) aims to lower the number of "unnecessary trips" that people make to obtain some small goods—groceries, books, documents, and dry cleaning—UShip matches people's desire for cheap shipping with delivery companies that want to make money.

Neither of these systems would exist without real-time information and the ability of the Web to connect strangers through common goals and aspirations, and it is through harnessing this information that they are able to utilize existing transportation infrastructures and vehicles in order to more efficiently deliver goods and to reduce what is termed *travel demand* in the city.[5]

On a larger scale, cities such as Florence, Italy, and New York City are both actively researching or integrating the deployment of digital transportation information systems that will nullify the need to produce additional physical infrastructures. Instead, virtual layers of digital information are being used to promote the efficient consumption of existing transportation systems over an entire city.

When Florence's city center was named a UNESCO World Heritage Site in 1982, the city became a physical frozen museum. Everything within the old city walls—the buildings, pavement, piazzas, and even the less successful postwar retrofits—became protected. But in many ways this historic honor was a double-edged sword: while UNESCO's decision has seen the inner-city prospering from tourism, traditional residents are moving out due to the difficulty of living in a frozen city that disallows changes in zoning and that can no longer adapt to the needs of its residents.

Now, however, the city is actively searching for ways to support local residents through the use of digital layers of information. Research carried out by MIT students in a Digital City Design Workshop about Florence in 2008[6] and projects such as SENSEable City Lab's Eyestop[7] (a series of bus stops that act as digital community notice boards and that provide real-time information about bus arrival, whether you have time for an espresso, and upcoming weather conditions) show that through accessing digital information, not only can we

Carlo Ratti, Nashid Nabian, and Christine Outram

make the consumption of transportation networks more efficient, but we can do it without widening roads or disturbing the heritage listed city.

Lastly, let us remind ourselves of Mayor Michael R. Bloomberg's thirty-three-point proposal for improvement of the public transit system in New York City. As a part of Mayor Bloomberg's 2009 campaign for reelection for a third term in office, the proposal, for the first time, incorporated a series of suggestions in terms of how the existing infrastructure could become more efficient and transparent to the riders: providing "countdown clocks" in subway stations that indicate when the next subway is arriving, the creation of an integrated New York transit RFID Smart Card, and increased NYPD control over transit system security, with a reference to the installation of surveillance cameras in subway tunnels, increasing bus service in off-peak times by using smaller vehicles that could break the catch-22 of "we made the bus infrequent because no one rides it because it's so infrequent," and making cross-town buses free, which would speed up service by eliminating fare collection.[8]

Although many dismissed the proposal as political grandstanding (Bloomberg had no payment plan for the transit platform that he unveiled), it is worth noting the principal goals of the plan symbolized an important shift in the way New York politicians focus on transit improvements—notably because the list did not include any new subway extensions, which are typically the mainstay of similar attempts to attract public support, and which are inevitably forgotten as soon as the campaign ends.

The cases of New York, Florence, FriendFreight, and UShip are some among many examples that show a gradual shift from the densification of public transport infrastructure and the continual purchase of more vehicles to meet peak demand loads to what we would like to define as an intensification approach, where adding the virtual depth of real-time information made available to users of transportation networks can make it more efficient and flexible for individuals and hence more desirable.

Toward a Future Rhizomatic Urbanism

In the final section of this chapter we discuss how the presence of on-demand vehicles and the ability for citizens to harness real-time transportation information on the go could facilitate a new multicentered dynamic urbanism.

Traditional multimodal cities—cities where citizens switch transportation modes to get where they need to be—require fixed physical hubs: a taxi stand, a central train station, an airport, a port, a shipping facility, and so on. The existence and distribution of these fixed hubs and their relation to economic growth and the supply and demand of goods and services are embedded in the theoretical literature of city creation. In particular central place theory (created by the German geographer Walter Christaller), with varying degrees of success, attempts to explain the historical physical layout of cities and asserts that settlements simply function as "central [fixed] places" providing services to surrounding areas.[9] However, what central place theory does not account for, and which we believe is vital to understanding new multimodal transportation systems, are the temporal aspect of city development and the dynamic way in which we interact with cities as we go about our daily lives. In addition, we disagree with the fact that the nodes in the central place theory network are often thought to cover nonoverlapping service areas—since considerations of distance and the cost of commute were thought to discourage citizens from traveling between one node area and another.[10]

In contrast, as a layer of networked digital elements is increasingly blanketing our built environment and as we (mobile phones in hand) have a greater ability to extract and insert information about mobility in real time, we believe that fixed nodes, which only serve fixed-service areas, eventually will lose some importance in cities of the future. Instead, with real-time location and route information and on-demand vehicles that do not require specific parking locations, ad hoc transportation hubs can form and dissolve as required, creating dynamic nodes that will support a new series of micro-exchanges in the built environment and a truly ubiquitous multimodal system. We define this as a rhizomatic urbanism. Drawing parallels from the theories of Deleuze and Guattari, it is an in-between system that allows for multiple, nonhierarchical entry and exit points and that resists chronology and organization, instead favoring a nomadic system of growth and propagation.[11]

A few examples will help clarify this trend, and we close the essay by looking at Real Time Rome and the Open Bike and car2go services.

In 2006, MIT's SENSEable City Lab produced the project Real Time Rome.[12] In a world first, this project aggregated anonymous data from cell phones, buses, and taxis in Rome to better understand urban dynamics in real time. By revealing the pulse of the city, the Real Time Rome visualizations were able

Carlo Ratti, Nashid Nabian, and Christine Outram

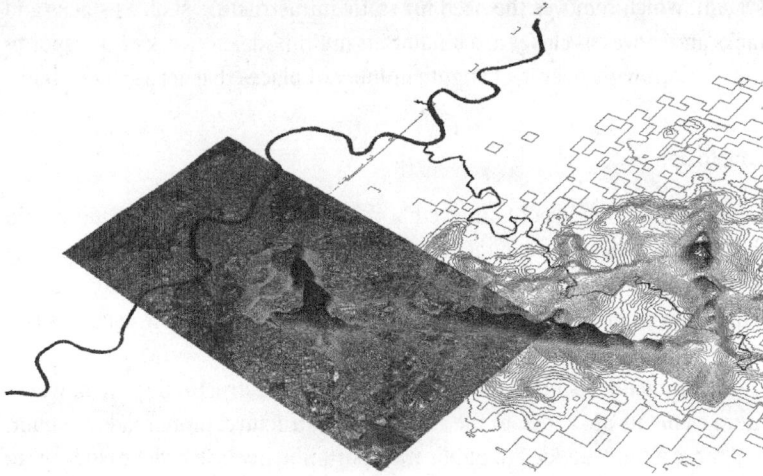

Fig. 2. Real Time Rome combines different datasets in a single interface: real-time data, GIS data, and raster images creating a topography of communication. (Carlo Ratti, © SENSEable City Lab, Massachusetts Institute of Technology)

to compare movement patterns of people with that of transportation in the city, as shown in fig. 2 where the higher contour areas represent the density of people in a given area in Rome (using anonymous and aggregated cell-phone records as a proxy for people density), while the dots represent buses, with the length and direction of their tail representing, in turn, the speed and direction. From this information the lab was able to understand that taxis and buses are not always where people are, opening up questions of how dynamic demand might be matched with dynamic supply "on the run" and in multiple and changing locations.

Meanwhile, two recently implemented systems—the Open Bike Share System[13] and car2go[14] are commercial examples of ubiquitous mobility that manifest the potential of a dynamic-hub system. Both services offer "floating" vehicles that do not need any special parking permits (the city of Austin, where car2go is implemented, supports the system and offers free parking for all vehicles). Both systems also make full use of real-time digital information for locating, booking, and payment, and the companies that provide the vehicles use an algorithm to determine the number of vehicles needed in a given geographic area and the likelihood that all vehicles are less than a ten-minute walk away from members of the service. In other words, this is a fully floating system, which removes the need for static infrastructure such as stacks and racks and moves us closer to a ubiquitous multimodal network of transportation options with an ever-changing number of places that act as ad hoc hubs.

Conclusion

Cities of today are hyperconnected both with their counterparts and within themselves—ideas and capital, human and material resources, are perpetually moving within and between physical urban infrastructures. The question at hand is, in what ways do the global infrastructures of mobility need to adapt to accommodate this accelerated rate of connectivity?

One immediate solution is that of physical infrastructural growth, where more elements are added to the existing infrastructure: more roads are built, and more units are added to public transportation fleets in order to meet peak demand load. Yet, in many cases due to both physical limitations posed by urban density or perhaps unexpandable boundaries of urban regions—due to topographical characteristics and economic considerations—expanding and adding to the existing infrastructure is not the optimal response.

A different set of closely related solutions looks at harnessing real-time information to make existing infrastructure as efficient as possible. What is ultimately certain is that the act of retrofitting our physical infrastructures of mobility with a digital infrastructure of real-time information will shift the urban paradigm of centrality from a single hierarchy of central places to a more dynamic configuration of fixed and ephemeral hubs that take shape and dissolve based on emergent conditions of mobility demand. With this shift will come a future, where transportation will be composed of many different solutions—bicycles, buses, trains, and even private vehicles—and what will tie it all together is a real-time information network that can be accessed from anywhere, anytime. Our new hybrid infrastructure of mobility—consisting of a physical network and a digital layer that augments it—will optimize performance and improve reliability while the seamless multimodal mobility that it provides will increase flexibility and open up a paradigm shift in how we think of centrality in an urban context.

Hence, the saying "all roads lead to Rome" (a fixed transportation hub approach) will be gradually replaced by a lengthier, but more accurate "all roads bind together many hubs and centers that dynamically re-create new patterns of mobility within the city based on real-time information." The rhizomatic networked city of dynamic hubs is not a tree, as Christopher Alexander might point out; it is much more effective if seen as a lattice where physical connections between each and every node are constantly optimized.[15]

Notes

1   Thomas B. Reed, "Reduction in the Burden of Waiting for Public Transit Due to Real-Time Schedule Information: A Conjoint Analysis Study," in *Vehicle Navigation and Information Systems Conference Proceedings* (New York: Institute of Electrical and Electronics Engineers, 1995), 83–89.

2   For excerpts of Hugo Gernsback's piece see "Gernsback Imagines Life 50 Years Hence 1925)," Paleofuture, September 19, 2009, http://www.paleofuture.com/blog/tag/moving-sidewalk.

3   Christine Outram and Francesco Calabrese, "FriendFreight: Leveraging Real-Time Location Information for a Sustainable Community-Based Goods Delivery Service," in *Movement-Aware Applications for Sustainable Mobility: Technologies and Approaches*, ed. Monica Wachowicz (Hershey, PA: Information Science Reference, 2010), 175–94.

4   See UShip, http://www.uship.com/.

5   Outram and Calabrese, "FriendFreight," 175.

6   Giandomenico Amendola, Anne Beamish, Dennis Frenchman, and William J. Mitchell, *Technological Imagination and the Historic City: Florence* (Naples, Italy: Liguori Editore, 2009).

7   See EyeStop, http://senseable.mit.edu/eyestop/.

8   Michael Barbaro and Sewell Chan, "Mayor Proposes Free Crosstown Buses," *New York Times*, August 3, 2009, http://www.nytimes.com/2009/08/04/nyregion/04bloomberg.html (accessed April 21, 2011).

9   Stan Openshaw and Yannis Veneris, "Numerical Experiments with Central Place Theory and Spatial Interaction Modelling," *Environment and Planning A* 35, no. 8 (2003): 1389–403.

10 Walter Christaller, "How I Discovered the Theory of Central Places: A Report about the Origin of Central Places," in *Man, Space, and Concepts in Contemporary Human Geography*, ed. Paul Ward (New York: Oxford University Press, 1972), 601–10.

11 Gilles Deleuze and Félix Guattari, *A Thousand Plateaus: Capitalism and Schizophrenia*, trans. Brian Massumi (Minneapolis: University of Minnesota Press, 1987).

12 See "Real Time Rome," http://senseable.mit.edu/realtimerome/.

13 See Open Bike Share System, http://www.cphbikeshare.com/winners.aspx.

14 See car2go, http://www.car2go.com/.

15 Christopher Alexander, "The City Is Not a Tree," *Design* (London: Council of Industrial Design, no. 206, 1966).

The Future of Personal Urban Mobility
An Engineer's Perspective

Sven Beiker

Today's city traffic is often described in the following ways: too dirty, too loud, too congested, and too dangerous. There are simply too many cars taking up limited urban space, causing too many delays and too much frustration for residents. Scientifically speaking, transportation has three major problems: (1) vehicles are not optimized for city movement; (2) drivers are not efficiently operating their vehicles; and (3) urban mobility is overly dependent on personal vehicles. The solution to these problems is fairly straightforward, and it would make this essay rather short: Remove all automobiles from the city and offset the loss by developing more public transportation, bike paths and walkways. However ideal this solution may sound, it is not the most realistic approach. The following essay discusses a multifaceted solution that incorporates personal vehicles into urban transportation design. The automobile, after all, cannot be quickly dismissed. It is much more than a mere mode of transportation; it provides freedom, independence, and flexibility. This essay explores these attributes of automobiles, along with future directions and potential solutions for urban mobility.

If a personal vehicle is simply a means of getting to and from destinations, it would not be one of the biggest investments we make in our lives (second only to the home), an investment we use only 8 percent of the time (privately owned automobiles remain parked approximately 92 percent of the time).[1] To better understand this phenomenon, we can deconstruct the word *auto-mobile* into its two parts. The Greek prefix *auto* refers to the "self" or "one's own"; it can also mean "spontaneous." The word *mobile* refers to the ability "to move freely or easily." Taken together, the word *automobile* refers to a (luxury) device that enables drivers to determine their own trajectories in time and space.

Ease of movement may be a trait of modern, industrialized, or developed societies, but it has been present throughout human history. Mobility, especially *auto-mobility*, has been an important value for centuries. Thousands of years ago, the ability to move easily in a self-determined direction provided an important socioeconomic advantage, particularly during times of war. The problem today, however, is that we have replaced horses and oxen with sedans and sport utility vehicles. Moreover, we are using this automobile transportation for business *and* recreational purposes. As a result, personal transportation has become both a necessary commodity and a social entitlement. To worsen matters, there is little reflection on the adverse effects of widespread automobile transportation. For example, if we move our own 75 kilograms of human body weight (more or less) around in a device that weighs more than twenty times that much, and if we multiply this combined weight by the thousands of others with whom we share the road—creating congestion in our cities and beyond—what does it all add up to?

The Problem

The conventional automobile weighs approximately 1,500 kilograms, yet it is used to transport approximately 75 kilograms; this is the crux of the problem. By the numbers, the vehicle is mechanically and energetically inefficient, resulting in toxic exhaust gases, loud noises, and other pollution problems. Furthermore, the personal vehicle is used for the majority of mobility needs in many countries, resulting in street congestion, traffic jams, and gridlock. Interestingly enough, the *auto-*, or "spontaneous" and "self," aspect of our mobility contributes to unpredictable driving conditions, resulting in approximately 33,000 fatalities—along with other automobile-related accidents and injuries—in the United States every year. While vehicular traffic is congested, dirty, loud, and dangerous in general, these attributes are only exacerbated in dense urban areas.

Possible Solutions

To devise solutions for personal urban mobility, we must acknowledge the status quo:

- Automobiles cause numerous problems, especially in urban areas.
- A world without personal automobiles is unrealistic, as it would ignore or otherwise deny fundamental social values.
- Solutions for personal urban mobility are urgently needed; otherwise, we all lose.

As previously mentioned, the words *dirty, loud, congested,* and *dangerous* are often used to describe the problems of city traffic. Conversely, the words *electrification, automation, communication,* and *commoditization* are fitting words to describe potential solutions. Each of these words signifies a multifaceted field of inquiry pursued by academics, industry professionals, and public administrators. We will take a look at each of these fields and will discover that the problem-solution relationship in this case cannot be expressed in a neat 4x4 matrix. On the contrary, we must integrate all four fields to produce an efficient, sustainable, enjoyable, and safe urban mobility.

Electrification

Many people are talking about *electric, electrified,* or *plug-in* vehicles. Each is a type of vehicle that can improve urban driving efficiency. (By *urban,* I'm referring to relatively slow, short-distance, variable-speed driving.) The internal combustion engines of these vehicles, although sophisticated, are not very efficient at covering different mobility profiles. To be clear, these engines can move vehicles at almost any acceleration, speed, and distance (assuming they are powerful enough), but they are rather inflexible, in terms of the driving conditions and terrain they can accommodate. In other words, one can either have a very small engine best suited for city driving, or one can have a more powerful engine capable of pulling a two-thousand- kilogram boat trailer up a long hill without slowing down in traffic—but one cannot have both and maintain efficiency. In comparison, an electric motor can operate at different speeds with different loads; thus, it has great overall efficiency. Furthermore, an electric motor tends to be quieter than its gasoline—or diesel-powered— counterpart.

An electric motor *can* be cleaner, as well. To discuss this in all relevant detail, another essay or even book would be necessary. To summarize: When we consider the manufacturing of a vehicle (especially the battery of an electric vehicle), the generation of energy for propulsion (especially the electricity from nonrenewables), and the operation of the vehicle (especially moving around heavy batteries), we cannot easily claim that an electric vehicle is cleaner or even more sustainable than a conventional vehicle powered by a combustion engine.[2] While the overall efficiency and sustainability of an electric vehicle is difficult to compare with that of a conventional vehicle—and, in some cases, the results are not as favorable as one might think—other problems, such as so-called range anxiety, further complicate matters. As long as electric vehicles have been researched, produced, and operated, their range specifications, expectations, and concerns have been scrutinized. While the mantra for conventional vehicles is "no replacement for displacement," the mantra for electric vehicles might be "no replacement for capacity." (By *capacity*, I'm referring to the energy content of the battery in kilowatt-hours.) One might argue this is a necessary trade-off, as drivers cannot have it both ways. Vehicles can either be sustainable or independent, but not both. As previously mentioned, however, the prefix *auto* in the word *automobile* refers to the independence vehicles afford us. This independence is often the reason we purchase automobiles in the first place.

While electric vehicles may not be as sustainable and as flexible (in terms of mobility range) as we had hoped, there are solutions to these considerations, and these solutions are well suited for urban settings. For instance, electric vehicles might not need to carry large, heavy batteries if their existing batteries could charge while operating. The solution would involve a wireless transfer of electricity from the road surface to the vehicles. This would allow the vehicles to move freely (without cables) and would not deplete the batteries, as the energy for propulsion is sourced externally. Pilot programs are already underway. The infrastructure needed to support wireless power transfer would cost a couple million dollars per lane mile, which is not insignificant, but mobility is a luxury, and transportation infrastructure is always costly. Ultimately, this development would combine the best of both worlds—high efficiency and unlimited range—to yield cleaner, quieter, and spontaneous mobility.

Automation

The car does the driving in *autonomous*, *driverless*, or *self-driving* vehicles. One might enter the destination into the vehicle's navigation system, and the automobile will perform the steering by activating satellite navigation (to determine the vehicle's location), electronic mapping (to determine the route to the destination), and many different computer vision systems (to detect obstacles to avoid through electronic steering, braking, and accelerating). Today, a vehicle can automatically control velocity, following distance, and lane placement, but its preprogrammed system cannot always respond to unforeseen incidents, such as persons crossing the street, vehicles disobeying traffic rules, faded road signage, or inclement weather. Engineers hope to address all of these challenges, of course, but the urban setting will inevitably present other problems. While we can rule out many unexpected happenings on an interstate highway, the situation in a dense city is very different and much more complex. City officials may have to deploy certain systems, such as vehicles, infrastructure, and user communities, in limited and restricted ways to test driverless technology. For example, automated vehicles may only be able to initially shuttle shoppers between stores, cafés, and parking structures in designated areas at very slow speeds. Once safety standards are met, some of these restraints might be lifted, allowing automated vehicles to move at faster speeds within designated lanes, similar to bike lanes, of city streets. They also might be able to cover more ground by traveling to nearby hotels, train stations, or apartment complexes. Eventually, automated vehicles might be able to use major artery roads and drive at regular speeds alongside human driven vehicles.

These automated cars will inevitably make driving less demanding. One might then assume there will be more vehicles on the road, exacerbating the traffic problem. It is actually unclear if vehicle automation will lead to more congestion, as the computers on board these vehicles will allow for better traffic coordination. To understand this, one needs to realize that searching for parking accounts for approximately 30 percent of inner-city traffic. Furthermore, a good amount of urban land is dedicated to parking lots. If automobiles can serve as moving parts of a centrally controlled transportation system (as opposed to serving as individually owned and operated free agents), then fewer vehicles can accommodate the same number of passengers. Smartphone applications can dispatch automated vehicles; once these vehicles transport passengers to their destinations, they can move on to serve new passengers— eliminating the need for parking. Thus, the overall number of vehicles on the road might not increase. At the same time, the sensors and collision avoidance systems on board these vehicles may enable them to travel closer together, freeing up even more road space.

Although automated vehicles have the potential to make urban personal mobility safer and more efficient, much of this technology still needs to be researched, tested, and certified. In the end, automation just might be the key to combining the best of both worlds: the efficiency of public transportation and the flexibility of the personal automobile.

Communication

"Vehicle-to-vehicle communication," "vehicle infrastructure integration," or the "Internet of cars," are all phrases coined over the past decade to signify promising ways to increase safety and efficiency of road traffic. Some of us may ask, "Why is my phone so smart but my car so dumb?" While this thinking is understandable, it is actually incorrect. A vehicle—equipped with hundreds of sensors, tens of computers, and a varied assortment of communication networks—is incredibly knowledgeable. The automobile, however, is a very introverted object, meaning it keeps all information to itself; it doesn't share information with its peers or with back-end central servers that could monitor and manage traffic. While every home, office, store, and factory are connected to the Internet these days, there are a number of reasons why automobiles are not fully connected—yet.[3]

One challenge is to find a universal standard so all vehicles speak the same language, regardless of brand and age. In this case, drivers won't have to decode vehicle communication and risk the distraction that comes with multi-tasking (already an immense traffic safety problem). Furthermore, all of this communication will need to be wireless, which presents additional challenges regarding infrastructure, creating reliable connections, and safeguarding data and communication ports. We also need to consider who will pay for the communication to and from vehicles. Drivers may be willing to pay for entertainment and other information transfer over the network, but not necessarily for the transfer of safety updates.

If we can resolve all of the aforementioned problems, and if vehicles can communicate with each other and with a centralized control infrastructure, then certain applications, similar to the collision avoidance systems in aircrafts, can produce automatic stops at red lights, curve speed control, or activate hazard warning lights, for example. In cities, pedestrians and cyclists can wear transponders to send warnings to approaching vehicles. Centralized traffic management can control the speed of vehicles in certain city sectors to prevent or mitigate congestion. While vehicle automation will require a substantial amount of regulatory work and infrastructure implementation, it is relatively safe to assume that a significant push in this direction will occur over the next ten years. The urban setting is most conducive to this development, as the wireless communication infrastructure is already in place (and sometimes overloaded, which needs to be considered). Regardless, we can assume that communication between vehicles and with centrally controlled infrastructure will make traffic safer and more efficient. This is the future of personal urban mobility: a connected vehicle that, in theory, will deliver the best of both worlds—real-time entertainment for the driver and safety for everyone.

Commoditization

Carsharing, de-motorization, and *car-free* seem to describe a trend suggesting the end of car ownership, or "worship," as we know it. Our relationships with our vehicles are undoubtedly changing, but we need to consider the demographics of personal mobility. Young people are obtaining their driving licenses later in life, according to recent research. These young people, who seem to prefer the Internet over the automobile, are gravitating more toward carsharing than ownership. Alternatively, many elderly people are keeping active lifestyles well into their eighties, for which the personal vehicle is a travel requirement.

The meaning and message of vehicle ownership has also changed. From "I can afford it" (the luxury choice) to "I care, therefore I sacrifice" (the sustainable choice) to "I can do without, and it is actually very liberating" (the non-ownership choice), automobiles are now used to make personal statements. Forgoing ownership altogether is more prevalent in urban areas, where cars are more often defined by their inconveniences (such as scarce parking, congested streets, and vandalism) and alternative mobility options are more prevalent. A rejection of the personally owned vehicle, however, is not necessarily a rejection of the automobile in general. This explains the recent boom in carsharing, which suggests some of us still want access to auto-mobility without the trouble of ownership.

The need for an alternative to vehicle ownership is more prevalent in urban areas where population density and mobility demand per area are higher. In an urban setting, it is easier to maintain a carsharing system with a thousand diverse vehicles in different locations serving a population of twenty thousand residents per square mile (San Francisco) than it is to maintain one vehicle in a single location serving a rural or suburban population of twenty residents per square mile (Shasta County, California). In terms of congestion, carsharing reduces the number of vehicles meeting the mobility needs of the city. As a result, fewer vehicles are parked in the streets, freeing up space for other personal mobility options, such as biking or walking. As these mobility modes become more convenient and accessible, more residents might consider them viable vehicle alternatives; increased engagement with these alternatives could free up even more space. Beyond urban areas, however, people may still choose owning a vehicle over renting.

With this split situation, the keyword *commoditization* is a bit misleading, as it does not represent a universal trend (which is the case with *electrification, automation,* or *communication*). While personal mobility is moving in the general direction of commoditization, it is not safe to assume all of us will reject ownership in the future. After all, the word *mobile* in *automobile* refers to the ability "to move freely and easily," so renting a car by the hour contradicts our basic understanding of the vehicle. One must schedule a rental in advance. Furthermore, one must pick up and return the rental at designated times and locations. The entire process takes the spontaneity out of the automobile. On the other hand, renting might give one access to a wider variety of vehicles than ownership, and the location of a rental vehicle might be more convenient than that of a parking spot. In these ways, one might actually gain more flexibility, freedom, and ease through sharing or renting a car. Moreover, the integration of scheduling, dispatch, or on-demand systems through smartphone applications has the potential to enable even greater spontaneity and ease.

As discussed, the commoditization of personal urban mobility can lead to less congestion and noise, and more efficiency and safety, on city roads. In these ways, it can combine the best of both worlds: the convenience of personal mobility without the hassle of owning and maintaining a vehicle.

Integration

Thus far, we have discussed how automobile electrification, automation, communication, and commoditization can improve personal urban mobility in distinct ways. I argue that an integrated approach, an approach combining all four fields of inquiry, can further improve efficiency, sustainability, and safety in urban mobility.

The integration of communication and automation will enable vehicles to avoid collisions and other accidents. Traffic- and weather-related updates can trigger automated responses within vehicles. Moreover, vehicles will be able to share information (such as location, velocity, and trajectory) with each other. This is important, as this shared firsthand information from vehicular sources will be more accurate than secondhand information obtained from onboard sensors.

Automation and electrification inevitably complement each other. If automated driving will assist with accident avoidance, then passive safety components can be designed much lighter. A lighter vehicle will require less energy for propulsion, making the vehicle more efficient. The battery capacity will then offer more driving range.

The integration of communication and commoditization already make it possible to conveniently reserve a shared vehicle using a smartphone application or to instantaneously rent and pay for a vehicle via wireless communication, such as with Lyft, Uber, carma, RelayRides, or other on-demand ridesharing. Taking this connected lifestyle further, one can imagine matching the travel plans of different commuters via social networking platforms for the purpose of coordinating ridesharing opportunities based on travel needs, personal interests, and vehicle availability. For example, the Los Angeles_REDCAR prototype presented at the Mobility & the City Colloquium sponsored by the AIA San Francisco in 2010.

The ultimate vision for personal urban mobility—the electrified, automated, connected, and shared vehicle—would integrate all four fields of interest previously discussed. Such a vehicle would be available on demand via smartphone. It would automatically proceed to a user's location. It would then transport the user along an optimized, energy-conserving route. Once the destination is reached, it would proceed to the next user—or it might return to a charging station to replenish its energy storage. Meanwhile, the user (or, in this case, the passenger) would enjoy a relaxed commute in a quiet, efficient, and safe vehicle. If the user must travel beyond the urban area, where the infrastructure for wireless charging, automated driving, and online control is not readily available, then the user could opt to take control of the vehicle and operate on battery power. The infrastructure needed to deploy this concept might be complicated and costly, but the large number of potential users and improved driving conditions in urban settings could justify the effort.

Public Transportation

As discussed, the electrification, automation, communication, and commoditization of the automobile has great potential to substantially improve personal urban mobility. This, however, is only one half of the overall solution. Public transportation is also an extremely efficient and safe mobility solution. It should not, however, simply coexist or compete with automobiles. The two mobility options need to be integrated. While buses and trains are the best options for transporting large groups of commuters to destinations along fixed routes, automobiles are better suited for commuters who need to access out-of-the-way locations, particularly in their own time. Fortunately, all of the integrated personal mobility solutions mentioned above can extend to include public transportation. For instance, the integration of automobile communication and commoditization can enable users to access and coordinate with bus and train travel schedules. This integration can be seamless so that efficiency, sustainability, and movement are optimized for the benefit of the individual, society, and environment.

Conclusion

Personal urban mobility faces many challenges regarding efficiency, sustainability, and safety. Moreover, personal automobiles provide drivers with freedom and ease, and these highly regarded values cannot be easily ignored. Integrated solutions involving electrification, automation, communication, and commoditization could, however, address some of the problems presented by personal automobiles in the urban context. They could help improve traffic and free up space for alternative personal mobility modes, such as walking or biking. As discussed, they could yield extremely efficient, safe, and convenient ways to move around. While much more research and regulation is necessary to realize such integration, initial steps are already underway. Ultimately the electrified, automated, connected, and shared urban mobility concept of the future will have to be part of an even larger network: a fully integrated system of public transportation and personal mobility

Notes

1   See Ruth Eckdish Knack, "Pay as You Park: UCLA Professor Donald Shoup Inspires a Passion for Parking," Planning: American Planning Association (May 2005), http://shoup.bol.ucla.edu/PayAsYouPark.htm. Also see Donald Shoup, "Cashing Out Employer-Paid Parking," http://shoup.bol.ucla.edu /EvaluatingCashOut.pdf (accessed May 15, 2016).
2   At present, the limitations for electric vehicle batteries include excessive weight, limited life span, and expense—usually around $12,000 to $15,000, or one-third the price of the vehicle, among other factors.
3   As of 2016, vehicle-to-vehicle (V2V) communication is in limited use. The State of California has plans to legalize car-to-infrastructure (C2I) communication in 2017. Other states are expected to follow.

Part III

Hard Systems

In this final section, we turn our attention to hard systems, synthesizing the findings from the previous sections by considering the significance of new mobility strategies on urban form. The essays identify specific issues in urban studies that concern the relationship between changing social dynamics, evolving technologies, and the built environment. Some of the contributions are speculative and future oriented; others are written by practitioners based on empirical research. Together, the essays in hard systems explore the catalytic effects of networked technologies on the city, investigate future implications, and extend the discussion at a global-metropolitan scale.

The Automobile, the City, and the New Urban Mobilities

Frederic Stout

The very act of thinking about the "new urban mobilities"—and especially the connections between the emerging intelligent technologies of transportation and the larger issues of renewable energy development, sustainability, climate change, and the exercise of basic urban functions—demands a new level of understanding, both practical and ideological, of how urban communities progress over time and how those processes in turn contribute to ongoing personal, social, political, and cultural transformations. Keeping those human concerns primary in discussions of policy and infrastructure is exactly what Lewis Mumford meant when he insisted to an audience of urban planners in 1937 that the principal responsibility of their profession must always be to nurture, not frustrate, what he called the "urban drama": the day-to-day life of urban individuals, families, and communities as they go about the diurnal tasks of living, working, raising families, and governing themselves.[1]

From the earliest times and increasingly, mobility has been an important urban value, no more so than in the twentieth century when the affordable personal automobile became common. With astonishing rapidity, the automobile replaced horses with horseless carriages, competed with trolleys and horse-drawn omnibuses for the provision of mass transit, and made suburbs so accessible to urban centers that a fundamentally new kind of city—the vast, interconnected metropolitan region—came into existence as the dominant paradigm of human settlement. It seems fitting, therefore, that an examination of the history of the automobile's impact on cities in the twentieth century would be a convenient entryway into an understanding of the new forms of urban mobility that will characterize the twenty-first. Today, there is a clear movement away from autos in favor of walking, cycling, and an intensified commitment to mass transportation solutions to the problems of congestion and pollution. At the same time, both a global economy and a global urban network are emerging, digital communication dominates flows of information, millions of rural in-migrants flow into the burgeoning megacities of Asia and Latin America, and in the West a new "creative class" called the "millennial generation"—those born in the 1980s and 1990s and now coming of age in the 2000s—stands ready to inherit the global-urban Earth with all its problems and all its promises. Who will not agree that we are at an important transition point leading to a new urban paradigm?

The conversation about current and emergent urban mobilities will inevitably—and perhaps justifiably—be dominated by specialists in transportation technology, by urban transportation planners, and by public policy experts. What an urban studies generalist can contribute is an interdisciplinary perspective on the larger contexts that surround and encompass the machines, the plans, and the policies. And if looking at the past impact of the private automobile on cities of the twentieth century is a useful way of approaching the issue of what the future impacts of new forms of urban mobility might be, we will need to consider the issues along three dimensions of analysis:

1. The effects of mobility technologies on the essential functions of urban social life—the *citadel* functions of law and governance, the *market* functions of economic production and commerce, and the *community* functions of individuals, families, neighborhoods, and local cultures;
2. The influence of urban globalization on the mobility aspirations of two key constituencies who will be the consumers of the policies and technologies of the future—the emerging urban middle class in the formerly underdeveloped regions of the world and the new millennial generation in the developed world;
3. The ways in which the urbanization process itself, along with appropriate urban design and development policies in both the public and private spheres, can—and likely will, over time—respond to many of the challenges posed by the issues of urban sustainability, population growth, and social equity.

This last point is especially important. The conversation about urban mobilities today is driven not just by exciting new developments in transportation technologies, nor even by overarching concerns about climate change and sustainability, but by the astonishing rapidity with which the demographics of urbanization have transformed, and continue to transform, human history.

For the past two hundred years, the percentage of the human population that may be categorized as urban has skyrocketed: the United Kingdom reached the milestone of 50 percent urbanization sometime in the mid-nineteenth century, the United States reached that point by 1920, and the planet as a whole became majority-urban sometime in 2009. And the best current projections suggest that the world may become 70 percent or even 80 percent urban by the end of present century.[2] Absent these facts, speculations about new urban mobilities would be of limited interest or relevance. Surprisingly, however, there is some reason to believe that the current urbanization trends themselves—along with wise policies and sensible designs—will help to solve many of our current economic, social, and environmental challenges. It is in this larger context that reassessing the historical relationship between the automobile and the city—as case study—will hopefully enlarge our understanding of the importance of all forms of urban mobility and help us formulate the necessary wise policies and sensible designs that the urban future demands.

Rethinking the Common Wisdom about the Automobile and the City

In recent years the relationship between the automobile and the city has become highly problematical. The common wisdom seems to be that automobiles were one of those technological mistakes of modernism that have had an overwhelmingly negative effect on the course of human development. According to this view, cars have been responsible for untold deaths from accidents and for chronic diseases caused or exacerbated by tailpipe exhaust. Worse, the widespread adoption of the private automobile is said to have destroyed sensible, efficient transit systems—the Los Angeles Red Line, for example—and created an auto-centric civilization characterized by unbearable congestion in the central cities and life-wasting social anomie in the sprawling suburbs. In support of this argument, critics regularly rehearse the accusatory narrative of a scandalous "transportation conspiracy"—that General Motors, Firestone Tire, and Standard Oil secretly bought up all the privately owned electric trolley lines in major American cities and converted them to diesel bus systems to maximize their private profits by criminally subverting the common good. This story was first advanced in a 1974 report to the U.S. Senate Judiciary Committee by Bradford Snell,[3] a government antitrust attorney, and gained further credence by an article in *Harper's Magazine* in which journalist Jonathan Kwitny charged,

"Mass transit didn't just die, it was murdered."[4] The story resurfaced in 1988 as the plot line of the popular cartoon-noir movie *Who Framed Roger Rabbit?* and, in 1996, in the documentary *Taken for a Ride*, which was shown on the American Public Broadcasting Service (PBS). And not surprisingly, the issue still lives on a matter of heated debate on the Internet to this very day.

A review of the facts tends to deflate the argument a bit. General Motors did indeed aggressively market its buses as an alternative to electric trolleys nationwide during the 1920s and 1930s. The Los Angeles Red Line was not one of the systems they purchased, but GM was prosecuted in 1947 under the 1890 Sherman Antitrust Act for attempting to monopolize urban transportation nationwide and for illegally restricting the purchase of new buses by the systems it owned to GM products. Although the company was found not guilty of the primary charge of conspiring to monopolize transportation, it was found guilty of the lesser charge of buying their own buses, for which it was fined a grand total of $5,000. It is perfectly understandable that many Americans at the time may have thought the new steel and glass buses were much cleaner and more modern than the old trolleys, and plausible arguments were advanced that diesel buses, not being on fixed tracks, were a much more flexible and adaptable system for growing cities than the electric trolleys with their overhead wires. Within academia and the larger world of intellectual discourse, however, the corporate criminality charge and even more extreme arguments were and still are regularly advanced that automobiles, buses, and the corporations that make them have destroyed the very fabric of our urban civilization—single-handedly creating poverty, social class divisions, racism, ill health, premature death, and almost certain ecological collapse in the near future.[5]

Of course, it is undoubtedly true that automobile accidents do account for some fifty thousand accidental deaths yearly in the United States alone. Gridlock caused by automobile commuting and center-city traffic congestion have indeed become significant time wasters and sources of pollution. And, increasingly, cars are seen as the centerpiece of a carbon-based economy that contributes to climate change and that promoters of sustainable urban development hope to replace with alternative sources of energy and new approaches to planning that valorize urban densities, mass transit, and walking-city values over mindless suburban sprawl and robotic automobile dependency. This is why more and more cities and regional planning agencies are adopting transit-first and bicycle-friendly policies. But the implementation of these policies has unfortunately sometimes led to situations where many drivers feel that they have become victims of a virtual "war against the automobile." This sense of frustration and dissatisfaction was nicely expressed in a recent letter to the editor of the *San Francisco Chronicle*: "I am very confused. To be green, the city has requested that residents should . . . use Muni [the local bus and trolley system], bike, walk or take a taxi. Bike lanes have taken away parking places. Now car shares will be given preferred special slots, taking away another 900 spaces. [But] Muni service is often unreliable, scofflaw bikers are given carte blanche, taxis are a rare commodity and car-share space is exclusive. These policies force drivers to pollute . . . . How green is that?" (July 25, 2013). With popular anger running high among the motoring citizenry, perhaps it may well be time to call a truce in this "war" and attempt to achieve a more balanced understanding of the present and future role of cars, trucks, and buses in the urban environment worldwide.

Urban mobility by way of personal automobiles—once cars stopped being an extravagant toy of the super rich and became an essential tool for all but the very poor—accounted for an extraordinary advance in the ability of city dwellers of the advanced industrial nations to navigate their own immediate neighborhoods, to access all corners of their metropolitan regions, and to engage in complex manufacturing and commercial activities leading to unprecedented and widespread prosperity.[6] Automobiles did indeed eliminate some of the social and recreational aspects of city streets, but that in turn encouraged the construction of urban parks and playgrounds.[7] The interstate highway system in the United States—inspired by the *autostrade* and *Autobahnen* of Europe—may have cost billions of dollars in public outlays, but it led to a new stage of economic integration and opened up the entire North American continent to the national distribution of commodities and manufactured goods by trucks and to middle-class family vacations in station wagons and SUVs.[8] The personal mobility provided by automobiles played an important and liberating role for women and youth as both the "flappers" of the 1920s and the young baby boomers of the 1960s used cars to escape the confines of patriarchal domesticity.[9] Trucks, tractors, and automobiles transformed agriculture and eliminated much of the isolation of rural life. And in the urban centers themselves, city taxicabs became an accessible form of spontaneous, unscheduled transportation for millions and provided an entry-level occupation for thousands of immigrants and otherwise unemployed workers.[10]

Today, a combination of social and technological advances are making cars safer, cleaner, more energy-efficient, and more accessible than ever before. And at the same time, an emerging global economy is spreading middle-class aspirations, and the promise of middle-class comforts, to tens of millions of new urbanites in the burgeoning megacities and urban regions of Asia and Latin America. All reliable projections indicate that the foreseeable future will require more cars—along with more walking, biking, and mass transit options—not fewer.

In the end, an intelligent reassessment of the relationship between the automobile and the city must be based on two fundamental propositions: first, that many of the perceived shortcomings of the automobile as a form of urban transportation are accurate and need to be seriously addressed; but second, that the automobile is nonetheless likely to be around for some time—not any longer as the single dominant element of mobility but certainly as one useful part of the multimodal transportation mix of the urban future. Much of the common wisdom today tells us that the automobile became in the twentieth century humanity's technological master. The challenge is to look beyond that critique, much of it exaggerated, and again make the automobile—indeed all forms of urban mobility—humanity's servant.

From Auto-Utopia to Auto-Dystopia

Historically, the automobile was one of a handful of technical inventions that together had a transformational effect on the modern industrial city. Electric lights opened up the night to both work and play. The telephone expanded the range of communication both within and between major urban centers. The elevator dramatically increased urban densities and created efficient, high-rise downtowns. And in the twentieth century, the automobile helped to bring unprecedented mobility, prosperity, and suburban comfort to millions. The automobile opened entire metropolitan regions—not just those areas served by mass transit lines—to commercial and residential development by the middle class.[11] In addition, cars became deeply imbedded in the popular culture as a symbol of freedom and personal identity.[12] And especially with the introduction of Henry Ford's "Universal Car"—the Model-T—manufacturing, maintaining, and fueling cars and trucks became the driving forces behind an enormously successful consumer-based industrial economy. Indeed, "Fordism"—

the practice of mass-producing inexpensive, well-built products while paying the workers living-wage salaries that permitted them to aspire to middle-class status—became a norm in modern industrial practice worldwide and was even admired and envied by Lenin's economic planners in the Soviet Union and helped to inspire Hitler's Volkswagen project in Germany.[13]

Almost from the first, however, the relationship between the automobile and the modern city has been, to say the least, uncomfortable. Whether because of traffic and congestion, or public safety, or air pollution, or suburban-sprawl threats to sustainability, the private automobile is frequently seen as the enemy of efficient economic development, public amenity, and responsible governance. Increasingly, cities are at pains to restrict automobile use in favor of bicycling, walking, or public transit options; parking has been made more expensive and less available as a matter of policy; and some of the more visionary planning theorists propose transforming city streets into auto-free pedestrian malls and whole cities into auto-free utopias.[14] In this context, it is instructive to review the role that mobility played in earlier utopian urban planning proposals of the modern era and note how automobility helped to create what many regarded as a utopia of prosperity, independence, and spatial freedom in the first half of the twentieth century . . . and how auto-utopia began to be perceived by many as an auto-dystopia during the second half.

The earliest of the several urban utopias that actually influenced the direction of modern urban planning practice—Ebenezer Howard's Garden Cities of 1898 and Arturo Soria y Mata's Ciudad Lineal of approximately 1892—were, of course, proposed before the widespread popularity of the automobile. Nevertheless, both of those late nineteenth-century visions emphasized technologies of mobility as integral features of the urban plan: railways and canals in Howard's case, a potentially endless trolley line in Soria's. Later, the two most influential urban utopias of the mid-twentieth-century era—Le Corbusier's techno-elite skyscraper cities of the 1920s and 1930s (one of which was funded by the Voisin Motorcar Company) and Frank Lloyd Wright's radically decentralized Broadacre City proposal of 1935—relied heavily on privately owned automobiles as the basic form of transportation.[15] The influence of the two starkly contrasting visions—Corbusier's glorifying the central city, Wright's emphasizing rural values—were intended to lead to very different results. But as history actually unfolded, cities in Europe and America adopted both mass transit solutions (buses, subways, and trolleys) and automobiles (private cars and taxis) to satisfy their complex urban transportation needs. In Europe, transit systems like the London Underground or the Paris Metro led the way. In the United States, automobiles predominated even in dense cities like New York and Chicago. Indeed, if "mass transit" means moving masses of people, then in America the automobile became the most popular and most successful form of mass transportation. To this day, all forms of scheduled, fixed-route mass transit—trolleys or buses—account for less that 7 percent of American vehicle miles traveled.[16]

Simply put, the automobile revolutionized America and the world—profoundly affecting the house and family, the city and suburb, and the very essence of the modern metropolitan way of life. In center cities worldwide, the high-rise apartment, the taxi, and the subway or bus line became almost essential elements of urban life. Elsewhere, particularly in suburbia, the detached home and the private car became a social norm deeply imbedded in the larger culture. Some have argued that it was the 1939 New York World's Fair and the "Futurama" exhibit that established the pinnacle of auto-utopian optimism.[17] Others favor the Detroit-style chrome-and-fins auto-fantasies of the 1950s for that distinction.[18] But the spirit of the historical moment was perhaps best captured in the carefully considered assessment offered by John B. Rae in his 1971 study, *The Road and the Car in American Life*. The automobile, Rae wrote, was "an instrument of social revolution" that "can and does provide mass transportation for people and bulk transportation for goods; if these were its sole functions, it would be an invaluable supplement to other forms of transportation. But these are the lesser part of what the motor vehicle has to contribute. The major part is that it offers individual, personal, flexible mobility as nothing before it has ever done and as nothing else now available now can do."[19]

Rae's positive assessment did not go unchallenged for long. The auto-utopia visions of the early twentieth century may have been glowing, but soon there developed a very contrary vision: the automobile as parasite and the auto-centric city as a social and environmental catastrophe. Questions of safety and tailpipe exhaust pollution played a part in the perceptual change, but only a part. Many point to the publication of *Unsafe at Any Speed* by Ralph Nader in 1965 as the turning point from auto-utopia to auto-dystopia, but seat belts and airbags actually solved many of the safety problems associated with cars in relatively short order. Similarly, cleaner fuel formulations and catalytic converters addressed pollution problems with great success beginning in the 1970s.

The larger, deeper cause of the changed perception of the automobile involved the conceptual history of suburbia and the suburban way of life—what Robert Fishman called the "Bourgeois Utopia."[20] In the auto-utopia phase of the relationship between the automobile and the city, a new, cleaner, more commodious metropolitan region comprising gleaming, high-rise downtowns and comfortable, leafy suburbs promised the elimination of slums and a better life for all. In the auto-dystopia phase, however, suburbia became a kind of social prison based on inequality and fear of the lower classes, mired in wasteful, unsustainable extravagance on the one hand and social irresponsibility on the other.

Clearly, the intellectuals' distaste for the automobile was closely tied to the automobile's role in fostering the development of suburbs at the expense of the inner city. Many popular books and respected academic studies have blamed automobiles for formless urban sprawl, social anomie, and the decline of community and civic engagement. In *The City in History*, Lewis Mumford called places like Los Angeles "anti-cities" because of their subservience to the automobile,[21] and the very titles of other books on suburbia capture the general tone of much of the commentary: *The Crack in the Picture Window* (1956), *The Split-Level Trap* (1961), *Bomb the Suburbs* (2001), *Bourgeois Nightmares* (2005), and even *Sprawl Kills* (2005)! In addition, as globalized urbanization in the form of the rapid emergence of new megacities in formerly underdeveloped regions of the world becomes the new focus of urban thinking, many environmental critics of the automobile-suburbia nexus are alarmed by the prospect of a growing demand for cars and suburban housing by millions of new middle-class consumers in Asia.[22]

While Mumford decried as "obsolete" those modern cities built solely "for the convenience of the private motor car,"[23] other critics, especially environmentalists, turned up the rhetorical heat. In 1975, Ernest Callenbach published the popular utopian novel *Ecotopia* in which the states of the Pacific Northwest secede from the Union and virtually abolish the private automobile . . . except, oddly, in the African American communities! In 1993, radical social critic James Howard Kunstler published a stinging critique of modern suburbia, *The Geography of Nowhere*[24] and titled his chapter on the automobile "The Evil Empire." Jane Holtz Kay subtitled *Asphalt Nation*[25] "How the Automobile Took Over America and How We Can Take It Back." And *The Automobile and the Environment*, a book for schoolchildren, assured its readers, "Making and using cars may be one of humankind's most polluting activities."[26] Thus, a widespread anti-automobile consensus was constructed in the public mind and laid the groundwork for urban transportation planners to escalate initially benign "transit first" policies into a planners' crusade to eliminate, as rapidly as possible, automobile dominance in the urban mobility network.

Now, however, as new mobility technologies and a new kind of urban world emerge, some may wonder if the planners' crusade was, if not misguided, at least short-sighted.

As Joseph Interrante has observed, the automobile was "an historically specific form of transportation, one appropriate to a particular stage in capitalist development . . . that is, the corporate development of new markets to provide new goods and services to an enlarged buying public."[27] To paraphrase Interrante, auto-suburbia may have been a historically specific form in the development of urban settlement patterns, one that was quite appropriate to its historical moment and that provided important benefits to humanity at a time when city-versus-country perceptions were rapidly giving way to more integrated, rural-urban middle-landscape ways of life. And as if to further emphasize their common commitment to mobility as a modern urban value, both Le Corbusier's high-rise central-city vision and Frank Lloyd Wright's decentralized Broadacre featured not only futuristic superhighways for speeding cars but another form of urban mobility as well: aviation. Le Corbusier inserted an actual airfield into the very center of his Contemporary City skyscrapers; Wright envisioned oddly shaped helicopters buzzing about in the skies above Broadacre.

The sources of this integrated, metropolitan-scale spatial pattern of urban settlement, made accessible by automobility, go even deeper than the twentieth-century visions of urban mobility technologies simultaneously creating center-city densities and suburban spatial breadth. The real source lies in what can almost be called a profound longing for the integration of urban and rural values in the intellectual life of the nineteenth century, a time when urbanization—what Frederick Law Olmsted called the inevitable "townward drift"[28]—was rapidly transforming the world. Ebenezer Howard, of course, based his entire Garden City vision on the idea of three "magnets"—the country magnet, the city magnet, and a city-country magnet that would combine the best features of both.[29] But the idea had been percolating even earlier. In 1893, a radical populist from Kansas, Henry Olerich, published a visionary tract entitled *A City-less and Country-less World*. A year later, in *A Traveler from Altruria* by William Dean Howells, a wise man from the utopian future explains, "Why, you know, we have neither city nor country in your sense, and so we are neither so isolated nor so crowded together."[30] Both Olerich and Howells, of course, may have been responding to the famous formulations of Marx and Engels in *The Manifesto of the Communist Party* of 1848—that the bourgeoisie had "created enormous cities" that "rescued a considerable part of the population from the idiocy of rural life" and that the proletariat, in their turn, would carry out a "gradual abolition of the distinction between town and country, by a more equable distribution of the population."[31] But even before Marx and Engels, the deep intellectual desire for what would eventually manifest itself as modern suburbia was a feature of intellectual life, at least in America. In 1844, Ralph Waldo Emerson confided to his journal: "I wish to have rural strength and religion for my children, and I wish city facility and polish. I find with chagrin that I cannot have both."[32] And even earlier, Thomas Jefferson had proposed a checkerboard plan for future city development, one that would be rigidly and regularly divided fifty-fifty between built space and open space.[33]

Thus, if the desire for suburbia—even sprawling auto-suburbia—can be understood not as a tragic mistake but merely as an artifact of a particular moment in the urban history of the twentieth century and the fulfillment of a deeply held desire of a society transitioning from rural to urban, then the conceptual groundwork is laid for understanding the new social and spatial accommodations that are likely to be developed as new urban patterns, with new kinds of mobility options, emerge in an age experiencing its own transitional moment—the movement from cities imbedded within a framework of modern nationalism to the new "metageography" of urban globalization.[34]

Mobility Technologies and Urban Globalization

Despite the widespread popularity of automobile-as-dystopia thinking today, automobiles are still a major form of personal transportation, suburbs continue to attract many young families, and *Car Talk* remains a very popular show on National Public Radio. Driving is still regarded by many as fun, and automobile manufacture and maintenance remain mainstays of our national/international economy. Indeed, one measure of the staying power to the auto economy is that although former GM chairman Charles Wilson, President Eisenhower's secretary of defense in the 1950s, was widely derided for declaring, "What is good for General Motors in good for America," President Obama, sixty years later, made rescuing GM and the rest of the American auto industry an urgent priority of his economic recovery program. And although the rising global demand for cars remains a cause for real environmental concern, that rising demand is increasingly seen as a legitimate, indeed irresistible, aspiration of the newly emerging global middle class. In India and China, this means a rapid expansion of automobile sales as economies once mired in poverty become at least marginally middle class, sometimes even affluent.[35]

In her pioneering work on global cities, Saskia Sassen has noted that urban globalization has created enormous wealth but that the wealth is very unevenly distributed with huge gaps between the super-rich and the super-poor.[36] This is a view that is widely shared, especially since the publication of *The Challenge of Slums: Global Report on Human Settlements 2003* by the United Nations Human Settlements Programme (UN-HABITAT), with its sobering findings that nearly one-third of the world's urban population live in slums and that fully one-half subsist on less than US$2 per day.[37] What this view misses, of course, is that rural village poverty may even be worse and that millions of peasants stream into the cities of the developing world in search of a better life. The rich and powerful firms that have established operations in the global cities need service workers of all kinds, and a low-level service job, however ill-paying, may often be the first step toward middle-class status for millions of urban in-migrants worldwide. For such new city residents, mobility is an immediate necessity upon arrival and one that continues as incomes slowly increase and as small-scale businesses grow. For many, this translates, at some point, into the desire to own an automobile or small truck.

Consider the production figures. In 2010, there were an estimated 40 million passenger vehicles in use in India, and the local automotive industry was producing some 3.7 million units per year.[38] In China, now the world's largest producer of automobiles, more than 18 million cars, buses, vans, and trucks were produced in 2010. There are currently more than 62 million vehicles already on the road in China, and that number is expected to increase tenfold by 2030 according to a McKinsey & Company report.[39] These are explosive levels of growth, and the statistics speak to both the success of the economic reforms of Deng Xiaoping in the 1980s and 1990s and to the mobility aspirations of millions of Chinese, many of whom have experienced unprecedented economic success over a relatively short period of time despite strong traditional and policy impediments to upward mobility.[40]

In the already advanced economies of Europe and North America, on the other hand, young members of the millennial generation seem to be taking a very different path. As one Stanford student recently put it, "We will be the first generation in automotive history to drive less than our parents. Our issues with cars and with urban mobility in general will be different from the past." And as another commented, "At the end of the 20th century, sprawling suburban environments only accessible by automobiles dominated the metropolitan region. This is the environment inherited by the millennial generation; this is the environment Millennials do not want."[41]

The literature on the millennial generation is still developing. Much of what exists is popular, anecdotal, and surprisingly political, with both free-market libertarians and Obama-era social liberals claiming the millennials as their own.[42] To date, much of the best information comes from the Pew Research Center and its series of reports exploring the new generation's behaviors, values, and opinions.[43] On the one hand, the millennials are called "confident, self-expressive, liberal, upbeat and open to change"—the very picture of what Richard Florida calls "the Creative Class."[44] But the whole picture is not so rosy. Good full-time jobs are scarce in the wake of the recent economic downturn, underemployment is rampant, and more than a third of the entire generation have had to move back in with their parents. Many recent graduates are burdened with heavy college debt, in some cases as much as $40,000 to $50,000. And the tendency to share apartments—and to spend more of their income on cellphone service than on private cars—seems to be driven as much by hard economic necessity as by the desire to live frugally and sustainably. Their hope is not to own a car but merely to have access to one, when one is necessary, through some form of carsharing or short-term rental. And it often seems that their vision of the good life is not to settle into a comfortable suburb but to move to a bustling city where rents may be high and streets congested, but neighborhoods are vibrant, Wi-Fi is available in the nearest coffee shop, and prospects of a better future are at least possible, even in a down economy.

The values and aspirations of these two emerging mobility constituencies— the new urban middle class in the megacities of the developing world and the creative-class millennials in the West—follow very different paths indeed, suggesting a kind of historical irony at play. And yet in both the advanced industrial world and in the emerging nations, the social and cultural effects of automobility seem to have increased apace with the new technologies of communication and online social interaction, developing the possibility of new kinds of "communities of mobility" to replace the locationally centered cultures of the past. As it happens, major social and technological developments are just emerging or already in place that will almost certainly affect urban automobile use worldwide. New small "city cars" like the ones imagined by the late William J. Mitchell in *Reinventing the Automobile*; electric cars, hybrids, and cars powered by natural gas or hydrogen fuel cells; self-driving "autonomous cars" that can be summoned by cell phone and that communicate with each another; both commercial and informal carsharing services that disjoin the convenience of car use from the burden of car ownership—all these innovations are rapidly emerging as options for urban automobility at precisely the same time that digital telecommunications are revolutionizing the way urban dwellers interact, recreate, and conduct business.

Today, the role of digital communications is particularly important to urbanists—whether historians, planners, or policy specialists. As cellphones and tablets reduce the need for the personalized physical mobility provided in the past by automobiles and transit in order to engage in some common social and economic activities, new forms of "virtual community" not tied to geography in the traditional sense have emerged to take their place. Manuel Castells has famously called this the distinction between the electronic "space of flows" and the more traditional, physical "space of places."[45] This new dual urban reality is nothing less than a revolutionary development in the history of humanity, but it is one that members of the new millennial generation, having grown up with computers, take for granted. They navigate the digital flows and the physical places—and code-switch between the two—with ease. Indeed, the need for the "personal and flexible" type of mobility that Rae identified as the automobile's great gift to urban civilization in the twentieth century may be greater than ever before, but now that need for mobility may be satisfied by other technologies. The city of the future that is emerging within the contexts of globalism—with instant digital access to every part of the earth and economically connected megacities that are actually vast urbanized regions organized into a new global "network of cities"[46]—will require a totally new range of mobility options. Cyber-cities will never completely replace traditional physical urban space, but many citadel functions, market functions, even community functions, are already being carried out through informational websites, Internet shopping, and social media. Cars, taxis, transit systems, walking, cycling, as well as the handheld mobile devices—all will be among the mobility options of the future and will very likely interact in ways yet to be imagined.

Planning the Future of Urban Mobilities in a Globally Urbanizing World

In this new historical moment, urban planning theory and practice need to adapt to the changing conditions of urban life. In a world where the far-flung ring of what were once bedroom suburbs have been transformed into what journalist Joel Garreau calls "Edge City"[47] and historian Robert Fishman calls "technoburbia," the daily commute has been radically reorganized, and the urban-suburban dichotomy has been replaced by a more seamless spatial pattern of metropolitan interconnections.[48] Now more than ever, new conceptual tools need to be developed to reimagine not only the modalities of transportation but, indeed, the very purpose of urban mobility itself.

Faced with these new realities, many see the New Urbanism and the Smart Growth movements as useful ways to plan for future urban growth. These new planning traditions make reducing our reliance on the private automobile— moving away from "the monoculture of the automobile" and the legacy of poor twentieth-century planning that made the automobile the *only* viable transportation option available to millions of urban and suburban residents—one of their central goals.[49] What Smart Growth and the New Urbanism propose is that future urban development, especially in the suburbs, be in the form of denser, multistory, pedestrian-friendly communities built around transit (usually light-rail) hubs—achieving a combination of private comforts and social amenities that recall the small towns and "classic suburbs" of the railroad and streetcar era before the dominance of the automobile that most of the major historians of American suburbia identify as the high-water mark of suburban living.[50] Many of the New Urbanite's transportation needs are met by walking, cycling, and efficient mass transit. And automobiles remain as one part of the multimodal range of options, but used only for the kinds of trips for which walking, cycling, or fixed-rail, fixed-schedule transit is inappropriate: multistop errands, vacation trips, and the many other types of travel that together constitute inhabiting the whole metropolitan region.[51]

The New Urbanism movement, especially on the West Coast, grew out of both environmentalism and the "systems thinking" revolutions that led to phenomena like *The Whole Earth Catalog* on the one hand and the Apple laptop computer on the other. Many early adherents of the movement were strongly influenced by intellectual traditions of bioregionalism, decentralization, small-is-beautiful economics, and even back-to-the-land, off-the-grid rejections of city life. Recently, however, a number of books have been published that argue that urban life is in fact the greenest mode of human existence and that population density, not Ralph Borsodi–style flight from the polluting city, provides the smallest carbon footprint per capita when compared to suburban, rural, or even wilderness-commune settlements.

In *Green Metropolis* (2009), David Owen, a writer for the *New Yorker*, tells how he and his wife, immediately after college, moved to a community where they did not own a car, walked or took public transit for all shopping and commuting, lived in a tiny shelter, and annually consumed a small fraction of the energy used by the average American. The name of the environmental paradise: Manhattan![52] Owen's thesis is both provocative and firmly supported by facts. The urban economies of scale really do make city life greener, on a per capita basis, than any other option and serve to fulfill the promise of Owen's subtitle: "Why Living Smaller, Living Closer, and Driving Less Are the Keys to Sustainability." In another recent book, *Triumph of the City: How Our Greatest Invention Makes Us Richer, Smarter, Greener, Healthier, and Happier* (2011), Harvard economist Edward Glaeser argues the essential pointlessness of developing new sustainability projects for dense cities since cities themselves embody the best of green development. "If the environmental footprint of the average suburban home is a size 15 hiking boot," he writes, "the environmental footprint of a New York apartment is a stiletto heel size 6 Jimmy Choo."[53]

The perception that dense urban life may actually be greener than other human settlement options is not entirely new. As long ago as 1985, architect and author Peter Calthorpe, one of the founders of the New Urbanism movement and a pioneer of the transit-oriented development (TOD) concept, wrote a short article for the *Whole Earth Review* entitled "Redefining Cities," in which he argued that our "image of the city as a cancerous lesion oozing with pollution and destroying the environment as its relentless growth paves the Earth is born of nineteenth-century industry" and that today, in reality, "the city is the most environmentally benign form of human settlement."[54] More recently, in *Urbanism in the Age of Climate Change* (2011), Calthorpe argues that "compact and walkable development . . . can have a major impact in reducing carbon emissions and energy demand" and that "urbanism is the most cost-effective solution to climate change, more so than most renewable technologies."[55] In a series of impressive charts, Calthorpe compares current sprawl development with current urban density and clearly demonstrates that "simple urbanism" is far more sustainable than "trend sprawl" in a number of important categories of resource consumption: water and energy use per household, greenhouse gas emissions, vehicle miles traveled, infrastructure costs, and so on. Adding the newest technologies and renewables—thereby creating "green urbanism"—makes the urban advantage even greater.[56]

Perhaps not surprisingly, the idea that the cities of the future will indeed be bigger, denser, greener, and more sustainable—"more like Manhattan," as Owen puts it—and that automobiles will soon share local streets with pedestrians, cyclists, and all manner of public transit is an idea that has captured the imaginations of many in the millennial generation as well as many practicing planners in Europe, the Americas, and Asia. The logic of the "urbanization solution" is beginning to take hold. As global urbanization rates swell to 70–80 percent, humanity's collective carbon footprint may well grow smaller, and the world will grow greener. And that is not all. People who live in cities have fewer children than rural people, so the pressures of a rapidly expanding global population will gradually ease. And if past history is any guide, levels of education, safety, and economic prosperity are also likely to increase.[57]

This kind of urban triumphalism is pleasing to the egos of urbanists, of course, but a word of caution may well be in order. Like anything else, taking advantage of the clear tendencies of global urbanization—and the vast elaboration of mobilities thereby implied—can be done well or poorly. For example, in *Arrival City* (2010)—an important new book arguing that the alarming global slums surrounding many of the world's great cities are actually breeding grounds for upward mobility—journalist Doug Saunders makes a clear distinction between successful "arrival city destinations" and failed ones.[58] The message is that wise, welcoming public policies and good, community-nurturing urban design are essential if positive, long-lasting outcomes for new immigrants to the city are to be achieved. Advocates of urbanism cannot fall prey to complacency and self-satisfaction. The urbanization process all by itself will not cause everything to come out well in the end. Ever and always, we have work to do, and we must be diligent.

An Agenda for Study and Action

If the increasing demands for urban mobilities are likely to continue as essential elements of urban life, then a number of issues will need to be addressed. Many of these are technical questions that automotive engineers and transportation planners are already working on, for example:

- How can we make cars less polluting and less dangerous while making transportation of all kinds cleaner, faster, and more accessible for new generations of urban mobility consumers?
- What kinds of new vehicles, engines, and clean fuels will we need? And how will a new refueling infrastructure be put in place?
- How can we go about reinventing the city taxi, both as a technology and a social institution? What other approaches to "personalized mass transit" are viable? How can we apply computerized scheduling technologies—and perhaps the creative merging of private taxi companies with public transit services—to avoid rush-hour shortages and make the delivery of mobility services more efficient and equitable across geographic and socioeconomic divides?
- More generally, how can policy makers reimagine the automobile as a form of mass transit when both entrenched interest groups and established planning practice rigidly separate private cars from public buses and trains? How can we prevent implementation issues from frustrating the achievement of real policy reform?
- How can we plan both our center-city and suburban communities to be more livable, more sustainable, and more open to cycling and walking?
- How can we design better streets and sidewalks to manage the many inevitable and potentially dangerous traffic interfaces between automobiles and pedestrians, automobiles and cyclists, and cyclists and pedestrians?

Other questions require a broader, more nuanced analysis:

- How will new multimodal approaches to urban mobilities affect housing, work, social interactions, and the economic and governance functions of urban communities?
- How will space-of-flows mobilities interact with space-of-place mobilities?
- And how can we rethink the way we plan our urban spaces to accommodate citadel functions, market functions, and community functions in an age when our cities are becoming seamless metropolitan regions . . . and our metropolitan regions are becoming interconnected nodes of an intensely networked but globally dispersed urban world?

Questions like these demand that we reconsider what exactly a city is . . . and what purpose urban mobility serves. To do that, we need to think about the meaning of the ultimate mobility word, the verb *to go*. In the age of the "space of flows/spaces of places" dichotomy, we still want *to go* to the party, and we probably need *to go* to the gym, but we no longer need *to go* to the store or *to go* to the library. Today, much to the dismay of brick-and-mortar retailers and librarians everywhere, we have the new mobility option of shopping for products and accessing information online. Increasingly, this is a characteristic shared by both the millennials of the advanced industrial nations and the rising middle classes of the developing world. And this expanded range of mobility options, in turn, transforms our very definition of "the city" and of "the urban personality" from local to global contexts of understanding.

In response to the overwhelming bigness of our big cities, and to the global reach of our urban networks, many people already identify with their small neighborhood units instead of the larger municipality, leading perhaps to a simultaneous decrease and intensification of civic engagement. If the cities of the world continue to grow and become globally interconnected—and if real social networks increasingly span continents instead of just city blocks—there is a clear possibility that online mobility can just as easily lead to alienation and isolation, resulting in new personal vulnerabilities and social disconnects, as to that increased inclusiveness that global urbanism potentially offers. The cultural tension between connectedness and disconnectedness, both on the personal and social levels, will be an ongoing struggle for both the millennial generation and the rising urban middle classes of Asia, Africa, and Latin America.

If the citadel, market, and community functions of cities are increasingly performed online—often spontaneously and on a twenty-four-hour basis— there may be significant gains in terms of efficiency but also losses in terms of the daily social interactions of Mumford's "urban drama." More than ever, we now need wise, nurturing plans and policies that keep humane values primary. And although policy implementation issues are always a problem, we can take some comfort in the observation that motivated consumers sometimes merely walk away from traditional systems and adopt new ones, on their own, that better meet their needs. Something like this seems to be already happening in the popular adoption of carsharing and ridesharing schemes outside the reach of existing regulations governing taxis and car rental services. And as with the newly emerging attitudes toward automobile ownership, home ownership may become less important—and homes smaller in square footage, especially for younger people still used to college dorm lifestyles—as more and more living functions become social and take place in shared space. The resultant loss of privacy may lead to pushback and the search for new ways to experience solitude. The danger will be a kind of systematic withdrawal from the physical and social space of the city, a process that may have already begun as evidenced by the way people talking on cell phones or listening to music walk the streets as if unaware of others around them.

In the end, the relationship between the city and the mobility technologies of the future will depend on how we respond to our understanding of our urban mobility history. We know how the automobile in the twentieth century was appropriate for its historical moment as the modern city moved from a city-and-hinterland model to a system of integrated metropolitan regions. We know how it was an innovative technological response to deeply felt human needs about nature and civilization expressed in visionary plans and utopian projections. But now a very different historical moment is clearly emerging with its own visions, problems, and aspirations. Our challenge is to make sure that the full range of transportation options, connected by and to the other mobility technologies of digital communication, will be seen the way Marshall McLuhan in the 1960s saw the technologies of media—that is, as vital, evolutionary extensions of humanity itself.

To achieve that positive result, what we must do now is examine the history, policy issues, and possible impacts of all forms of urban mobility on both current and emerging cities of the world to develop new ways of thinking about urban mobility in an era of global transformation. To fully understand the historical and cultural imperatives of the new urban mobilities, it will be necessary to engage in the widest possible range of interdisciplinary thinking and multidisciplinary research. In the end, a reassessment of urban mobility may lead to a reimagining of the very nature of the human community.

Notes

1   Lewis Mumford, "What Is a City?," in *The City Reader*, ed. Richard T. LeGates and Frederic Stout (London: Routledge, 2011), 93.

2   United Nations, Department of Economic and Social Affairs, *World Population Prospects: The 2012 Revision* (New York: United Nations, 2012).

3   Bradford Snell, *American Ground Transport: A Proposal for Restructuring the*

Automobile, Truck, Bus, and Rail Industries (Washington, DC: U.S. Government Printing Office, 1974).

4   Jonathan Kwitny, "The Great Transportation Conspiracy," *Harper's Magazine*, February 1981, 14.

5   Jane Holz Kay, *Asphalt Nation: How the Automobile Took Over America and How We Can Take It Back* (Berkeley: University of California Press, 1997); James Howard Kunstler, *The Geography of Nowhere: The Rise and Decline of America's Man-made Landscape* (New York: Simon and Schuster, 1993); Ralph Nader, *Unsafe at Any Speed: The Designed-in Dangers of the American Automobile* (New York: Grossman, 1965); Daniel Sperling and Deborah Gordon, *Two Billion Cars: Driving toward Sustainability* (New York: Oxford University Press, 2009).

6   Mark S. Foster, "The Automobile and the City," in *The Automobile and American Culture*, ed. David L. Lewis and Laurence Goldstein (Ann Arbor: University of Michigan Press, 1983), 24–36; Joseph Interrante, "The Road to Autopia: The Automobile and the Spatial Transformation of American Culture," in Lewis and Goldstein, *Automobile and American Culture*, 89–104.

7   Clay McShane, *Down the Asphalt Path: The Automobile and the American City* (New York: Columbia University Press, 1994), 57, 220–24.

8   John B. Rae, *The Road and the Car in American Life* (Cambridge, MA: MIT Press, 1971), 136–43.

9   David L. Lewis, "Sex and the Automobile: From Rumble Seats to Rockin' Vans," in Lewis and Goldstein, *Automobile and American Culture*, 123–33; Charles L. Sanford, "'Woman's Place in American Car Culture," in Lewis and Goldstein, *Automobile and American Culture*, 137–52; Cotton Seiler, *Republic of Drivers: A Cultural History of Automobility in America* (Chicago: University of Chicago Press, 2008), 36–68; McShane, *Down the Asphalt Path*, 149.

10 Reynold M. Wik, "The Early Automobile and the American Farmer," in Lewis and Goldstein, *Automobile and American Culture*, 37–47; Rae, *Road and the Car*, 160–61; Public Broadcasting System, "Taxi Dreams" (2001) http://www.pbs.org/wnet/taxidreams/index.html.

11 Rae, *Road and the Car*, 43.

12 Kenneth Hey, "Cars and Films in American Culture," in Lewis and Goldstein, *Automobile and American Culture*, 193–205; Gerald D. Silk, "The Image of the Automobile in American Art," in Lewis and Goldstein, *Automobile and American Culture*, 206–21; Julian Smith, "A Runaway Match: The Automobile and American Film, 1900–1920," in Lewis and Goldstein, *Automobile and American Culture*, 179–92.

13 Walter H. Nelson, *Small Wonder: The Amazing Story of the Volkswagen* (Boston: Little, Brown, 1965), 38–97.

14 James H. Crawford, *Carfree Cities* (Utrecht: International Books, 2002); Jan Gehl, *Life between Buildings: Using Public Space* (New York: Van Nostrand Reinhold, 1987).

15 Robert Fishman, *Urban Utopias of the Twentieth Century: Ebenezer Howard, Frank Lloyd Wright, Le Corbusier* (Cambridge, MA: MIT Press, 1977); George Collins, "The Ciudad Lineal of Madrid," *Journal of Architectural Historians* 2 (May 1959): 38–53.

16 Robert Puentes and Adie Tomer, *The Road . . . Less Traveled: An Analysis of Vehicle Miles Traveled Trends in the U.S.* (Washington, DC: Metropolitan Policy Program, Brookings Institution, 2008).

17 General Motors, *Futurama* (New York: General Motors Corporation, 1940).

18 Paul Ingrassia, *Engines of Change: A History of the American Dream in Fifteen Cars* (New York: Simon and Schuster, 2012), 57–80.

19 Rae, *Road and the Car*, 360–61.

20 Robert Fishman, *Bourgeois Utopias: The Rise and Fall of Suburbia* (New York: Basic Books, 1987).

21 Lewis Mumford, *The City in History: Its Origins, and Its Transformations, Its Prospects* (Harcourt, Brace & World, 1961), 509–11.

22 Sperling and Gordon, *Two Billion Cars*, 1–5.

23 Mumford, *City in History*, 510.

24 Kunstler, *Geography of Nowhere*.

25 Kay, *Asphalt Nation*.

26 Maxine A. Rock, *The Automobile and the Environment* (New York: Chelsea House, 1992), 25.

27 Joseph Interrante, "The Road to Autopia: The Automobile and the Spatial Transformation of American Culture," in Lewis and Goldstein, *Automobile and American Culture*, 90.

28 Frederick Law Olmsted, "Public Parks and the Enlargement of Towns," *American Social Science Association* (1870), in LeGates and Stout, *City Reader*, 323.

29 Ebenezer Howard, *Garden Cities of To-morrow* (London: Faber & Faber, 1945), 50–57.

30 William Dean Howells, *A Traveler from Altruria* (New York: Harper & Brothers, 1894), 187.

31 Karl Marx and Frederick Engels, *Manifesto of the Communist Party* (New York: International, 1932), 13, 30–31.

32 Ralph Waldo Emerson, *The Journals of Ralph Waldo Emerson*, vol. 6, 1841–1844 (Boston: Houghton Mifflin, 1911), 506.

33 John W. Reps, *The Making of Urban America: A History of City Planning in the United States* (Princeton: Princeton University Press, 1965), 317.

34 Jonathan V. Beaverstock, Richard G. Smith, and Peter J. Taylor, "World-City Network: A New Metageography?," *Annals of the Association of American Geographers* 90, no. 1 (2000): 123–34.

35 Tingwei Zhang, "Chinese Cities in a Global Society," in LeGates and Stout, *City Reader*, 590–98; Ke-Qing Han, Chien-Chung Huang, and Wen-Jui Han, "Social Mobility of Migrant Peasant Workers in China," *Sociology Mind* 1, no. 4 (2011): 206–11.

36 Saskia Sassen, "The Impact of the New Technologies and Globalization on Cities," in *Cities in Transition*, ed. Arie Graafland and Deborah Hauptmann (Rotterdam: 010 Publishers, 2001).

37 United Nations Human Settlements Programme (UN-HABITAT), *The Challenge of Slums: Global Report on Human Settlements 2003* (New York: United Nations, 2003).

38 China Association of Automobile Manufacturers, "Automotive Statistics" (2013), http://www.caam.org.cn/english/.

39 China AutoWeb.com, "How Many Cars Are There in China?," http://chinaautoweb.com/2010/09/how-many-cars-are-there-in-china/; BusinessGreen.com, "China's E6 Electric Car: 'We're Not Trying to Save the World—We're Trying to Make Money," April 3, 2009, http://www.businessgreen.com/businessgreen/news/2239795/china-e6-electric-car-trying.

40 Han, Huang, and Han, "Social Mobility."

41 Frederic Stout, personal communication with two students in Urban Studies 167: The Automobile and the City (winter 2012), Stanford University.

42 Madsen Pirie and Robert M. Worcester, *The Millennial Generation* (London: Adam Smith Institute, 1998); Jarrett Walker, "Public Transit: When the Millennials Rule the Bay Area" *San Francisco Chronicle*, August 4, 2013.

43 Pew Research Social & Demographic Trends, "Millennials: Confident. Connected. Open to Change" (Washington, DC: Pew Research Center, 2010).

44 Richard Florida, *The Rise of the Creative Class: And How It Is Transforming Work, Leisure, Community and Everyday Life* (New York: Basic Books, 2002).

45 Manuel Castells, "Space of Flows, Space of Places: Materials for a Theory of Urbanism in the Information Age," in LeGates and Stout *City Reader*, 572–82.

46 Beaverstock, Smith, and Taylor, "World-City Network."

47 Joel Garreau, *Edge City: Life on the New Frontier* (New York: Doubleday, 1991)

48 Fishman, *Bourgeois Utopias*, 182–207.

49 Congress for the New Urbanism, "Charter of the New Urbanism," www.cnu.org/charter.

50 Sam Bass Warner, Kenneth T. Jackson, Robert Fishman, and Robert Bruegmann.

51 Peter Katz, *The New Urbanism: Toward an Architecture of Community* (New York: McGraw-Hill, 1994), xi–xx, xxi–xxiv.

52 David Owen, *Green Metropolis: Why Living Smaller, Living Closer, and Driving Less Are the Keys to Sustainability* (New York: Riverhead/Penguin, 2009), 1.

53 Edward Glaeser, *Triumph of the City: How Our Greatest Invention Makes Us Richer, Smarter, Greener, Healthier, and Happier* (New York: Penguin, 2011), 14.

54 Peter Calthorpe, "Redefining Cities," *Whole Earth Review* 45 (March 1985), 1.

55 Peter Calthorpe, *Urbanism in the Age of Climate Change* (Washington, DC: Island Press, 2011), 4.

56 Calthorpe, *Urbanism*, plates 1–7, pp. 20ff.

57 Glaeser, *Triumph of the City*, 1–15.

58 Doug Saunders, *Arrival City: How the Largest Migration in History Is Reshaping Our World* (New York: Pantheon, 2010), 1–94.

Rethinking Urban Utopias
A Manifesto for Self-Supported Infrastructure, Technology, and Territory

Mitchell Joachim

At some level, urban design engages a position that promises a better tomorrow. For centuries, notions of utopia have informed evolving societies, offering maximal solutions to existing real-world problems by tackling upheaval with orderly retribution.[1] In nearly all their variations, fictional utopias (and anti-utopias) and real-life utopian communities, such as the Shakers, offer an exaggerated answer to a crisis by calling attention to a problem. Today, however, utopian intentions have shifted from the idealized or grandiose to merely earnest and good.[2] Thus, as urbanist Alex Krieger asserts, a broad vocation such as urban design is defined more by a scrupulous sensibility than an exclusive authority.[3]

To guide our discussion of the making of urban utopias, this essay is divided into five parts: (1) an introduction and theoretical background, (2) definitions and methodologies, (3) a case study demonstrating the scope and aims of the new discipline of Urbaneering, (4) a discussion of the issue of scale in today's global setting, and (5) a look at future challenges and implications for urban design.

Urbaneering—A New Profession for the Design of Cities

A current question among the planning professionals is "Who will be the primary authority in the making of extraordinary future cities?" We propose the answer is Urbaneers. Urbaneering is a burgeoning discipline based on design that negotiates a complex mix of technology, theory, and practice and is committed to reinventing our cities to balance the requirements and resources of the planet with humans' needs and desires. Urbaneering undertakes a radical

THE FIELD OF URBANEERING

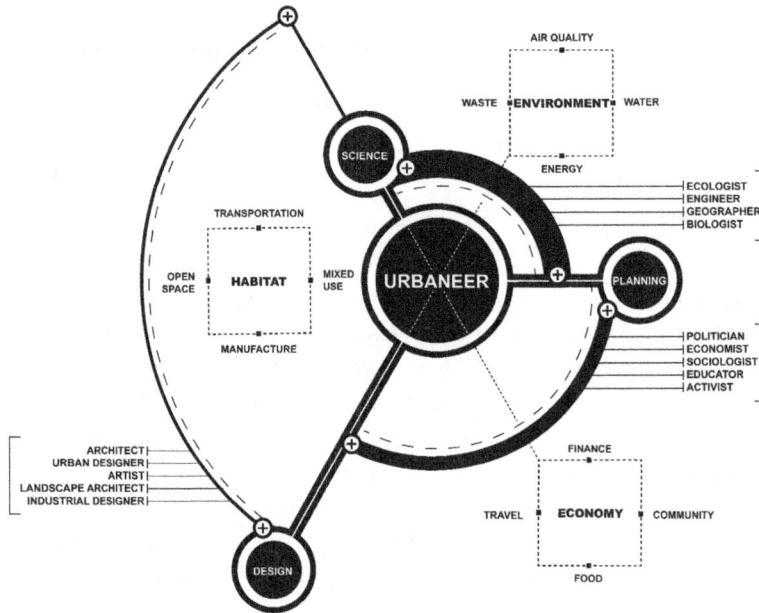

Fig. 1. The interdisciplinary field of Urbaneering. (Terraform ONE ©: Mitchell Joachim, Maria Aiolova, Melanie Fessel, Caleb Lowery)

reconsideration and redevelopment of traditional interdisciplinary urban design.

Background

Although urban design has been recognized as a discipline since the mid-1950s, the field has so far failed to significantly respond to contemporary challenges. The originators of urban design, such as José Luis Sert, Kevin Lynch, and others, could not have imagined social networks, smart phones, climate dynamism, our current energy addiction, or global economic calamities—all of which require new approaches and methodologies. As an alternative, Urbaneering involves city design that takes on board a huge range of new ideas, including crowdsourcing, hackathons, localized energy, shared transport, e-government, high-throughput computation, biotechnology, and ecology. Urbaneers focus as much on cities' ecosystems and infrastructure—areas ripe

Mitchell Joachim

Fig. 2. Green Brain Park Space combines multiple functionalities by providing bike paths, agriculture, leisure activities, and algae production in one space. (© Terraform ONE: Mitchell Joachim, Maria Aiolova, Melanie Fessel, Dan O'Connor, Celina Yee, Alpna Gupta, Sishir Varghese, Aaron Lim, Greg Mulholland, Derek Ziemer, Thilani Rajarathna, John Nelson, Natalie DeLuca)

for improvement—as on more conventional subjects like buildings and public space. As a catalyst to reimagining the city, Urbaneering strives to create a new field of inquiry that expands far beyond the traditional ends of city design.

One of the problems is that the profession of urban design is at an impasse. In the developed world it has been unable to mend the rift between theory and practice, as expressed in debates such as the one between Landscape Urbanism and New Urbanism. Landscape Urbanists' concepts favor the landscape over architecture in city planning.[4] In contrast, New Urbanist schemes promote historical, pedestrian-centered neighborhood developments.[5] As examples, consider the neotraditionalist town extension of Poundbury near Dorchester, England, endorsed by New Urbanist Prince Charles, and the high-tech interactive open space zone of Schouwburgplein in Rotterdam, designed by the

Fig. 3. Urban stackable car with solar recharge port. (© Terraform ONE: Mitchell Joachim, Maria Aiolova, Melanie Fessel, Philip Weller, Ian Slover, Landon Young, Cecil Howell, Andrea Michalski, Sofie Bamberg, Alex Colard, Zachary Aders)

Landscape Urbanist firm West 8. Both of these design factions have their merits, yet the debate is largely academic, restricted to architects and planners. The public that uses and occupies these spaces is largely disinterested in the discussion. Urbaneering sidesteps the dichotomy between tradition and newness and strives to devise a holistic idea for the future sustainable city by taking into consideration the past while being committed to new models and solutions.

Urbaneering undertakes a diverse range of projects as a prescription for maximal design. Totalized schemes rethink all scales of involvement from the doorknob to democracy. Urbaneering projects can range from new materials and enclosure systems to new mobility strategies for megacities. Currently, a few Urbaneers have shaped phytoremediation ponds, living woody plant structures, rooftop farms, soft cars and buses, urban junkspace, and citywide action plans. To inspire interdisciplinary innovation, Urbaneers encourage people to switch roles, so that architects might design cars, automotive engineers devise ecosystems, and ecologists draw up buildings.

At the core of Urbaneering is a variety of utopian agitation that dispels the elitist myths of modernism with populist objectives. An Urbaneer replaces implausible rules and master planning with suggestive memes and polemical models. For example, taglines such as "city beautiful," "garden city," or "smart growth" are used to rally the public around open-ended, symbolic gestures and phrases. Because these memes are not fully explicit, room exists for broad cultural interpretation. It is what many communities yearn for: a strategy to define their own urban spaces within specific objectives and contexts.[6] Thus the Urbaneer's aim is to support citizens to become part of an advanced intellectual initiative that reconceptualizes the city.

Projects such as London's Canary Wharf, Potsdamer Platz in Berlin, New York's Highline, Masdar City in the UAE, and the Eco-city project in Tianjin, China, already demand fresh directives and solutions. Within the academy, a recent thrust has recognized the importance of sustainable planning frameworks for sustainable ecodistricts. Those frameworks primarily assert that all necessities for urban health and well-being are provided within a closed-loop system. In an ecological city, food, water, air quality, energy, waste, mobility, and shelter are radically restructured to support life in every form. Infrastructure is celebrated not only as the connector but also as the new center.

Methodology

So how does Urbaneering work—what is its methodology? While research and analysis are standard in Urbaneering, new design methods are required to communicate that information. Analytical diagrams combining ecology and urbanity, called *ecograms*, serve to prioritize design directives. Light and air are among the primary causal factors that respond to context in such ecograms. Equally, encapsulation of the program is correctly orchestrated via any low-energy embodied volumes or more densely utilized loft spaces. For example, highly malleable spaces support growth, with elaboration and magnification of character at its limits. Ecograms reflect the plurality inherent in complex urban systems and serve to clarify the relationships between urban and ecological factors.

Beyond the research and developing the ecogram, Urbaneers collectively possess a set of proficiencies that merge previously disparate occupations, and in this way strive to meet the constantly changing needs of urbanization. One historical example of a proto-Urbaneer is Frederick Law Olmsted (1822–1903), a nineteenth-century activist who combined journalism, social action, and landscape architecture to a single political end. One of his greatest

Fig. 4. S.O.F.T. Mobility, Blimp Bumper Bus. (© Terraform ONE: Mitchell Joachim, Maria Aiolova, Melanie Fessel, Philip Weller, Ian Slover, Landon Young, Cecil Howell, Andrea Michalski, Sofie Bamberg, Alex Colard, Zachary Aders)

achievements is, of course, New York's Central Park.[7] The future city not only requires a new breed of communicator, but also one who is skilled in the sciences beyond what is typical of today's planners, civil engineers, architects, and activists. Diverse knowledge must be synthesized by incorporating all aspects of urban existence. Where municipal problems normally take multiple disciplines to solve, Urbaneers look to merge the edification and expertise needed to re-form the city of today for the utopia of tomorrow.

As an example, consider Brooklyn 2110, City of the Future, in which Terreform ONE's design strategy replaces existing dilapidated structures with habitable infrastructure sustained by a vertical agricultural system. Former streets become arteries of livable spaces embedded with renewable energy sources, soft cushion-based vehicles for mobility, and productive green rooms. The

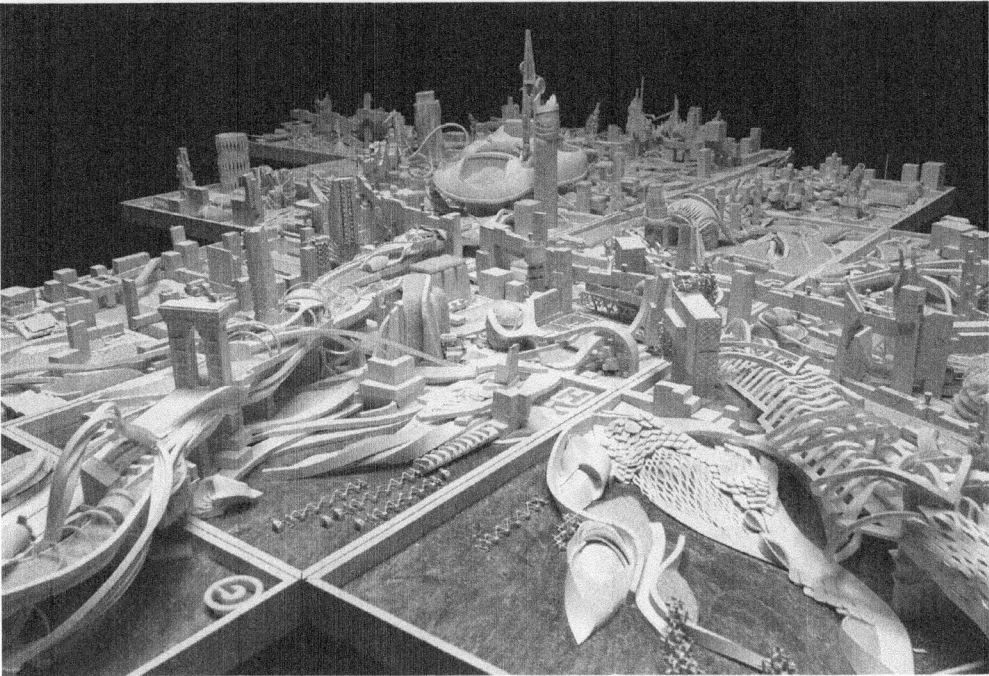

plan integrates the former street grid as the foundation for up-to-the-minute information networks. By reengineering the obsolete streets, it becomes possible to install radically robust and ecologically active smart pathways. In this proposal, all possibilities are considered; Terreform ONE designs the scooters, cars, trains, and blimps, as well as the streets, parks, open spaces, cultural districts, civic centers, and business hubs that comprise the future metropolis.

As a speculative proposal, Brooklyn 2110 affords an initial platform for discussion by modeling different scenarios for tomorrow's city. In this example, ecological design is not only a philosophy that inspires visions of sustainability but also a focused scientific endeavor. The mission is to ascertain the consequences of fitting a project within our natural environment. Solutions are derived from numerous examples: living material habitats, climatic tall building clusters, and mobility technologies. Current research attempts to establish new forms of design knowledge and new processes of practice at the interface of design, computer science, structural engineering, and biology. Urbaneers expect the future will necessitate marvelous dwellings coupled with a massive renewable/recyclable resource net.

Case Study: Rapid Re(f)use—The Infrastructure of Smart Waste

Imagine our colossal municipal landfills as a proximate and logical resource for building future urban and peri-urban structures. What type of technology will be required to reuse their contents? Now that the bulk of humanity has chosen to settle in urbanized areas,[8] waste management needs radical revision. The United States is the leading generator of waste, producing approximately 30 percent of the world's trash and tossing out 0.72 metric tons per person per year.[9] *Value* has devolved into rampant waste production—overpackaged, inexpensive products intentionally designed to be used briefly and then discarded. As Heather Rogers shows in *Gone Tomorrow: The Hidden Life of Garbage*, a culture of throwing things away is unsustainable, yet we continue to follow that path.[10] Where does it end? The first step is reduction—a massive discontinuation of objects designed for obsolescence. The second step is the development of a radical reuse plan.

Since the topic of mobilities includes waste transportation, one approach is to design waste to work within a closed system, as is found in natural ecological systems. Terreform ONE's concept is to reallocate resource streams to flow in a positive direction.[11] In this scenario, waste is not merely recycled through infrastructural mechanisms but instead upcycled in perpetuity. Consider New York City, where 10,000–12,000 US tons of waste are disposed of every day, enough paper products alone to fill a volume the size of the Empire State Building every few weeks.[12] Terreform ONE's Rapid Re(f)use project proposes capturing this resource, reducing waste, and redesigning New York's refuse infrastructure. The initiative envisions a vertical city constituted from its own discarded materials—all the trash entombed in the Fresh Kills landfill. Theoretically, this method could produce, at minimum, seven entirely new Manhattan Islands at full scale.

How would this work? Combining the existing technologies of 3D printers and equipment used in industrial waste compaction would yield machinery able to rapidly process trash into building materials. Nothing drastically new needs to be invented. Rather, instead of machines that crush discarded objects into cubes, we would have compaction devices with adjustable jaws that could craft "puzzle blocks" ready for assembly into structures. The blocks of waste material could be predetermined, using computational geometries, to form domes, archways, lattices, windows, or whatever patterns are needed. Different materials would serve specified purposes: transparent plastic for fenestration, organic compounds for temporary, decomposable scaffolds, metals for primary structures, and so on. Eventually, the future city would make no distinction between waste and supply.[13]

Although the envisioned city would be constructed from trash, it would not be ordinary trash, but "smart refuse" that becomes "smart units" through artificial intelligence. Each individual component would be enhanced with a modicum of CPU (central processing unit) power. Brief durational events would endow these smart units with "experiences" needed for their evolution. One significant factor of the city composed from smart refuse revolves around "post-tuning," meaning that unitized devices with artificial intelligence would learn over time and slowly adapt to the formal and material qualities of a neighborhood.[14] Thus, artificial integration into the city texture would gradually evolve. Eventually the responses would become more attuned to the needs of the urban dweller.

The Rapid Re(f)use proposal imagines the possibility of a smart, self-sufficient urbanism in perpetual motion. Science contends that perpetual motion is impossible because it necessitates a machine that produces more energy than it consumes. Cities, however, in many ways are more analogous to complex ecologies than machines. Ecologies are capable of achieving a continuous balanced state, or even a positive intensification. If ecological models are productive indefinitely, then logically urban models can follow. In this way, a Rapid Re(f)use city could enable a condition of "positive waste"—one that produces more energy from renewable sources than it consumes. In this scenario, nothing is thrown away. Every item of trash would be a vital piece of stored energy, poised for reuse in a cyclical nutrient stream.[15]

Rapid Re(f)use, then, is imagined as a city that not only has zero impact but that also makes a positive contribution to the environment. This is the steady state of a truly interconnected, metabolic urbanism. The concept of positive waste could become a reality that addresses our socio-ecological needs—perhaps not a utopia, per se, but a place where everything has value and nothing is wasted.

The Necessity of All Scales: Planetary Design in the Age of Global Connection

Globalization has a final outcome; it's not an unending process. Humanity is headed into the age of globality, the final state of globalization. Globality is the endgame, an all-inclusive terrestrial status.[16] Theorists such as Saskia Sassen and Keller Easterling describe a condition where information flows originating from financial, legal, and military sources create new spatial agglomerations and extraterritorial zones.[17] In this fully connected world, populations will compete with everyone, everywhere, for everything, at all times, at all scales. Conversely, a state of planetary equilibrium could influence the major sectors of industry, resource management, infrastructure, technology, energy, and governance with profound, and positive, transformations.

In this saturated condition of globality, what are the urban design priorities? Effects of scale are constantly transferred between the irreducible and the colossal. As globality operates at all scales simultaneously without privileging any one form, implying measureless shifts in size, small changes ramify into massive results, and vice versa. In this brave new world, thinking inside strict categories of scale becomes not only outmoded but also counterintuitive. Charles and Ray Eames demonstrated this principle in their documentary *The Powers of Ten*, in which scale is conveniently defined in neat square frames.[18] The point of the film is to bridge the different perceptions of scale cohesively. The Eames' aim was to empower people to visualize the ranges of observation melded into a single point of view. Nothing happens in only one frame of space or time.[19]

Neither can effects be contained in discrete locales. As a subcomponent of complexity (in the scientific sense), the chaotic nature of the universe—and especially its quality of having small, apparently insignificant changes with far-reaching effects (e.g., the butterfly effect)—applies. Case in point, when postwar cities set up a centralized fossil fuel–based energy system, the unintended global climatic effects were not fully understood at the time.[20] If the earth is understood as a closed system, then traditional boundaries and categories are insufficient. Design needs to keep pace by breaking out of emblematic questions of size, especially as it relates to our planet. One size does not fit all—rather all sizes fit one. Any scale is best perceived holistically in relationship to other scales.

The condition of globality and scale necessitates a restructuring of the design professions as we know them. It requires a new breed of designers who can speculate and produce at the nano-scale up to feats of geoengineering and beyond. These thinkers can be referred to as *planetary designers.*

As part of a globalized, connected, meta-Pangea community, design is obliged to be pervasive. It simply cannot relegate itself to any one scale or project scope. If it is so constrained, its relevance and instrumentality are greatly diminished. The principal operations of scale and systems that employ it obfuscate the complicated reality of design problems, and the more such systems are used, the more designers fail to envision the whole picture, so important with the design of urban infrastructure.

Conclusion

Faced as we are with increasing climate change, the reinvention of urban design could not be more timely or important. In 1989, in his book *The End of Nature,* Bill McKibben documented the then-latest scientific evidence about carbon emissions, depletion of the ozone layer, and a harrowing array of other ecological concerns, and outlined the inexorable changes that human activities have wrought on our planet.[21] The situation has, of course, only worsened over the following decades. Although human actions have been altering the environment for centuries, in the past those depredations were relatively localized. The consequences of greenhouse gas emissions and ozone depletion are global. Furthermore, the industrial mindset that defines natural resources as products and profits of economic development denies our very real dependence on nature for our existence. McKibben argues that society has lost something of irreplaceable importance: nature as a quasi-celestial source of ultimate meaning and value. He refers to this as an apocalyptic calamity.

In this context, sustainable designers and planners are concerned with revealing "truth windows" to avoid negative consequences. They highlight ecological processes in their proposals so that users of the environment can experience, comprehend, and appreciate the multiple scales of those processes. In practice, revealing ecological processes has included capturing storm water on the surface of the land before it drains away into sewers or planting a row of trees in an urban plaza where a creek once existed. Ecological processes may be persistent, in the sense that they can continue to subsist without the management of society, or they could be deeply artificial, engineered systems that need relentless human supervision if they are to survive in an urbanized context. Ultimately, the intention is to make the scales of ecology visual and thereby reveal an interdependent balanced system.

Architecture has long recognized an immeasurable ecological quality that goes well beyond the borders of the building site. It's also clear that ecological principles comprise a web of interconnected concepts; in this web, architecture cannot exist within a single scale. Thus, design boundaries must be planetary—encompassing everything from a single biological cell to the outer edges of the atmosphere. The issue of scale also serves as a constant reminder of the widespread implications of our actions. Yet it is ironic that design disciplines, project scopes, and programmatic language are all defined in terms of size, a redundant supposition in the age of globality.

If we are to make a concerted attempt at sustainable urban agendas, professionals and activists must come together to make collective decisions, as actions are no longer locally bound. In this sense, ecological infrastructure with innovative directives becomes a means to the end—that of bringing together technological, social, and ecological knowledge from all disciplines to shape a broad range of ultimate circumstances. We designers must take action and modify our stance on all scales and morphologies to have a positive effect on the global community.

Notes

1   Stamatina Th. Rassia and Panos M. Pardalos, eds. *Cities for Smart Environmental and Energy Futures: Impacts on Architecture and Technology* (Heidelberg: Springer, 2014, http://www.onleihe.de/static/content/springer/20131024/313763/v313763.pdf.

2   James C. Collins, *Good to Great: Why Some Companies Make the Leap . . . and Others Don't* (New York: Harper Business, 2001).

3   Alex Krieger and William S. Saunders, eds., *Urban Design* (Minneapolis: University of Minnesota Press, 2009).

4   Charles Waldheim, ed., *The Landscape Urbanism Reader* (New York: Princeton Architectural Press, 2006).

5   Peter Calthorpe, *The Next American Metropolis: Ecology, Community, and the American Dream* (New York: Princeton Architectural Press, 1993).

6   For aspects related to DIY urbanism, see Celeste B. Pagano, "DIY Urbanism:

Property and Process in Grassroots City Building," *Marquette Law Review* 97(2): 335–89.

7   Charles E. Beveridge and Paul Rocheleau, *Frederick Law Olmsted: Designing the American Landscape* (New York: Universe, 1998).

8   United Nations, "World's Population Increasingly Urban with More Than Half Living in Urban Areas," July 10, 2014, http://www.un.org/en /development/desa/news/population/world-urbanization-prospects-2014 .html (accessed June 29, 2015).

9   Environmental Protection Agency, "EPA's Report on the Environment: Highlights of National Trends," 2008, https://cfpub.epa.gov/roe/documents/ROE _HD_Final_2008.pdf.

10 Heather Rogers, *Gone Tomorrow: The Hidden Life of Garbage* (New York: New Press, 2006), 54–67, 104–32.

11 Mitchell Joachim, Maria Aiolova, Melanie Fessel, Philip Weller, Ian Slover, Emily Johnson, Landon Young, Cecil Howell, Andrea Michalski, Sofie Bamberg, Alex Colard, and Zachary Aders for Terreform ONE (Open Network Ecology), Ecological Design Group for Urban, Infrastructure, Building, Planning and Art.

12. Sarah Crean, "Talking Trash: 212 Things Worth Knowing about NYC's Garbage," New York Environment Report, July 21, 2014, http://www .nyenvironmentreport.com/talking-trash-12-things-worth-knowing-about -the-citys-waste-stream/.

13 Terreform ONE is not the only one to have conceived this idea. While we were conceptualizing Rapid Re(f)use, we visited the Walt Disney Imagineering headquarters in Glendale, California. Our group prepared a presentation that would unpack a comprehensive view of their version of the future: a world free of carbon loading in the atmosphere and abundant in self-sufficient lifestyles. We were crestfallen when Ben Schwegler, mastermind and chief imagineer, pulled back the proverbial curtain to reveal Disney Pixar's current project: *WALL-E*, a film about a solar-powered, curious, obedient, highly evolved robotic trash-compaction-and-distribution device. We had been beaten to the punch. WALL-E's name is an acronym for Waste Allocation Load Lifter Earth Class. Left behind by mankind, he toils with trillions of tons of nonrecycled inner-city trash. Not only is WALL-E a highly advanced rubbish manager; he also is a mechanized and inventive architect. While WALL-E is only fiction, the science behind the film bears further investigation. What is preventing us from recycling trash into building material?

14 "Cities are not machines and neither are they organisms and perhaps re-

semble them even less. Rather than communities of non-thinking organisms undergoing inevitable phases until they reach a certain iron limit, cities are the product of beings capable of learning. Culture can stabilize or alter the habitat system, and it is not clear whether we wish it to be otherwise." Kevin Lynch in *A Theory of Good City Form* (Cambridge, MA: MIT Press, 1984) 26–27.

15   William McDonough, "Waste Equals Food: Our Future and the Making of Things," in *Awakening: The Upside of Y2K*, ed. Judy Laddon, Tom Atlee, and Larry Shook (Spokane, WA: Printed Word, 1998), 5–57.

16   According to Keller Easterling, extraterritorial places are positioned outside of the sovereignty and jurisdiction that surrounds them or that are contiguous to them. International ownership treaties demarcate airports and ports, international waters, international seabed, the moon, outer space, international zone, the United Nations, Antarctica, and extraterrestrial real estate. Jurisdictionally ambiguous, they are infused with myths, desires, and symbolic capital. See Keller Easterling, *Extrastatecraft: The Power of Infrastructure Space* (Brooklyn, NY: Verso 2007).

17   Other examples include the behavior of interrelated economies during the 2008–09 financial crisis and ongoing industrialization. Easterling, *Extrastatecraft*.

18   Ray and Charles Eames, *A Rough Sketch for a Proposed Film Dealing with the Powers of Ten and the Relative Size of Things in the Universe* (1968), and *Powers of Ten: A Film Dealing with the Relative Size of Things in the Universe and the Effect of Adding Another Zero* (1977) (documentary films).

19   More recently, Rem Koolhaas and Bruce Mau emphasized scale in their book S, M, L, XL, yet also alluded to the in-between thresholds and differentiation of projects. Rem Koolhaas and Bruce Mau, S, M, L, XL (New York: Monacelli Press, 1995).

20   Today rapid migration compounds that effect; for example, between 2000 and 2010 the population of Karachi, Pakistan, expanded by 80.5 percent. Wendell Cox, *Demographia World Urban Areas*, 9th ed. (Belleville, IL: Wendell Cox Consultancy, 2013).

21   Bill McKibben, *The End of Nature* (New York: Random House, 1989).

Urban Mobility in the Informal City

Alfredo Brillembourg and Hubert Klumpner

Cities around the world are growing rapidly; a projection that we have all heard time and time again. However, the necessary follow-up questions are heard far less frequently. Which cities are growing? Which specific parts of cities are growing? One cannot possibly hope to accommodate the urban growth that is currently underway, and that which is yet to come, without delving deeper into these questions.

All cities are not created equal, at least not in size. While megacities, the likes of Tokyo, New York, Cairo, Mexico City, and Lagos, will likely always experience a certain level of incoming immigrants bound for their centers in search of the opportunities associated with urban living, these are not the areas where mass flocking will occur in the next few decades.[1] Midsized cities are the sites of extreme peaks in the number of urban inhabitants. Most of the fastest growing cities in the world at the moment—Beihai (China), Ghaziabad (India), Lubumbashi (Democratic Republic of the Congo)—fall into this category of midsized cities, and it is toward these environments that architects and urban planners must turn their attention to best serve the expanding urban, global population.[2] The question of which cities to focus on has now been answered. However, it is the second question of where, specifically, within these cities do we see extreme growth patterns, and how should new demands on infrastructure and mobility best be accommodated, that is the focus of this essay.

"One billion people live in squatter communities worldwide, a number expected to double by 2030."[3] This effectively means that 50 percent of total urban growth will be informal. Christian Werthmann of the Harvard Graduate School of Design emphasizes, "Only an estimated 5% of the design profession is occupied with the phenomenon of informal urbanism. An imbalance does

Fig. 1. Metrocable des Caracas, Venezuela, provides public transportation for those who live in mountainous regions. The system was built as a tool for social reform with stations set up to accommodate a variety of services such as daycares, libraries, police stations, markets, and theater. (Photograph by Daniel Schwartz, U-TT and ETH; © Urban-Think Tank)

not only exist in the global distribution of material wealth, but also in the provision of design capital."[4]

As this informal sector within the urban framework of midsized cities continues to grow, innovation and exploration in the fields of infrastructure are desperately needed. Informal communities are drastically lacking in adequate healthcare facilities, available public space, sustainable housing, water and sanitation facilities, the list of basic services continues. Though the lack of all of these contributes to the maintenance of the stratification between classes, no single actor plays a more dominant role in the divide between the haves of the formal city and have-nots of the informal city than unemployment. It is understandably difficult to have a job when physical mobility between where positions are located (formal city) and where those in search of gainful employment are located (informal city) is limited. Mobility between the informal and the formal cities must also be a part of the investment made in informal infrastructure in the future.

Alfredo Brillembourg and Hubert Klumpner

Informal settlements tend to be not only separated by a clear divide in socio-economics but also physically separated by a change in geological makeup as well. Flood plains, steep slopes, and marshlands are environments not easily navigated and are typical areas of informal growth. Retrofitting these areas with infrastructure models that were originally suited for formal cities—roads, tramways, subways, railways—in many cases is neither innovative nor sufficient. Creating modes of transit both throughout these settlements and between the informal and formal sectors of the city, as connectivity should always be a goal of infrastructure development, must originate from a bottom-up design strategy. As the formal world aims to become increasingly "intelligent" in its urban design—green designs, increased sustainability, minimized carbon footprints—one must rethink what it means to design "intelligently" in varied environments with varied needs and varied levels of preexisting development. One cannot design for a city without visiting it. One cannot assume knowledge of the needs of a city until knowing its residents. One cannot possibly hope for sustainability without getting the on-the-ground community involved firsthand. Bottom-up, adaptable design is "intelligent" design in informal cities just as much as, say, taking into account the "influence of the filler–bitumen ratio on performance of modified asphalt mortar" is "intelligent" design in formal cities.[5]

Smart City versus the Growing, Learning City

The terms *smart* and *intelligent* have become part of the language of urbanization policy, referring to the use of IT (information technology) to improve the productivity of a city's essential infrastructure and services and to reduce energy inputs and CO_2 outputs in response to global climate change. LED lighting, electricity-powered cars, facial recognition security surveillance, home automation, tintable smart glass, space-saving folding vehicles, and fuel cell technology are just a few examples from the past three years of technological innovations that cities are incorporating in an effort to become "smarter."[6] Implementing many of these technologies in the growing informal sectors of midsized cities would be about as far from "smart" as possible. A car that can shrink to half of its size when parked is about as useful in the favelas of Sao Paulo (where passageways are rocky, steep, and far too narrow for most vehicles) as a submarine is to the landlocked country of Mongolia. There are clear limitations to design solutions that depend heavily on advanced technology. This speaks to the need for a rethinking of what "smart" design and development truly are.

What, then, would constitute "smart" design in informal cities? One example, related to housing in particular, is modular design. By effectively solving problems of construction and deployment in the design stage, modular housing can be extremely effective in the informal setting. This tactic allows for the negotiation of existing buildings and steep slopes. Small, workable units allow the owner of a home to also be the investor and the builder of a project. This allows for low costs, community involvement, and maximum catering to the needs of the residents. Additionally, and potentially most importantly when keeping in mind inevitable expansion, modular constructions allows for add-ons as they become necessary. A unit built of two modules for a family of five can be expanded upward with an additional module should relatives move in and the family expand to eight, for example. There is unquestionable "intelligence" is such a highly adaptable design.

"Informal economies supply 60 percent of jobs in the Global South."[7] With such staggering statistics, it is reasonable to project that housing needs in these areas will increase at an astounding rate. How can urban areas accommodate such an influx of inhabitants in a "smart" way? In Caracas in 2005, Urban-Think Tank partnered with St. Mary's Anglican Church to provide emergency housing. The goals of the project were clear: housing needed to be low-cost, quick and easy to construct, expandable, and sustainable. The solution was a "growing house." "The intention was to design the concrete frame, electricity, drinking and wastewater services at each level, and then allow the users who will inhabit the apartments to fill in block closures and complete the designs themselves. Expanding a concrete frame vertically and using a steel shelf-type system in between the floor gave the design flexibility for future adaptation. This idea was inspired by both the real examples of squatting in buildings under construction and by the 1980s New York artist loft scheme that left raw space to be fitted out by the user. The project also incorporated a kindergarten, a café, meeting halls, and several shops, giving the premises space to create a working community.[8] In this case, the benefits to modular design (low costs, adaptability, resident autonomy) as a means to accommodate informal expansion spoke for themselves.

It is not the case that cutting-edge technology has no place in the informal

Alfredo Brillembourg and Hubert Klumpner

city. IT can contribute to successful development in favelas and barrios as well as metropolises. It may simply be a matter of in which stage in the process it is implemented. While the implementation of advanced technology might be the end result in a cosmopolitan area that struggles with vehicle congestion—putting folding cars in Los Angeles, for example—it might serve the informal sector better if placed at the beginning of the design process. Algorithms that assess risk zones, track social movement, map topography, and posit future growth can provide developers with invaluable insight into construction needs as well as limitations.

When it comes to "intelligent" infrastructure specifically, transit systems must avoid being imposing, destructive, and invasive. In short, they must not go against the grain. In the specific case of San Agustin, a barrio of Caracas, the provincial government proposed the construction of a road through the slum that would require tearing down 30 percent of housing and the bringing of cars into what was essentially an exclusively pedestrian community. In July of 2003, Urban-Think Tank organized a symposium at Caracas's Central University to protest the government road plan and begin the process of exploring other possible solutions. The symposium resulted in the creation of a task force consisting of an organized group of community volunteers and the U-TT team. In relatively short order, the task force selected, from among several suggestions, a cable car system that traveled across the barrio and connected to the city's formal public transportation at the foot of the barrio. It was of the utmost importance that whatever system was to be put in place not only increase internal mobility within the settlement but also make external mobility easier. This plan was seen by the community as well as the design team as being ideally suited to the terrain, minimally invasive, accommodating of the existing fabric of the settlement, highly sustainable, and flexible. In a word, smart.

Emerging Mobility Solutions from the Informal City

In addition to being minimally invasive, "intelligent" infrastructure in informal settings must multitask. Torre David, a forty-five-story office tower in Caracas designed by the distinguished Venezuelan architect Enrique Gomez, was almost complete when it was abandoned following the death of its developer, David Brillembourg, in 1993 and the collapse of Venezuela's economy in 1994. Pushed out of their hillside barrios by a series of floods and landslides

Fig. 2. Torre David in its urban context. As of 2012, over 750 families, approximately three thousand residents, inhabit the first twenty-eight floors of this abandoned structure. (Photograph by Daniel Schwartz, U-TT and ETH; © Urban-Think Tank)

between 2007 and 2010, squatters headed to the city's center for refuge.[9] They found it within this colossal tower. As of 2012, over 750 families, approximately three thousand residents, inhabit the first twenty-eight floors of this structure. Its unfinished layout provides a world of possibilities. Squatters have established different ways of dividing space, sectioning off public and private areas, providing general services to the tower's community—grocery stores, athletic facilities, barber shops, day cares—and communal kitchens. Some see the structure as nothing more than a vertical slum, a "crude patchwork of improvisation, a blemish on the face of Caracas.[10]" Thousands of others call it home. The inquisitive may be wondering why only the first twenty-eight floors have been inhabited. Would spreading out not provide increased space for each family? Improve sanitation? The answer is both shocking and logical: residents have only settled so far up because this skyscraper has no elevator system.

This informal vertical community is in dire need of increased and improved transportation systems. Residents didn't need an architect to make that clear. Highly adaptive by nature, the community came up with a mobility solution of their own. The parking structure built next to the building was not originally attached to the tower for safety reasons. However, those living in the upper levels of the building have put down foot bridges from each floor of the spiraling parking garage to Torre David itself. Motorcyclists play the role of taxis drivers and transport walkers, by way of the garage, up and down the first ten floors.

The "intelligence" of this adaptation of what was intended to be automobile infrastructure does not stop there. Squatters have seen further potential for this parking garage. Shops have begun to pop up within the garage, transforming its intended single use into a multipurpose environment. Shopkeepers have realized that there are profits to be made on last-minute purchases. All of a sudden, one's last mile home becomes a key player in informal economic networks. This informal blending of transit and commerce may be the way of the future with respect to infrastructure and urban mobility.

Torre David is not the only structure in the city that has made transportation-specific infrastructure into so much more. Today, retrofitted parking garages are a new vernacular in Caracas (an oil-based economy that over-anticipated the amount of automobile dependence that would arise after the millennium) and have been occupied by Chinese restaurants, dry cleaners, doctors' offices, hairdressers, nightclubs, real-estate agents, and much more.[11] This adaptive

Fig. 3. Torre David has no parks in the vicinity, so the youth play soccer within the abandoned structure. (Photograph by Iwan Baan; © Urban-Think Tank)

Fig. 4. Retrofitted parking garages may be occupied by restaurants, dry cleaners, offices, and more. Caracas, Venezuela. (Photograph by Daniel Schwartz, U-TT and ETH; © Urban-Think Tank)

approach to parking structures offers small businesses a cheap and central location and allows customers to drive right up to the storefront. This innovation converts the *drive-in* to a *drive-up* typology. But why stop at the interweaving of transportation and commerce?

Growing midsized cities will inevitably face housing crises over the course of the next decade. Why not look to preexisting infrastructure for the solution? Herzog & de Meuron, experimenting with this typology, recently designed a top-end 65-million-dollar parking structure in Miami. It impressively combines parking with a penthouse apartment, designer clothing store, and a posh event space.[12] While this specific example is one from the formal sector of the city, housing units within parking garages are indeed feasible in a less formal setting as well. That said, the process of incorporating living arrangements into these structures, originally intended for transportation-related use, is not without its challenges. Ventilation, sanitation concerns, use of public space, and security all need to be addressed in the long run. What if the parking garage, in addition to providing basic shelter, had designated spaces for urban agriculture, sports facilities, sustainable energy production, and new services such as a large social space, kitchen, library, laundry unit, classroom, and workshop? Public services, such as a health clinic or sports facilities on the roof, would attract a wider mix of users and address whatever stigma might be attached to the garage.[13] The potential positive externalities are boundless! Similar to the case of housing discussed earlier, the success of this system lies in its modular formatting. As individual homes or facilities are being constructed, the rest of the parking complex remains fully functional. Displacement is minimal. The true "intelligence" of this design lies in its ability to anticipate the direction that urban living may be heading. As cities increase their interest in reaching a postcarbon energy system, making use of what already exists rather than the practice of demolition and new construction will surely become commonplace. This method recycles resources and minimizes the carbon footprint left behind by construction processes.

Transportation systems in both formal and informal cities are strongest when integrated into programming that catalyzes human interaction. As a typology, this parking garage adaptation could function like a street in the sky. Such treatment could allow infrastructure hubs to become pivotal spaces in the city, connecting different urban planes and adapting to various modes of transport and needs. Infrastructure initially intended for transit becomes the destination rather than simply a means to an end.

Centering around this theme of infrastructure and urban mobility as being "so much more" than it currently is, U-TT designed a cityscape model of what Sao Paulo's formal sector could look like in the year 2030 for Audi's Urban Future Initiative exhibition in 2012. Foot bridges connecting the tops of skyscrapers, elevators on the exterior of buildings traveling up to helicopter landing pads on some structures and down into the main subway system beneath others, bus and tramways integrated and accommodating of bicycle transit, metro cables traveling high above roads that are currently congested, ramps providing access to different elevation levels of transit both inside of buildings and externally. Rather than a city having a single transportation center, urban infrastructure would act like satellite dishes all over the city forming many hubs. Rather than having almost no choice but to go to the central hub to engage in certain direction and medium transfers (from a north-south trajectory to an east-west or from subway to bus) one would have multiple points of mass integration (hubs) better connecting the city. Essentially, U-TT's vision for formal mobility sees the future of urban infrastructure as trading in decentralization for localization.

Looking Forward

James Shore, a software development team leader, preaches a practice that is well aligned with how informal development should be treated going forward: "Incremental design applies the concepts introduced in test-driven development to all levels of design. Like test-driven development, developers work in small steps, proving each before moving to the next. This takes place in three parts: start by creating the simplest design that could possibly work, incrementally add to it as the needs of the software evolve, and continuously improve the design by reflecting on its strengths and weaknesses."[14] Design that follows this vein of thinking allows for the creation of infrastructure that is never necessarily finite. Rather, it has adaptive traits that make possible a metamorphosis of function as different needs present themselves. A structure intended as temporary housing for cars in a vehicle-heavy era may need to transform into a market one day, a school the next, a nightclub when the area changes its age demographic, and a retirement facility a few years down the line. With the rate of expected growth in informal cities, the best design projects are those that can be seen as "works in progress"; not because they are incomplete, but because they are able to evolve and multitask along with the communities that they serve.

Stepping back from the idolizing of technological advancement as our only way toward progress, it becomes clear that there is value in the downgrading of infrastructure (technologically speaking) as well. Poor areas of cities tend to be in the most need for improvements in mobility (both physical and social mobility). Problem-solving urban design needs to be case-specific and localized to particular situations rather than a swiftly repaired, "one size fits all" generalized approach. In informal urban areas, implementing a regulated tuk tuk or motorcycle taxis system may do more for people than a tram system that displaces 40 percent of an informal community. Urban infrastructure in the future must be the meeting point between upward social mobility for the poor and downward adaptability of today's obsession with advanced technology.

Fig. 5. Audi Parangole Axonometric, São Paulo, Brazil. Rather than cities having a single transportation center, urban infrastructure could act like satellite dishes distributed all over the city forming many hubs. (© Urban-Think Tank, for Audi Future Initiative 2012)

Ultimately, the success of "intelligent" infrastructure in informal cities is dependent upon how well it meets case-specific needs, how much it involves the on-the-ground community, how easily adaptable it is (to the constant and rapid growth seen in informal environments), and how well it can multitask. Once all of these parts come to together, formal cities may find themselves lacking in comparison and may seek to borrow transportation methods from the informal sector. In fact, such is already the case. If you have ever tried to get around New York's Times Square on a Friday or Saturday evening, your best bet is not to hail a taxi or trudge into the depths of the subway. Your fastest and most cost-effective choice is to hop on the nearest rickshaw and have the young man steering it run you to your desired destination. Able to weave through narrow openings unnavigable to a car, all while avoiding the expensive and environmentally damaging use of gasoline . . . Times Square starts to sound quite a bit like Brazil's favelas.

Notes

This essay was written with the assistance of Lindiwe Rennert, ETH/U-TT researcher.

1   City Mayor Statistics, "Some 640 Million People Live in the World's 300 Largest Cities." http://www.citymayors.com/features/largest_cities.html.

2   City Mayor Statistics, "World's Fastest Growing Cities and Urban Areas from 2006 to 2020," http://www.citymayors.com/statistics/urban_growth1 .html.

3   Christian Werthmann, "Green Infrastructure in the Non-formal City," seminar course SCI 0644500, Harvard Graduate School of Design, spring 2012.

4   Ibid.

5   Hongsheng Qiu, Ximing Tan, Shu Shi, and Heng Zhang, "Influence of Filler–Bitumen Ratio on Performance of Modified Asphalt Mortar by Additive," *Journal of Modern Transportation* 21, no. 1 (2013): 40–46.

6   Rick Delgado, "20 Smart City Technologies for 2013 and Beyond," Freshome, May 1, 2013, http://freshome.com/2013/05/01/20-smart-city -technologies-for-2013-and-beyond/.

7   Alfredo Brillembourg and Hubert Klumpner, *Moderating Urban Density* (exhibition) (Berlin: Aedes, 2006).

8   Ibid.

9   Alfredo Brillembourg and Hubert Klumpner, *Torre David: Informal Vertical Communities* (Zurich: Lars Muller, 2013).

10 Ibid.

11 Alfredo Brillembourg and Hubert Klumpner, with Alice Hertzog and Daniel Schwartz in association with ETH Zurich Department of Architecture and Urban-Think Tank. *Beyond Torre David: Informal Vertical Communities* (exhibition) (Berlin: Aedes Gallery, 2013).

12 Robert Wennett, *1111 Lincoln Road*, http://www.1111lincolnroad.com.

13 Brillembourg and Klumpner, *Beyond Torre David*.

14 James Shore, *The Art of Agile Development* (Santa Rosa, CA: O'Reilly Media, 2008).

The Paradox of Urban Mobility and the Spatialization of Technological Utopia

Chamee Yang

A city made for speed is made for success.
　—Le Corbusier, *The City of To-morrow and Its Planning*

Mobility: a cornerstone of the smart, sustainable city.
　—Schneider Electric, Arup, and the Climate Group, "Urban Mobility in the Smart City Age"

Long before Le Corbusier claimed speed to be a necessity for humankind's progress, the goal of overcoming the friction of space has always been one of humanity's biggest aspirations. The evolutionary history of technologies of transportation and communication reflects how our desire to control space has gradually found its way into supposedly "annihilating space" with the instantaneity of today's electronic technology.[1] And contemporary cities, composed of various modes of mobilities that mediate movements of bodies, material goods, knowledge, and ideas, are pressed to optimize themselves in response to the growing need for sustainability and efficiency, to facilitate and expedite certain forms of mobility in the hopes of their own growth and betterment.

In fact, there has recently been a conspicuous increase of public discourse that sets out mobility as the leitmotif of urban problems. This epochal representation of the contemporary city often urges us to respond to the pressing challenge of "speeding up" the city and reducing our dependency on natural resources. Here, urban mobility is emphasized as both a primary challenge for a city's continued growth and as a tool to enhance economic, social, and environmental well-being. Through focusing on mobility, this new growth paradigm of the city seeks to adapt to a global reality where information science and technology are the clean and sustainable growth factors.

This essay's first aim is to examine a broadly generalized view of *mobility* and explore its multiple and ambivalent consequences. Rather than seeing mobility merely as a matter of origin and destination, or as a matter of speeding up and setting free, I seek to understand it as a useful concept that reveals a series of contradictions that structure social exclusions that are latent in the technologies and the surrounding circumstances that inform their use. In particular, I anchor my argument to the notion of the "paradox of mobility"[2] as it relates to the dialectics of mobility and immobility that contribute to the human experiences of space. As Stephen Graham and Simon Marvin have rightly pointed out, this paradox also captures the socially embedded nature of urban network infrastructures, which mediate both connections and disconnections among different social agents.[3] While facilitating mobility presupposes systemic "stability,"[4] mobility discourse, with its emphasis on dynamism, simultaneity, and speed, often obscures this underlying rigidity, order, and rationality.

I further argue that the deliberate focus on the process of transition replete in the popular discourse on mobility and networked infrastructure corresponds with governments' strategy of claiming its affinity with the global capitalist market, while, at the same time, the strategy relies on differentiating its population. This association reinforces the technologically deterministic assumptions that posit technological innovation as a solution to urban problems, evoking a utopian vision of future cities engineered and optimized to be secure, orderly, and materially abundant.

Lastly, the essay provides a focused observation of "U-City" (Ubiquitous City)," which has been taking place in the Songdo district of Incheon, South Korea. This case study, within the context of East Asian developmental politics, foregrounds the city planners and policy makers' aspirations to materialize a utopian idea through the means of the latest technological innovations. Numerous strategies of "mobilizing" the city resources have been implemented in order to achieve "economic revitalization" and win global recognition. Among these strategies are special zoning policies that advance a public-private partnership between the city administration and (global) corporations. However, the realization of an egalitarian and harmonious image of utopia has been subverted by the social exclusion and control exercised by the very system that claims this futuristic ideal as its present goal.

Paradox of Mobilities and the Technology That Disappears

In *Urban Mobility in the Smart City Age*, a collaborative research report put together by Schneider Electric, Arup, and the Climate Group, mobility is described as "the ability of people and goods to move around an area, and in doing so to access the essential facilities, communities and other destinations that are required to support a decent quality of life and a buoyant economy. Mobility incorporates the transport infrastructure and services that facilitate these interactions."[5]

In particular, the report suggests that the systems of "smart mobility" provide a means for cities to respond to the pressures of accelerated urbanization so that they can sustain growth. Smart mobility services typically operate from a central command center to access and use radio-frequency identification (RFID) technology and travelers' global positioning system (GPS) data to coordinate transportation flow by enabling smart parking, smart ticketing, journey planning, and bicycle and carsharing. These services are advertised as reducing road congestions and alleviating travelers' frustrations. This mobility-centered technological optimism echoes throughout related industry publications, including a multinational network production company like Cisco's 2013 white paper on the enterprise potential of "mobile innovation": "Organizations must find ways to do more for their customers in order to take advantage of this massive mobility progression—all made possible with high-performance, high-intelligence solutions that open new business models and create better experiences."[6]

Proponents of networked mobility's salutary potential commonly suppose that a city's improved modes of mobility will synergize with one another to catalyze its growth and subsequently win global recognition and investment. The conviction is based on the economic calculation that a resource provided to ensure the public good mobility deserves to be facilitated through investment. Cisco's calls for new solutions to meet the expectations of "clients" and "customers" reveals a motive to advance urban mobility that is intimately tied to a capitalist motive to foster their related businesses. However, Cisco's public relations approach appeals to political normativity in suggesting that the company's investment in the network services is beneficial to urban residents' well-being and even to the city's transparency of governance. Cisco's white paper does not neglect to include the promise of a safe and secure environment for future generations.

The utopian rhetoric of networked connectivity and mobility saturating the popular discourses such as the above profoundly reduces the range of mobility concepts that might otherwise multiply, even if they did so in contradiction to one another. Mobility, in a broader sense, refers not only to the mechanical modes of transportation but also to the movement of different objects, such as capitals, goods, bodies, and information, each moving with a variety of speeds, scales, and motives. In sociology, for instance, the concept of *social mobility* is understood as the degree to which an individual can move from his or her initial, stratified position to another that is perceived as having either a lower or a higher hierarchical value.[7]

More importantly, considering the fact that the networked infrastructures of mobilities management is becoming a default across a number of basic urban functions beyond transportation, including disaster prevention, retail commerce, energy management, and financial transactions, it is crucial that we recalibrate the concept of mobility applicable to those wider domains.

To demonstrate the possibilities of this concept, I now take up three inter-related domains in the hypertechnologized city within which to discuss the *paradox of mobility*: (1) the domain of human body, within which the accelerated virtual mobility confines bodily mobility into fixed locations; (2) the domain of human consciousness, within which the ubiquitous and pervasive presence of technology becomes more invisible (e.g., networked sensors and fibers built into urban infrastructure automatically monitor, record, and control individual activities without one's knowledge); (3) the domain of capital. Cities often attempt to increase their competitiveness through special zoning policies that legitimate selective investments in the urban infrastructure in order to stimulate market sectors such as tourism. However, a number of studies have pointed out the fast circulation of capital that these zoning policies enable can lead to uneven "splinters" in the local region.[8] From a local administrative per-spective, the ultimate goal of these policies is not enabling constant mobility of capital but providing a persistent "stickiness" that attracts and fixes capital to the region. Given the paradoxes that manifest in each of these domains, it is crucial that we ask the proponents of new urban mobility programs the question of what may inadvertently move with whatever they hope to mobilize, what the movement trajectory might be (from where to where), and what may be lost along the way.

Virtual Mobility and Corporeal Stasis

A tech-centered vision of urban planning often assumes a natural affinity between the virtual mobility of information and the material mobility of people, the combined effect of which will eventually improve urban functions and subsequently increase the well-being of urban inhabitants. However, it is difficult to dismiss outright the truism that nothing is gained without the loss of something else. According to Paul Virilio, what will be gained inevitably from information and communication technologies (ICT), such as an instant and real-time access to the "information superhighway," is dis-information.[9] For Virilio, the sense of universal time that the electronic media enables is nothing other than an epic tyranny, which fundamentally disorients our senses and our control over the reason. Our bodies—plugged into various interfaces including keyboards, keypads, earphones, screens, and all sorts of artificial prostheses—are virtually moving at the speed of light; this cybernetic extension of the body into the network gives us a sense of instant connectivity and interconnectivity. However, through a number of his aphorisms, Virilio argues convincingly that the illusion of virtual ubiquity conjured through networked urbanism is predicated on the passive and static position of human bodies.

I find an instance of this corporeal paradox of mobility in the U-City service in New Songdo City, South Korea, which offers domestic and public welfare services that are enacted by the wide-ranging use of "telepresent" technologies. Utilizing interactive screens, RFID tags, and a centralized data-gathering and processing center, the city's domestic and urban spaces are equipped with a variety of functions. U-Life Solutions, a smart home service launched in 2011 by a joint venture between Cisco and New Songdo International City Development LLC, is currently being tested by one hundred city residents.[10] The system provides remote education, health, and beauty counseling services through Cisco's HD video system, TelePresence. Residents can sit in front of their TV and chat with English tutors, take one-on-one yoga lessons from professional instructors, and even consult with doctors for aesthetic plastic surgery. TelePresence's subscription-based menu of programs is bundled with the purchase of extra equipment, including an HD camera, remote control, table microphone, and codec, all charged to the citizen-consumer's monthly utility bill. Similarly, U-Life Solutions also offers u-shopping, u-golf, and u-parking services, all of which are managed by an integrated information control center: the UMC, or U-Life Management Center.

Cisco's TelePresence system is also said to transform the way children are educated at school. Chadwick International School in New Songdo City is the first international school to enroll domestic students from preschool to the twelfth grade. Students are said to attend classes "with" their classmates in Palos Verdes, California, in Cisco's TelePresence room via real-time video connection.[11]

With just a few clicks and gestures, it is possible for the residents of U-City to control their access to multiple "telepresent" persons and spaces. Since information is supposedly moving in one's stead, it becomes unnecessary to leave the house to visit marketplaces, hospitals, and banks in person. There is even no need to take out the trash, thanks to an underground garbage disposal system that sucks it out of the house.

In such advanced networked systems, information comes to serve us in personalized and customized forms. In-person interpersonal communication is replaced by "face-to-face" online chats, which give the illusion of connectivity, participation, and community. This deluge of screens and spectacles creates a "fantasy of abundance"[12] in the domain of our consciousness, seeming to illustrate the infinite and free range of choices offered within hands' reach. A few tapping gestures on our tablets and smartphones encourage us to believe that we are enhanced, connected, and even empowered while we are nevertheless physically passive, static, and separated by actual distance.

One of the primary goals of government in embedding centrally governed data streams into our everyday spaces is the drive for efficiency. However, one cannot overlook the fact that this intense mediality of interaction is somewhat antagonistic to the basic idea of what city is: a site of tactile interactions and exchanges. As neighborhood crossroads become Internet transits, urban travelers become anonymous passengers. The virtual mobility achieved through telepresence technologies protects us from the feelings of isolation that result from social atomization by replacing local reference and history with spectacles—from which we are supposed to "actively" seek the pleasures of living in a high-tech city.

The Illusion of Liberty and Ubiquity of Control

The new set of U-City urban services being piloted in New Songdo City provides a means of carrying out our daily chores in the most effortless and liberating way. Simultaneously, however, these civic, or home, automation technologies sense and track (and may store and report) our everyday activities. Moreover, they are maintained and controlled by assiduous human labor that has been "invisibly" encoded into the networked infrastructure. Government urban services automation policies are rationalized through a rhetoric of urgency about the public's need for improved convenience and safety. According to a local survey conducted by Hanhwa group in Korea, the residents of New Songdo City are said to share a particularly high interest in protecting the place with the utmost security.[13] In fact, public safety through a networked security system is the benefit that U-City planners emphasized the most conspicuously throughout their proposal.

The U-City proposal suggests that Songdo's special focus on security maintenance will be realized by adapting the city's ubiquitous technology to that purpose. A ubiquitous city is one in which all the major urban functions (e.g., residential, medical, retail, and governmental) are digitized so that data is shared and integrated seamlessly across platforms. Officials in Songdo also initially proposed offering free public Wi-Fi as well, so that anyone in the city could access the Internet from anywhere at any time. Currently however, there are only a few free Wi-Fi zones operating, and these are not in residential areas but in tourist hotels, tourist information offices, district offices, and university campuses.[14]

In a 2005 New York Times interview, Anthony Townsend called Songdo's U-City "a uniquely Korean idea," fully supported by its "historical expectation of less privacy." As a result, he noted, Songdo had "fewer social and regulatory obstacles" to implementing ubiquitous technology.[15] A wide and pervasive use of RFID technology is indeed what makes Songdo incomparable to other cities in the world. RFID chips have been implanted in public recycling bins as well as in residents' private cars, multipurpose smart cards, and children's bracelets, fully adapting the city to the ideal U-City, where an unmanned machine remotely monitors, records, and controls every inch.

In 2010, IBM Korea announced that it would test its new smart CCTV (closed-circuit television) system in Songdo. Security cameras equipped with

Fig. 1. An inside look at the U-City control tower where patterns of micromovements in the city are monitored and managed. (Incheon Free Economic Zone Authority)

user-recognition technology not only record but also automatically react to any unusual levels of heat or movements in a scene. Government officials of Songdo legitimated the blanket use of surveillance technologies by citing the improvements they offer to public safety through enabling more efficient prevention of and response to fire disasters, hit-and-runs, and violent crimes.[16] Songdo is also where Cisco's experimental "Smart + Connected City" idea has been most freely deployed and fully tested. Its traffic solution, for instance, combines a number of technical components including IP (Internet protocol) cameras, license plate readers, and a unified data-processing center to identify real-time traffic conditions and to analyze the traffic-flow patterns in the city.

In public space, individuals are linked to a central data management center by smart cards that each person carries. A smart card can be used to unlock doors to buildings, travel on subways, borrow free public bicycles, make purchases at department stores, pay parking meters, and so on. In private spaces, on the other hand, smart meters record energy consumption and activity patterns from each household and building so that the exact average amount of electricity can be predicted and supplied. These intelligent domestic services can do more than assist with household economy or sustainable living. Parents can attach RFID chips to their children in order to locate and keep track of them when they are out of school. This child safety service, now in the beta-testing stage, will eventually be provided by subscription.

The paradox of advanced surveillance technologies is that their ubiquitous presence is invisible to the naked eye. While their technological mandate pervades literally everywhere, their operations become naturalized in urban dwellers' everyday context. As early as 1991, Mark Weiser predicted in *Scientific American* that ubiquitous technologies such as these would become the "most profound form of technology" in modern life. As their interfaces become the environment itself, technologies ultimately disappear from our consciousness, both individual and collective.[17]

Such a disappearance, according to Weiser, is a "fundamental consequence not of technology but of human psychology."[18] Technology does not disappear; it simply becomes better hidden. We are seldom reminded, for example, of the presence of the numerous kinds of software upon which we rely for our daily productivity and entertainment unless a program "asks" us to perform a version upgrade or intrudes on our activity with an error message. It is worth noting, however, that while technology can temporarily disappear from the boundaries of consciousness for users and consumers, behind the scenes assiduous human labor is required to constantly maintain and upgrade it. As the networked environment becomes such an integral part of our lives that we come to accept it as invisible and, at times, effortless, as in U-City Songdo, we should remember that the system still demands human intelligence and labor.

More problematically, the invisible technologies enabled by networked infrastructures, pervading all sorts of daily practices, give people the illusion that they are controlling their lives freely and independently. However, this illusion of liberty is achieved only when we yield the locus of control for our lives elsewhere. Samuel Nunn conceptualizes this surrender as a "paradox of solipsism."[19] The notion of solipsism is that the only thing that is real is what one sees and experiences. The self, the key agent that perceives its reality, is supposed to use technology in order to make its everyday life more efficient and convenient. However, the twist in this solipsist thinking, according to Nunn, is that something other than oneself is actually in charge of controlling one's reality. One's interaction with reality is mediated through external technological processes, which remains invisible, inexplicable, and thus unquestioned.

Technocratic governments tend to reinforce this paradox of solipsism by obscuring their highly regulated and rationalized management of systems of surveillance. Their rhetoric often celebrates technological novelties in a tone that is meant to convince people that the system advocates for their freedom and well-being. However, in such popular discourses, it is difficult to locate the actual price we must pay to maintain the system. It is seldom questioned how data will be gathered and processed, by whom the data will be managed, whether it is possible to opt out of the system without penalties, what the surveillance is securing ourselves from, and who will eventually profit from such invisible processes.

Technocratic governmental rhetoric often further obscures the power dynamics of these automated technologies through portraying them as "value-neutral" technologies that are codified in ways that prevent any intervention or partial judgment. However, the claim for value-neutral technologies is itself an intensely political rhetoric. It is because the tendency to regard technology as something that exists outside of politics is related to a perspective that sees an appeal to technology as a means of evading political controversies and contestations.[20]

Global Mobility Splintering the Local

In the year 2002, Incheon, a city located forty miles southwest of Seoul, South Korea, was officially granted the national government's permission to establish the Incheon Free Economic Zone (IFEZ). FEZ refers to a specially demarcated territory within which certain exemptions from taxes and other legal duties are awarded to international companies that conduct business and invest in the area. The Songdo (20.6 square miles), Yong-jong (8.42 square miles), and Chung-ra (6.87 square miles) districts of Incheon were designated as special zones, with each district having its own designated focus: Songdo on the high-tech industry and international business, Yong-jong on transportation and import/export, and Chung-ra on leisure and tourism.[21]

In order to increase international investment, each FEZ exempts companies from paying corporate income tax for the first three years and allow them to pay half the usual rate for the next two years. Labor management is deregulated, allowing employers to offer unpaid holidays and lifting any obligation for employers to employ veterans, the disabled, and the elderly. Each FEZ also provides exceptions to regulations that would otherwise prevent foreign investors from establishing schools, hospitals, and pharmacies that can be used by domestic residents. Cable networks offer 10 percent more foreign channels than is standard, and English is allowed for the processing of public documents.[22]

Located seven miles from Korea's Incheon International Airport in Yongjong, Songdo aspires to be an *aerotropolis*, a "gateway to more than ⅓ of the world's population in just 3.5 hours of flying time."[23] Its strategic location makes it easy for commercial travelers to access other megacities in East Asia, including Shanghai (1 hour), Tokyo (1.5 hours), Hong Kong (2.5 hours), and Singapore (5.5 hours). Thus, both in terms of policy and location, the Incheon Free Economic Zone has been positioned to serve as a central node in the mobilization of global capital.

This zoning strategy, unprecedented in Korean history, reveals a form of governance that "selectively" liberates special zones to differentiate various segments of population,[24] offering different privileges and imposing different restrictions based on residents' creativity, innovativeness, and "smartness." By granting authority to foreign investors and entrepreneurs, the government reveals its intention to treat people differently, depending on their profitability and their affinity for the global financial market. Graham and Marvin refer to this as a "networked paradox of global connection and local disconnection."[25] That is, economic development tends to follow a spatial pattern in which physically distant but socioeconomically "close" places converge even as they are distanced from physically close but socioeconomically "remote" places.

In light of the Incheon Free Economic Zone policies, Songdo's active adoption of surveillance technologies seems less politically neutral. Mounted license-plate readers at the city's entrance points and widely distributed CCTVs in public spaces suggest instead a governmental strategy of mobility management and boundary maintenance that favors residents who serve FEZ objectives. The city has effectively prioritized and enhanced one population's mobility over any others'[26]: FEZ insiders over outsiders; the capital, information, and technology haves over have-nots; young entrepreneurs and professionals over the elderly, less skilled, and undereducated.

Ultimately, a city's technological development plans reflect the ways in which its leaders and innovators conceive of social order. Deliberately or not, when cities develop technical infrastructure on a large scale, every design decision city planners make profoundly influences how their residents consume, move, work, and communicate. In the process by which such decisions are made, "different people are differently situated and possess unequal degrees of power as well as unequal levels of awareness."[27] In other words, people have uneven chances of being heard and unequal abilities to affect political decisions that impact their daily existence. Explicit political practices and institutional policies can differentiate between or unite people, but so do more implicit means of ordering and differentiating modes of mobility. Spatialized forms of power, for example, may be insinuated into "tangible arrangements of steel and concrete, wires and transistors, nuts and bolts."[28] Consequently, any choices related to urban infrastructure must be explored critically for their sociopolitical dynamics.

Urban Planning's Predispositions toward Technology

In the previous section, I examined three major domains within which the paradoxical systems of mobilities manifest: the human body, human consciousness, and capital. To provide a framework for a critical discussion of networked urban infrastructure across these mobilized domains, I borrow theories of media and technology from the fields of history and philosophy. My aim is to understand technology not as a value-neutral field of applied science focused solely on innovating past practical challenges, but as a socially constructed field of knowledge, practice, and instrumental capacity that has embedded within it enduring social forms and protocols. This critical examination of technology requires that we attend to the broader field of "technical arrangements"[29] that relate to specific forms of social power and authority, while assuming that the development and implementation of technologies "always already" rely on contested interactions between subjects who are equipped with unequal degrees of knowledge and power.

The workings of a technocratic society's dominant ideology are exposed through the ways in which it becomes both embedded in technological innovation and obscured through its rationalization. To more fully understand this process, it is useful to trace the constituitive choices that have dynamically shaped an associated set of technologies and guided their application in a specific region of intensive capital development: the city, taking up the case of Songdo in particular. Therefore, in this section, I tease out and discuss two interrelated rhetorical tendencies that have been often associated with emergent technology: technology as the key enabler of social change and progress, and technology as a symbol of the future. In the case of Songdo, such technocratic rhetoric implicitly grants technical development a prerogative, thereby legitimating the government's strategies of control and differentiation. Thus, the simplified, if not exaggerated, utopian vision of technologically enhanced urban design requires a serious and critical questioning of its sociocultural implications.

Technological Determinism

Cities today play reciprocal roles as central platforms of technical innovation and spaces of technological consumption. These reciprocal roles are reflected in Songdo IFEZ's new urban policies, which conceive of the city as both a business- and foreigner-friendly environment and a test bed for the new urban network services developed by its global corporate research and development centers. This dual conception of the city manifests explicitly in Songdo developments such as Smart Valley. The name suggests an explicit desire on the part of city planners to replicate Silicon Valley in establishing a South Korean high-tech consortium of corporate research and development (R&D) centers. According to Songdo's master plan, the high-tech Smart Valley business district occupies its most densely populated area. It is also located at the heart of the city, which is indicative of "utopian" Songdo's real focus: business.[30]

Owing to the special zoning policies of IFEZ, Songdo's Smart Valley was able to host several corporate headquarters and R&D centers, many of them the branch offices of Korean *chae-bol* companies (i.e., large, family-owned conglomerates). As of 2013, these included Samsung Biologics, Celtrion, Donga Pharmaceutical, Amko Solara's Korean branch office (alternative energy and lighting system), Cisco's Korean branch office, Daewoo International (international trade business), and Posco Engineering (engineering and construction). In addition to enjoying a corporate tax exemption and a number of policy-based benefits, these already prosperous companies are also allowed to own and manage privatized retail spaces such as the NC-Cube Shopping Center, Lotte Complex Shopping Mall, and Hyundai Department Store.[31]

This preferential investment in the high-tech industry and ICT-based urban infrastructure reflects Korea's national economic policies, which began promoting the postindustrial "knowledge economy" in the 1990s and have recently recast that present vision of future prosperity as the "creative economy." In early 2014, President Geun-Hye Park's annual public speech strongly emphasized information and communications technology (ICT) and its commercial application: "I ask that we all put our efforts into innovating our way toward achieving the miracle of a creative economy. Science, technology, ICT, and cultural content, the vitamins of a creative economy, are our strengths. . . . I will shift all regulatory systems to encourage investment and to overcome economic hurdles in our nation."[32]

South Korea's strategic dependence on science and technology to drive economic growth is not entirely new. The rapid economic recovery of a resource-poor country like South Korea has often been attributed to its concentrated investment in labor-intensive manufacturing industries such as textiles, steel, automobiles, and electronics. However, this alone cannot account for South Korea's success. In 1997, its industrial economy was impacted by cheap labor in South Asia and China as well as the intervention of the International Monetary Fund (IMF) and other global financial authorities (during a period often referred to as the "IMF crisis" or "Asian financial crisis"). In response, Korea adopted neoliberal economic reforms and shifted its focus to the high-tech industry as a new engine of growth.

In South Korea public nostalgia for progress and economic development has a unique association with a narrative in which technology is harnessed to achieve domestic economic growth. In other words, the dominant cultural narrative associates a strategically rationalized view of innovation with a collective desire for well-being. The problem with such an enthusiastic and deterministic approach to technology is that it reifies technology as an unproblematic and autonomous force that drives daily life and shapes urban areas. The prefix buzz of u- and smart- everything assumes that technology will make things unquestionably different, new and better. For city administrators and developers, it might be tempting to believe in the revolutionary potential of technology bringing about significant improvements in urban governance, such as in how people move around the city, and what neighborhood areas look like. Their public relations communications contribute to and recirculate other popular discourses' enthusiasm for the transformative potential of technology (e.g., "the iPhone revolution"; "ubiquitous technology" that makes "our city safe and green"), casually coupling technology and an anticipated or perceived positive social change.

What this technological optimism dismisses is the "tendency of newer networks to overlie and combine with, rather than replace, earlier networks."[33] In the case of Songdo, for instance, what is left out of the praise for the propagation of "walkable" neighborhoods is that in order to access them residents must travel significant distances by car or public transportation (the Incheon subway line, public bus service, or water taxis along the canals). Moreover, in suggesting that the development of a networked infrastructure serves only to promote the public good, the rhetoric and practice of the government elide a number of questionable sociotechnical arrangements. Among these is that the government seeks to ensure progress through authoritarian regulations and financial policies. Equally important is that government support for smart urban development is largely concentrated in large corporations, in the form of public-private partnership (in which the public sector outsources services to the private sector). Finally, this government-led technocracy legitimates the relative dispossession of older neighborhoods and disenfranchises labor from other market sectors such as agriculture, fishing, and manufacturing.

It may be that South Korea's unique cultural tendency to put collective interests ahead of individual rights, including the individual right to privacy, has led to the widespread adoption of surveillance technology in Songdo and other urban areas as they develop. Anthony Townsend suggests that the cause lies instead in the nation's drive for prosperity, saying, "Korea is willing to put off the hard questions to take the early lead and set standards."[34]

In the latter half of the twentieth century, South Korea's technological development policy has been characterized by the process of "compressed modernity."[35] This unique form of South Korean modernity has involved statistically rapid and extensive economic growth that monopolizes domestic financial resources in favor of *chae-bol* companies and makes use of exploitative labor management. Driven by a pro-efficiency approach to economy, and motivated to catch up with already developed Western counterparts, the authoritarian and despotic government of South Korea from the early 1960s through 1987 sanctioned policies that were especially antagonistic to women and unionized labor. The government's subsequent neoliberal turn during the 1990s further strengthened the alliance between the state and the global financial market. Having inherited this developmental strategy, the current government's investment in technological entrepreneurship and its promotion of a "creative economy" explicitly reinforces the neoliberal trend of deregulating and privatizing public assets. In this vein, the U-City project in Songdo IFEZ can be seen as the latest and the most vivid example of neoliberal growth coalition politics, which prioritize the technological innovation and capitalist interests over citizens' equal rights to access social infrastructure and to benefit from equitable urban development.

In sum, technology, as a political phenomenon, exists inside, rather than outside, society. Behind so-called intelligent machines exist largely invisible human intelligence and labor, embedded in the specific sociocultural context and institutional arrangements that inform their practice. Rhetoric that represents technological development as autonomous obfuscates the actual process of governance and its systematic exercise of control and differentiation. Through employing this kind of rhetoric, and deferring to the rationality of technology, governments such as South Korea's attempt to relieve themselves of any responsibility for confronting political controversies.

Utopian Ideals and Discourse of the Future

To displace tensions over economic and related social policies, technocratic governments rely not only on narratives that portray technological development as autonomous but also on those that are excessively future-oriented. At the Incheon Global Fair and Festival held in 2009, a local event prepared to promote the identity of the new city, organizers displayed the slogan "Lightening Tomorrow: Come and See the Future City."[36] As an ideal urban "vision of tomorrow," Incheon was represented as a place where all the citizens of the world would come together to create a peaceful and harmonious community. This vision of a technocratic utopia vividly epitomizes the particular urban ideal that has been deployed in the planning of Incheon's Songdo district. Songdo presents itself as an ambitious forerunner that leads the future, facilitating global harmony, offering green and healthy living (Songdo may be translated as "Island of Pine Trees"), and promoting regional economic growth.[37]

However, the problem with such utopian thinking is its distorted focus on the end result rather than the process. As Martin Meyerson points out, the practice of urban planning has "either ignored the means . . . or has concentrated on the efficacy of means to the exclusion of ends."[38] Any practice of planning necessarily involves looking ahead to the future. At issue is how, from the immanent here and now, we are going to access that desirable place that has yet to come. This strategy of squarely optimizing a city to fit an ideal model

Fig. 2. Songdo Tribowl Gallery, Incheon, South Korea. (Chamee Yang)

that is based on a limited number of simplified principles inhibits planners (and their fellow proponents) from attending to the conflict, ambiguity, and indeterminacy that are characteristics of actual social life. Engineers tinker with the algorithms and protocols that parse and process data across the smart city's infrastructure based on an understanding of the city not as it is, but as it should be. Flows of movements, among other forms of mobility, are calculated, predicted, and optimized. It is like playing an urban construction and management simulation game (e.g., SimCity) on a real-life scale—a game, however, that can be played only by those who can afford to invest.[39]

If we agree to regard the U-City project as a particularly contemporary conjuncture within the longer history of modernist urban planning practices, there seems to have emerged an interesting and yet uneasy overlap between urban planning, architecture, and computer science. It is as if urban planning is attempting to resemble an applied science, as the rationalist tendency of modernist planning gives way to computer science's disciplinary authority over information science through data mining and algorithms. From this perspective, urban space serves merely as a test bed for experimentation,[40] a copy-and-pastable template from which an immaculate model of the city can be mechanically reproduced. In that shining portrayal of Songdo's future, planning objectives (safety, cleanliness, and business-friendliness) are linked with the actual city's physical design and policies. Abstraction and optimization govern the process by which this technological utopia is spatialized. What is more, in urban planning, an excess of futurism in a project narrative can denote an attempt to compensate for a lack of deliberation by exaggerating the virtues of the end product.

Technocratic utopia's fixation on rationalized control and internal security makes it callous to social struggles from the outside. In the case of South Korea's IFEZ, the name "New Songdo City" already represents a desire to semantically differentiate the district from other districts of Incheon. Its image of rationalism and exclusivity erases any traces of conflict and anomaly. This is a feature of what David Harvey calls the "degenerate utopia," where "the dialectic is repressed and stability and harmony are secured through intense surveillance and control. . . . [I]t offers a futuristic utopia of technological purity and unsurpassed human power to control the world."[41] This kind of utopia is "degenerate" in the sense that its elite maintain a guarded posture that remains ignorant and indifferent to the existing state of affairs on the outside, while refusing to internalize or allow any critique in order to perpetuates the system of exclusion upon which their class advantages are predicated. The utopian elite knows all too well that they are protected within the pure, sanitized, and smart space they have wrought through technological virtuosity.

What remains is an urgent need for urban planners and the partners in government and enterprise to more carefully consider and discuss the consequences of altering fundamental features of urban sociopolitical culture. The discussion has to include deeper reflections on the form of citizenship, as well as the form of governance, envisaged in technical and spatial arrangements. More importantly, any future proposition for urban development has to consider affordability and accessibility in the here and now for all residents and the relationship of new development to existing neighborhoods.

Conclusion

In this essay, I set out to deconstruct the popular tropes of smart urban mobilities and to manifest a set of systematic paradoxes that are inherent in the networked urban infrastructures. My argument demonstrates how, in their drive to promote the city, proponents of new urban mobilities deploy the rhetoric of liberty, security, and sustainable growth, while the actual government policies supported by this rhetoric entail systematic contradictions that confine human bodies in relative stasis, differentiate populations based on their profitability, and legitimate pervasive forms of surveillance.

I further call into question the underlying predispositions that might maintain and reinforce such contradictions, employing South Korea's techno-utopian Incheon Free Economic Zone district of Songdo as one such case. On the one hand, in the popular discourse that concerns new urban mobilities, I identify a tendency toward technological determinism that may have the effect of limiting the public's focus to a direct and linear course of causes and effects. On the other hand, I find the developmental government's wishful thinking on technological development and utopian planning practices to be yoked to an enthusiasm for social transformation, which the public may share and find appealing. This dual-pronged rhetoric of new urban mobilities stands to contribute to sustaining a social system that callously differentiates between populations and legitimates unequal access to social infrastructure developments.

Emergent technology has often inspired utopian rhetoric about how it will lead to progressive social change. Its series of failures to achieve that end contradicts this promise. Yet developmental governments continue to incorporate emergent technology, including new mobilities, into urban planning in response to a structural necessity of the capitalistic system, which is driven to constantly reproduce itself. However, as Stephen Graham reminds us, to attempt to decouple technology from the matter of politics and to define cities "generically and one-sidedly as endogenous engines of growth" is to "ignore other formative aspects of urban history: economic and ecological parasitism, forms of socio-political exclusion and a dependence of commercial exchange."[42] We must acknowledge that technological means and its proposed ends are distinct phenomena. As Philip D'Anieri suggests convincingly, we should attend "not only to creating a vision but to understanding which elements of that vision are realized and especially which motivations and organizing principles are retained."[43] Otherwise, "the utopian vision can become simply a cover story for business as usual."[44]

Notes

1   Originally conceptualized by Karl Marx, "annihilation of space by time" is a process pertinent to the natural tendency of capital to move beyond a spatial barrier to exchange and circulate the excess product. Since circulation requires surplus labor and costs, the efficient means of communication and transport becomes a necessary physical condition for advancement of the capitalist mode of production. During the industrialization process, the invention of the telegraph and railroad played a critical role in overcoming spatial barriers, generating the emergence of a new perception of space and time, where the absolute power of natural space became subjected to the rationalized scheme of mechanical time. According to David Harvey, this diminution of spatial barriers by technical means, however, provoked instead an increasing sense of nationalism and localism to separate and to defend oneself from one another.

2   Paul Virilio, "Speed and Information: Cyberspace Alarm!" CTHEORY, August 27, 1995, http://www.ctheory.net/printer.aspx?id=72.

3   Stephen Graham and Simon Marvin, Splintering Urbanism: Networked Infra-structures, Technological Mobilities and the Urban Condition (London: Routledge, 2001), 13.

4   Mimi Sheller and John Urry, eds. Mobile Technologies of the City (London: Routledge, 2006), 5–6.

5   Schneider Electric, Arup, and the Climate Group, "Urban Mobility in the Smart City Age," http://digital.arup.com/wp-content/uploads/2014/06/Urban-Mobility.pdf, 4.

6   Cisco, "Mobile Innovation: Transforming Customer Expectations," 2013, http://www.cisco.com/c/dam/en/us/solutions/collateral/executive-perspectives/executive-perspectives/mobile_experience_pov.pdf (accessed November 19, 2014).

6   Cisco, "Mobile Innovation: Transforming Customer Expectations," 2013, http://www.cisco.com/c/dam/en/us/solutions/collateral/executive-perspectives/executive-perspectives/mobile_experience_pov.pdf (accessed November 19, 2014).

7   Seymour Martin Lipset and Reinhard Bendix, Social Mobility in Industrial Society (Berkeley, CA: University of California Press, 1959), 1–2.

8   Graham and Marvin, Splintering Urbanism, 33.

9   Virilio, "Speed and Information."

10   Ross Arbes and Charles Bethea, "Songdo, South Korea: City of the Future?" *Atlantic*, September 27, 2014, http://www.theatlantic.com/international/archive/2014/09/songdo-south-korea-the-city-of-the-future/380849.

11   *Korea Herald*, "Chadwick Offers Unique Chance for Global Education," June 27, 2013, http://www.koreaherald.com/view.php?ud=20130626000939.

12   Jodi Dean, *Democracy and Other Neoliberal Fantasies: Communicative Capitalism and Left Politics* (Durham, NC: Duke University Press, 2009), 42.

13   *Digital Times*, "International City Incheon Born Again to Song-do U-City" (Korean), December 23, 2012.

14   Songdo initially prided itself in the fact that the ubiquitous network infrastructure in the area was financially and physically independent from the private sector, such as companies like SKT, KT, or LG U Plus. According to Mi-ran Moon (author's personal communication) from the IFEZ office, this has been the very foundation on which free provision of public service was viewed to be feasible and legitimate in Songdo. This publicly developed and owned network infrastructure, however, was met with challenges at the stage of its actual utilization. Private telecommunication service companies were quick to put the brakes on the initiative, stating that Korea Communications Commission (KCC) prohibits the "external" use of the facilities by any individual or an organization that interferes with their business.

15   Pamela Licalizi O'Connell, "Korea's High-Tech Utopia, Where Everything Is Observed," *New York Times*, October 5, 2005, http://www.nytimes.com/2005/10/05/technology/techspecial/koreas-hightech-utopia-where-everything-is-observed.html?_r=0.

16   Another example of actual public service using smart CCTV was found in the Seocho district in Seoul, where the cameras provided twenty-four-hour monitoring of senior citizens who were living alone. The installation of heat and gas sensors at their residences meant that they were also able to be aided with timely treatment and care when an emergency situation occurred.

17   Mark Weiser, "The Computer for the 21st Century," *Scientific American* (September 1991), 94.

18   Ibid.

19   Samuel Nunn, "Designing the Solipsistic City: Themes of Urban Planning and Control in *The Matrix, Dark City*, and *The Truman Show*," CTHEORY, February 7, 2001, http://www.ctheory.net/articles.aspx?id=292.

20   Andrew Barry, *Political Machines: Governing a Technological Society* (London: Athlone Press, 2001), 7.

21   Incheon Free Economic Zone, "IFEZ Outline," http://www.ifez.go.kr/frt/ biz/contents/CTS_0000000000000001/getContents.do (accessed April 24, 2016).

22   Bae-Gyoon Park, "Spatially Selective Liberalization and Graduated Sovereignty: Politics of Neo-liberalism and 'Special Economic Zones' in South Korea," *Political Geography* 24 (2005): 856–58.

23   Songdo IBD, "About Songdo Location," http://songdoibd.com/about/ #location (accessed April 24, 2016).

24   Park, "Spatially Selective Liberalization," 852.

25   Graham and Marvin, *Splintering Urbanism*, 13.

26   David Murakami Wood and Stephen Graham, "Permeable Boundaries in the Software-Sorted Society," in *Mobile Technologies of the City*, ed. Mimi Sheller and John Urry (London: Routledge, 2006), 188.

27   Langdon Winner, "Do Artifacts Have Politics?," *Daedalus* 109, no. 1 (1980): 127.

28   Ibid., 128.

29   Ibid., 123.

30   Rachel Keeton, *Rising in the East: Contemporary New Towns in Asia* (Amsterdam: SUN Architecture, 2011), 318.

31   Financial News, "Benefits for Companies Moving into Smart Valley in New Songdo City" (Korean), May 9, 2014.

32   Geun-Hye Park, "The Three-Year-Plan for the Economic Innovation in Korea," Annual Public Presidential Statement, February 25, 2014.

33   Graham and Marvin, *Splintering Urbanism*, 22.

34   O'Connell, "Korea's High-Tech Utopia."

35   Kyung-Sup Chang, "Compressed Modernity and Its Discontents: South Korean Society in Transition," *Economy and Society* 28 (1999), 30–55.

36   The future city fair in Incheon was organized according to four major themes: intelligent city (ubiquitous technology), dynamic city (business and trade hub), eco-friendly city (green technology), attractive city (cultural heritage, sea).

37   One of the facts that constitute the myth of Songdo is that the city was built on land initially reclaimed from the Yellow Sea. Building the entire city from scratch certainly would have encouraged utopian thinking for the planners. Their principles of an idealized city employed from the early design of the city to the current networked public services pivot on the issue of the city's safety, cleanliness and business-friendliness.

38   Martin Meyerson, "Utopian Traditions and the Planning of Cities," *Daedalus* 90, no. 1 (Winter 1961): 181.

39 Ava Kofman, "Les Simerables," *Jacobin* no. 15–16, https://www.jacobinmag .com/2014/10/les-simerables (accessed November 19, 2014).

40 Orit Halpern, Jesse LeCavalier, Nerea Calvillo, and Wolfgang Pietsch, "Test-Bed Urbanism," *Public Culture* 25, no. 2 (2013): 272–306.

41 David Harvey, *Spaces of Hope* (Berkeley: University of California Press, 2000), 167.

42 Stephen Graham, *Cities under Siege: The New Military Urbanism* (London: Verso, 2011), 79.

43 Philip D'Anieri, "A 'Fruitful Hypothesis'? The Regional Planning Association of America's Hopes for Technology," *Journal of Planning History* 1, no. 4 (2002): 287.

44 Ibid.

Conclusion

Networked Urbanism and Everyday Mobility in the City

Over the next twenty-five years, transportation infrastructure will change at every level and geographic scale in response to wireless information technologies, fossil fuel economy, and neoliberal forms of regulation.[1] That change will necessitate a significant investment in how cities are conceptualized and organized. While the focus of this collection of essays is not on sustainable design per se, the immense task of creating sustainable cities is critical to whatever future form networked mobility takes. Along with solving environmental issues, new forms of mobility will need to address factors related to social equity and equal access as income disparities continue to widen. Neither policy makers nor developers can afford a narrow view; the intelligent city must be approached holistically. Urban mobility, thus, is not a discrete problem to be solved; rather, it must be seen as a connective system that impacts the entire city and the everyday experiences of its inhabitants.

Of pivotal importance now is the investigation of urban solutions that meaningfully explore the mechanisms for exchange across, and transgression of, disciplinary boundaries. The mutual framing of challenges is one way to overcome conceptual differences—one that is especially important in the design of smart cities. The need is evident for appropriate frameworks and methods of research into urban design, because larger environmental concerns such as climate change have expanded the purview of architecture beyond a tabula rasa to include ecological factors. While this collection of essays enfolds a theoretical position inherent to productive research investigations, it concurrently advances the smart mobility project by way of applying "tactical prototypes" as a method. Emerging topics for contemporary architects might challenge quotidian commuting routines, as in Mitchell Joachim's "soft" mobile transport; others, such as Jordan Geiger, reimagine public space and practices. Carlo Ratti, Nashid Nabian, and Christine Outram use social data to inform the design of sustainable transit; and BIG proposes reprogrammable road surfaces to make them more flexible, multifunctional, and open to greater diversity of activity. Our challenge, both opportunistic and optimistic, has been to initiate a conversation on mobility as a means to identifying new locations for productive urban interventions. Proposals presented herein pose questions, imagine alternatives, and stage potentials, nudging the public toward increased participation and collective decision making.

The Mobility Assemblage

Since the 1930s, US governance has assumed the role of the private automobile to be dominant in planning decisions and geared such decisions toward the growth of an extensive automotive infrastructure, a trend that resulted in decreased investment in alternative modes of mass transit.[2] Auto-centric perspectives also contributed to larger, unequal urbanization processes, in which population density in the central city core was reduced while the occupation of peripheral areas increased. However, as Frederic Stout argues, current demographic preferences for urban living may be reversing that trend; generational aspirations express new attitudes toward residing in the city core, as well as a lessening inclination for personal car ownership.

Similar demographic trends are influencing automotive industries' research and development activities, with much discussion on how advances in technology, design, and operations will transform the automobile and its role in urban mobility. More significantly, those changes include the automobile's evolution from a stand-alone, independently operated vehicle to one that operates as part of a service network. Changes in automotive design, technology, and connectivity will also lead to crucial changes in investment, and some speculate that even in the context of a growing urban population these expenditures might not be as large as originally estimated. Such changes include less need for investment in new highway and street capacity, at least as measured by construction of lane-miles of concrete and asphalt, because it is predicted that existing infrastructure could be utilized more efficiently[3] (although that claim's accuracy remains to be proven). Nevertheless, much greater investment will be needed in the "soft" infrastructure of information and communications systems. In-pavement roadside sensors, the wireless infrastructure to support communications between individual vehicles and central servers, and the computational capacity to process, analyze, and act on massive amounts of data in real time will both need to be vastly increased. Cisco Systems estimates the Internet would need to expand by three to five times to meet these demands.[4] Moreover, further investment will be needed in electric power generation, transmission, and distribution systems and in electric vehicle–charging infrastructure.

For developing countries, we are also seeing a new wave of infrastructures for extremely contrasting urbanizing territories through the concept of micro-infrastructure. In this context the questions being asked are these: How small can we imagine infrastructure? How does this change the way we have traditionally thought about urbanization, site selection and location, and environmental resources? As an alternative to traditional fixed infrastructure, the concept of microgrids holds possibilities for developing world contexts and urbanizing territories that currently lack the ability to connect to centralized, existing sources of infrastructural energy or water. That also includes user-driven practices, such as "autonomous infrastructure," defined as a new model of urbanism that considers the integration of multiple infrastructural subsets in a single cohesive system that harnesses energy from local renewable resources.[5] The aim is to generate infrastructural frameworks in which the core organizational principles rely on alternative energy sources, such as solar power, waste-to-energy, and passive design techniques, each of which has specific urban as well as architectural implications. Such a system has the potential to engender highly autonomous urban morphologies adapted to local climatic conditions and social practices that in turn influence future visions for mobility and the energy needs of horizontal city forms.[6] As envisioned, autonomous deployment allows the network to grow organically, driven by network users, similar to the evolution of the Internet. While an autonomous infrastructure might not be a long-term planning solution, in developing countries it may better serve the needs of the populace than traditional fixed, centralized models.

Substantial investment to construct a comprehensive metropolitan smart mobility system such as those proposed by private corporations (Cisco and Siemens, among others) raises larger issues about private and public ventures. Many of those issues remain to be fully interrogated; nonetheless, within the smart city discussion there is a growing trend to conceptualize mobility as a utility or a service, one that is always on and available.

While alternative transit platforms, termed *informal transit* or *paratransit*, have long existed in the developing world under various local names—*jitneys, tuk-tuks, dalla-dalla, mototaxis, angkots, sheruts*—they are less prevalent in the United States, although their numbers are growing steadily.[7] In Boston, a novel paratransit platform, Bridj, employs software that analyzes real-time data to predict areas of peak demand. The collected geo-spatial data includes home and work ZIP codes and addresses, along with Foursquare check-ins, Tweets, and Facebook updates to gauge travel patterns while factoring in significant events, such as Red Sox games. This last step enables Bridj to adjust its schedules to demand and anticipate routes that need to be added, using smaller shuttles to serve less popular destinations.[8] In comparison with conventional bus transit, the benefits for riders are shorter travel times, greater flexibility, and convenience, although the service costs more.

Despite those advantages, in the United States and Europe, informal transportation modes such as Uber, Lyft, Carma, and BlaBlaCar are generating significant controversy due to their disruptive effects on formal, regulated systems. The legal implications are being debated in cities globally, with some instituting bans on this type of service. However, by covering areas where public transportation is infrequent or unavailable, informal modes ably address the first and last mile problem. Rather than replacing public transit systems, as some fear, informal modes may augment or extend public transit routes, thus making it possible for people to better take advantage of existing public infrastructure. In a world with twenty-four-hour traffic, cities need more, and more diverse, modes of mobility, not fewer.

Analysis of the effects of ubiquitous computing technologies on existing mobility practices becomes instrumental in future urban planning and design. Anthony Townsend cautions that at the infrastructural level the fragility of an overarching wireless network system (WNS) coordinating the agent systems limits its implementation. Thus the development of highly reliable and secure wireless network systems is crucial to the automobile's evolutionary networked development. Other concerns exist alongside that of WNS vulnerability. While a vision of a connected city allows for the expansion of differential pricing structures, it ignores the important issue of equal and universal accessibility.[9] It cannot be overemphasized that a connected city needs to connect *everyone*.

If, as the automotive industry predicts, mobility evolves into a service through the combined practices of microleasing and informal modes of transit, then what will be the implications for current models of public transportation? Will there be less investment in public transit in the future? For cities such as Paris, the choice is not either/or but both/and, resulting in more mobility choices for urban residents. According to Vincent Roumeas of Paris Region Entreprises, a strategic design emerges from an overarching vision of what constitutes a thriving neighborhood. Mobility is only one aspect of that vision; employment opportunities, affordable housing, and enhanced neighborhood culture and identity are others.[10] Building on the established Vélib' free bicycle-sharing program, the Autolib' Bluecar microleasing program has strategically placed locations throughout the densest Paris neighborhoods, resulting in greater personal vehicle accessibility, as well as one of the highest metro riderships in the world. Other cities have followed suit with the electric car2go, in addition to others. Whether the options are public, private, or public/private, what is critically important for both planners and policy makers is to ensure that microleasing systems are equally available and affordable.

Still yet another unresolved issue concerns the use of electronic banking via mobile computing devices. While smartphones are an element of quotidian social practices, as they allow for messaging, coordination, navigation, and geotagging, thereby enabling individuals to reserve or hail rides electronically from their phones, they are not equally distributed. The smartphone is evolving into a form of highly personal infrastructure, which potentially conflicts with previous notions of what is held in common or public. That shift in what constitutes "the public" is destabilizing historic democratic principles related to civitas and the rights of access to the city.[11] Furthermore, if microleasing and ridesharing assumes computer literacy, will it continue to serve increased numbers of elderly or other underserved populations who are among the highest users of public transit? These are important questions, because mobility and access are integral components of the urban public realm, suggesting that along with the push for open data, which is to say data that is freely available for all residents, there exists a concurrent need for software research and development based on actual user needs, rather than perceived market-driven objectives.

In sum, mobility is a diverse assemblage of human actants, social practices, and computational and physical resources. If organizations, both societal and governmental, are moving in the direction of networked infrastructural models characterized by individuality, mobility, and affinity, what might this mean for urban environments? A critical realization is that each of the topics—transportation, social equity, public space, urban infrastructure, and privacy—can no longer be understood in isolation. Each entity is connected to the others through networked systems and wireless infrastructural integration.

Access to Enabling Infrastructures

Discussions such as the preceding encourage designers to move beyond cars and devices toward larger questions concerning land use planning and society. Simply replacing a fossil fuel–burning car with an electric one—even one that can safely and efficiently drive itself and collaborate with other vehicles—will not be enough unless we adopt new ownership models and fundamentally change settlement patterns.[12] Armed with what we know now about networked technologies, how can that new knowledge be applied to create more open, accessible, and sustainable cities? While academic research is examining questions assembled by disciplines ranging from transportation planning to sociology and cultural geography, design research is still insufficient to develop plausible responses addressing the social demand for access. In the search to create greater access for urban residents, rethinking the automobile may not be enough.

The discussion of mobility extends beyond the notion of simply reaching a destination, of moving people from point A to point B. Rather, mobility encompasses a more expansive definition by including the user experience of the public realm—the qualitative experience of moving along sidewalks, streets, and subways. Mobility is also concerned with user health, safety, and well-being, in addition to the many ways it contributes to urban cultural identity. Transit infrastructure, as Chamee Yang discusses, though intending to connect residents, may actually disconnect them from other sociocultural opportunities. That view is reinforced by Geoffrey Thün, Kathy Velikov, Dan McTavish, and Sue Zielinski, who contend that transportation corridors often create physical geographies of disruption, since corridors act as barriers, simultaneously generating geographies of exclusion—economic, cultural, and health-related.[13] For Alfredo Brillembourg and Hubert Klumpner's Urban-Think Tank, the need to rectify existing social exclusions is a primary shaper of design decisions. Community involvement figures prominently in their research methodology vis-à-vis public workshops attended by architects, planners, activists, and neighborhood leaders.[14] Others, such as Thün and his colleagues, also use participatory methods, but they integrate demographic data analysis related to proximity, availability, and affordability of mobility factors into their proposals. Recognizing that mobility as a field of study is complicated by diverse situations and actors, Urban-Think Tank, as well as Thün et al., suggests that transit space itself could be reconceived as a novel social system.[15] The reconfiguration of transit stations and corridors might result in new formal typologies, such that public transit stations might serve as more than functional transfer points, instead acting as cultural destinations by providing a broad variety of activities.

Architectural programs derived through community workshops have the advantage of identifying user-generated programs specific to each unique culture and neighborhood. In these territories, responding to constituents' unmet needs for access to health care, fresh produce and other foods, and learning opportunities uncovers significant untapped design potential. In addition to metro or jitney transfer points, transit nodes could also house medical clinics, farmers' markets, classrooms and libraries, public media studios, free Wi-Fi, or community meeting spaces.[16] The exploration of architectural prototypes, at multiple scales and time frames, could be a productive means to create increased access to social and civic amenities within the space of mobility infrastructure.

As Ryan Chin of City Science Initiative explains, we must fundamentally rethink the urban structure of our cities, so that living and working are brought closer together, making us less reliant on the automobile. That approach requires walkable, high-density, mixed-use neighborhoods where the needs of every resident are met within a twenty-minute walk.[17] Indeed, such ideas are not novel but draw inspiration from the Russian Constructivists (1919) through the principle of "coupling," a strategy that combines multiple functionalities. It is typical of advanced transit-oriented developments (TODs): mixed-use developments combining residential, commercial, and public space, which maximize access to public transport through proximity. TODs have been around since the 1950s, and they offer several advantages: increased urban density, lower car-to-resident ratios, and better pedestrian access to public transit. Moreover, because TODs are generally located within a radius of a quarter to a half mile from a transit stop, they solve the first and last mile problem mentioned earlier.

Today, shared mobility expands the parameters of TOD requirements, as well as their typological configurations, allowing TODs to be located almost anywhere.

Innovative urban modes and models are required to make cities a more accessible and inclusive space for all inhabitants. Land use planners are reexamining current programs and pathways in various global contexts (North American, European, and Asian cities, as well as Southern Hemisphere favelas) to discover new spatial possibilities and ways to bridge the socioeconomic divide of mobility.[18] Such investigations seek to imbue the spaces of mobility with activity, life, and purpose, thereby contributing to greater well-being in everyday experience.

Privacy and Data Collection

Although we have been considering the primarily positive effects of the mobility project, some less visible and more controversial aspects increasingly compromise networked urbanism. As most are already aware, intelligent infrastructure translates into an expansion of networked standards of surveillance into our physical lives through wireless network systems (WNS), global positioning systems (GPS), and other sensor networks. As a result, physical space is being increasingly measured, quantified, and circumscribed by data. What has become a matter of concern is that this future assemblage of wireless sensor networks and urban space has the capacity to instantiate an extensive applied control topology that entangles sensors with data, personal information, and mapping—in other words, context. The placelessness of the early Internet has come full circle to where every nodal point can be located, interconnected, and known.

If the entire city effectively becomes a wireless sensor network system with data spontaneously generated from each point, then individuals can be geographically located and monitored at all times.[19] Information gleaned from mobile wireless networks includes with whom we come into contact and for how long, and ultimately what value we, as individuals, offer as a node in the network. Moreover, the broad mobility dynamics concerning our movement as a group become all-important data for determining the reconfigurable topology and routing protocols implemented by the network, its efficiency, and overall performance.[20] At the same time, accurate information is crucial for municipal transit planning agencies to schedule, maintain, and operate a transportation system, as well as to plan strategically for transit investment.[21] Nonetheless, the integration of networked communication into location-based protocols and the expropriation of that data to external sources, such as mobility providers, raise serious questions about individual privacy.

Furthermore, the mass popularity of location-based software has not gone unnoticed by commercial interests. Market forces embed software opportunistically for both political and commercial objectives. From game designers to online retailers, profit-seeking commercial entities are finding ways to leverage locative media through new cross-platform applications that pop up daily. Those applications and services concurrently seek increasingly sophisticated ways of collecting and monitoring personal data. In addition, location-based mobile applications record information about everyday sociality, as the metadata collected through user-generated content running on proprietary applications also becomes commercially lucrative.[22] Just as geographic, social, and even biometric data form the economic base of fixed Internet conglomerates (such as Facebook and Google), the additional geospatial data retrieved from mobile devices is associated with a significant market value. These realities all have consequences for our individual privacy.[23]

What appears to be an emphasis on mobility customization at the user end is actually veiling the commercial practice of personal data mining on the provider end. Users perceive a gain in control, whereas they are in fact being constantly monitored. "The extent, precision, and speed of this data gathering is unprecedented," according to Internet theorist Felix Stalder.[24] As our notions of access and mobility are being reconfigured, so too is individual privacy. Concern about the surveillance of individual and collective actions, communications, and movements by domestic security forces is warranted, both here and abroad.[25] As evidenced by wireless networked systems, technology has multiple dimensions and may be repurposed for different objectives. Networked systems can thereby be instrumentalized to increase urban access, as well as to limit it.

Urban Implications

Collectively, the essays in this collection establish an experimental framework for mobility as a means to visualize greater accessibility for all urban habitants. What unifies the collection is the conviction that social exclusion from access to resources (transit or otherwise) is best addressed by raising awareness of the functioning of infrastructures and making that information available to others. While many of the ideas herein are as yet unrealized, speculation on the future of cities does more than merely present possibilities. Alternative futures may spark discussion and create new participatory practices. For landscape architect and urban planner Kevin Lynch, cultural imaginaries play a significant role in understanding context and influencing the decisions that either enable or limit possible futures. Thus, a discussion of future cities provides a space for urban residents to reflect on their daily experience and, more importantly, to participate in decision-making processes. For decades, planning decisions were based on an incomplete understanding of the consequences of the automobile and use of fossil fuels, not only with regard to climate change but also in relation to population growth, suburban development, and industrial expansion. While we acknowledge past shortcomings, the adoption of networked participatory practices may be a productive way to involve all residents in decision-making processes. One aspect of DIY urbanism is that residents can enter into a collective conversation and deliberate on a city as an envisioned space different from what they inherited. Neighborhood discussions such as these can be one of the most important catalysts for fundamental change.[26]

Intelligent infrastructure is altering urban practices through ad hoc experimentation, commercial software development, and communities of participation; however, this position should not be confused with technological determinism. The objective of this collection is to look at these new conditions and reflect on how we can meaningfully engage with change and shape technology toward humanistic objectives. The processes of governance are complex, and ultimately there is neither a single method nor a simple technological solution for collective decision making. How we, as a group, decide to plan for and adopt technology is what ultimately changes governance.

The integration of networked technologies into everyday social practices causes us to reflect deeply on their protocols, platforms, and interfaces. The production of space is increasingly dependent on code, and code is being written to produce space. Networked mobility as a form of code is thus actively shaping sociospatial organization, processes, and economies, along with discursive and material cultures. Those effects are set to become increasingly pervasive as more and more everyday practices are threaded through networked platforms.[27] With that in mind, designers, both urban and software, have a shared responsibility to concentrate not only on problem solving but also on the social, political, and environmental consequences of their design decisions.[28] While the focus of this project is not on policy per se, a humanistic approach, defined as an ethical perspective that emphasizes the value and agency of human beings, individually and collectively, is integral to networked mobility. Ultimately, intelligent infrastructure compels not only urbanists but also architects, software engineers, public policy makers, and ordinary citizens to understand its future challenges and opportunities.

Notes

1   Nicholas Low, ed., *Transforming Urban Transport: The Ethics, Politics and Practices of Sustainable Mobility* (London: Routledge, 2012), 227.

2   Edward Weiner, *Urban Transportation Planning in the United States: A Historical View* (Washington, DC: U.S. Department of Transportation, November 1992).

3   Mitchell L. Moss and Hugh O'Neill, "Urban Mobility in the 21st Century: A Report for the NYU BMW I Project on Cities and Sustainability" (New York: NYU Rudin Center for Transportation Policy and Management, November 2012).

4   Cisco, "New Cisco Internet of Things (IoT) System Provides a Foundation for the Transformation of Industries," *Network*, June 29, 2015, http://newsroom.cisco.com/press-release-content?type=webcontent&articleId=1667560 (accessed August 10, 2015).

5   Lemire Abdul Halim Chehab and Mohamad Makkouk, "Autonomous Infrastructures," MArch Dissertation, Architectural Association, 2013.

6   According to E. S. Sousa, advanced fourth-generation wireless networks are based on the concept of autonomous deployment of the network infrastructure. There is a requirement for self-configuration of the air interface to facilitate deployment by the users, and the network operator has the task to manage the use of the spectrum by the networking elements. See E. S. Sousa, "Autonomous Infrastructure Wireless Network" (paper presented at Mobile And Wireless Communications Summit, Budapest, July 1–5, 2007), http://ieeexplore.ieee.org/xpl/login.jsp?tp=&arnumber=4299332&url=http%3A%2F%2Fieeexplore.ieee.org%2Fiel5%2F4299028%2F4299029%2F04299332.pdf%3Farnumber%3D4299332 (accessed January 3, 2015).

7   Aaron David Golub, "Welfare Analysis of Informal Transit Services in Brazil and the Effects of Regulation" (PhD diss., Institute of Transportation Studies, University of California, Berkeley, 2003).

8   See Katie Johnston, "Data-Driven Bus Service Set to Roll Out: Venture Aims to Predict Riders' Needs," *Boston Globe*, April 22, 2014, https://www .bostonglobe.com/business/2014/04/10/data-driven-pop-bus-service-launch -boston/yz4EjzZC9nXnl22O6JcV2I/story.html (accessed August 20, 2015).

9   Differential pricing structures are seen to encourage energy optimization toward greater sustainability. See William J. Mitchell, Christopher E. Bor- roni-Bird, and Lawrence D. Burns, *Reinventing the Automobile: Personal Urban Mobility for the 21st Century* (Cambridge, MA: MIT Press, 2010).

10   As reported in "Is Paris A Smarter City Than New York?," Paris Region Prime, August 23, 2013, https://blogprimehubtech21.wordpress.com/2013 /08/23/is-paris-a-smarter-city-than-new-york/ (accessed 1/10/2015).

11   The Twelve Tables of Roman law defined the right to use a road as a *servitus*, or claim. The *ius eundi* ("right of going") established a claim to use an *iter*, or footpath, across private land; the *ius agendi* ("right of driving"), an *actus*, or carriage track.

12   Ryan Chin, "Solving Transport Headaches in the Cities of 2050," BBC, June 18, 2013, http://www.bbc.com/future/story/20130617-moving-around -in-the-megacity (accessed 01/12/2014).

13   Geoffrey Thün, Kathy Velikov, Dan McTavish, and Sue Zielinski, "Protean Prototypes: Developing Access-Enabling Infrastructures for Chicago" (presentation paper, Taubman College, 2014), http://taubmancollege .umich.edu/research/research-city/protean-prototypes-developing-access -enabling-infrastructures-chicagoland (accessed January 15, 2015).

14   Audi Urban Future Initiative 2012. "Move Examines Urban-Think Tank's Research on São Paulo" (conference paper, October 17, 2012), http://audi -urban-future-initiative.com/mooove_cms/resources/media/pdf/urbanthink -tank.pdf.

15   Social geographer Jean Tricart contends that the "social content" of a city is the basis for reading it, and the study of social content must precede the description of the geographical artifacts. "Social facts, to the extent that they present themselves as specific content, always precede forms and function and, one might say, embrace them." Jean Tricart, *Cours de Geographie Humaine*, vol. 2: *L'habitat Urbain* (Paris: Centre de Documentation Universita- rie, 1963).

16   Thün et al., "Protean Prototypes."

17   Chin, "Solving Transport Headaches."

18   Audi Urban Future Initiative 2012, "Urban-Think Tank's Research."

19   According to Dan Work, PhD, transportation engineer, University of Illinois

at Urbana-Champaign, the concern is that individuals can be identified through any two repetitive location points, even if the data is anonymized.

20   Anthony Townsend, *Smart Cities: Big Data, Civic Hackers, and the Quest for a New Utopia* (New York: W. W. Norton, 2013), 273–75.

21   Data may be deposited and stored anonymously in a Colorado facility for use in related research studies.

22   Felix Stalder, "Between Democracy and Spectacle: The Front-End and Back-End of the Social Web," in *The Social Media Reader*, ed. Michael Mandberg (New York: NYU Press, 2012): 250.

23   Rachel O'Dwyer, "Network Media: Exploring the Sociotechnical Relations between Mobile Networks and Media Publics" (paper presented at 17th International Symposium on Electronic Art, Istanbul, September 14–21, 2011).

24   Stalder, "Between Democracy and Spectacle," 250.

25   While it is understandable for urban planners to collect and model data to understand the complex interactions of a city, this understanding would not apply to how repressive governments use those very same methods of data collection to discipline urban residents.

26   Hilde Heynen, "The Need for Utopian Thinking in Architecture" (paper presentation at Berlage Institute, 2003).

27   As social geographers Rob Kitchen and Martin Dodge argue, urban policy making requires an interdisciplinary approach. GIS (geographical information systems) software, digital modeling programs, and wireless sensor information now make it possible to build a model of the city from user interaction and to understand movement and circulation patterns in novel ways. This enables designers and planners to study the city from the bottom up; that is, from the actual everyday social practices of urban habitants.

28   Barry Katz, "Design and the Human Condition: An Untimely Meditation" (lecture, Hewlett Foundation, Menlo Park, CA, February 14, 2008).

Selected Bibliography

Alexander, Christopher. "A City Is Not a Tree." In *Design after Modernism*, edited by John Thackara, 67–84. London: Thames and Hudson, 1988. http://www.rudi .net/books/200 (accessed May 13, 2016).

Allen, Stan. "Landscape Infrastructure." In *Infrastructure as Architecture*, edited by Katrina Stoll and Scott Lloyd. Berlin: Jovis Verlage, 2010.

Allen, Stan, and Marc McQuade. *Landform Building: Architecture's New Terrain.* Munich: Schirmer/Mosel, 2011.

Al Sayyad, Nezar. *Cinematic Urbanism: A History of the Modern City from Reel to Real.* London: Routledge, 2006.

Amin, Ash, and Nigel Thrift. *Cities: Reimagining the Future.* Cambridge, UK: Polity Press, 2002.

Apogee Research, Inc. *Cost and Effectiveness of Transportation Control Measures (TCMs): A Review and Analysis of the Literature.* Washington, DC: National Association of Regional Councils, 1994.

Ascher, François. *L'âge des métapoles.* Paris: Éditions de l'Aube, 2009.

Banham, Reynar. *Los Angeles: The Four Ecologies.* New York: Harper and Row, 1971.

Barry, Andrew. *Political Machines: Governing a Technological Society.* London: Athlone Press, 2001.

Behnke, Robert W. *California Smart Traveler System.* Washington, DC: USDOT, Federal Transit Administration, 1992.

———. *German "Smart Bus" Systems: Potential for Application in Portland, Oregon.* Vol. 1: *Technical Report.* Washington, DC: Department of Transportation, 1993.

Benedict, Mark A., and Edward T. McMahon. *Green Infrastructure: Linking Landscapes and Communities.* Washington, DC: Island Press, 2006.

Beroldo, Steve. "Casual Carpooling in the San Francisco Bay Area." *Transportation Quarterly* 44 (January 1990): 133–50.

Bijker, Wiebe, Thomas P. Hughes, and Trevor J. Pinch, eds. *The Social Construction of Technological Systems: New Directions in the Sociology and History of Technology.* Cambridge, MA: MIT Press, 1987.

Booth, Rosemary, and Robert Waksman. "Analysis of Commuter Ridesharing Behavior at Five Urban Sites." Washington, DC: Transportation Research Board, 1985. http://trid.trb.org/view.aspx?id=270903 (accessed May 15, 2016).

Bratton, Benjamin H. *The Stack: On Software and Sovereignty.* Cambridge, MA: MIT Press, 2013.

Brenner, Neil, and Christian Schmid. "The 'Urban Age' in Question." *International Journal of Urban and Regional Research* 38, no. 3 (December 2013): 731–55.

Brill, Michael. "An Ontology for Exploring Urban Public Life Today." *Places* 6, no. 1 (1989): 24–31.

Brown, Hilary. *Next Generation Infrastructure: Principles for Post-Industrial Public Works.* Washington, DC: Island Press, 2014.

Brownstone, David, and Thomas F. Golob. "The Effectiveness of Ridesharing Incentives: Discrete-Choice Models of Commuting in Southern California." Berkeley: University of California Transportation Center, 1992.

Burke, Anthony, and Therese Tierney, eds. *Network Practices: New Strategies for Architecture and Design.* New York: Princeton Architectural Press, 2007.

Burrell, Jena. "Co-Evolution of the Mobile Phone and Users in Rural Uganda." Lecture presented at CITRIS, University of California, Berkeley, February 11, 2009.

Busbea, Larry. *Topologies: Urban Utopia in France.* Cambridge, MA: MIT Press, 2007.

Bush, Vannevar. "As We May Think." *Atlantic Monthly*, July 1945, 52–79.

Calhoun, Craig. "Community without Propinquity Revisited: Communications Technology and the Transformation of the Urban Public Sphere." *Sociological Inquiry* 68, no. 3 (1998): 373–97.

Cambridge Systematics. *Moving Cooler: An Analysis of Transportation Strategies for Reducing Greenhouse Gas Emissions.* Los Angeles: Urban Land Institute and Cambridge Systematics, 2009.

Castells, Manuel. *The Informational City: Information Technology, Economic Restructuring, and the Urban Regional Process.* Oxford, UK: Blackwell, 1989.

———. *The Rise of the Network Society.* 2nd ed. Malden, MA: Blackwell, 2000.

Certeau de, Michel. *The Practice of Everyday Life.* Berkeley: University of California Press, 2002.

Cervero, Robert. *Fostering Commercial Transit: Alternatives in Greater Los Angeles.* Policy Insight no. 146. Los Angeles: Reason Foundation, 1992.

———. "Transport Infrastructure and the Environment: Sustainable Mobility and Urbanism." Paper presented at *Urban Development for the Twenty-First*

Century, Second Planocosmo International Conference, Bandung Institute of Technology, 2013.

Cervero, Robert, and Bruse Griesenbeck. "Factors Influencing Commuting Choices in Suburban Labor Markets—Case Study of Pleasanton, California." *Transportation Research A* 22, no. 3 (1988): 151–61.

Chun, Wendy Hui Kyong. "Control and Freedom: Power and Paranoia in the Age of Fiber Optics." In *New Media/Old Media: A History and Theory Reader*, edited by Wendy Hui Kyong Chun and Thomas Keenan. New York: Routledge, 2006.

Cooper Marcus, Clare, and Carolyn Francis, eds. *People Places: Design Guidelines for Urban Open Space*. 2nd ed. New York: John Wiley and Sons, 1997.

Coward, L. Andrew, and Nikos A. Salingaros. "The Information Architecture of Cities." *Journal of Information Science* 30, no. 2 (2004): 107–18.

Crang, Mike, and Stephen Graham. "Sentient Cities: Ambient Intelligence and the Politics of Urban Space." *Information Communication & Society* 10, no. 6 (2007): 789–817.Accessed December 15, 2007. doi: 10.1080/13691180701750991.

Daliot-Bul, Michal. "Japan's Mobile Technoculture: The Production of a Cellular Playscape and Its Cultural Implications." *Media Culture Society* 29, no. 6 (2007): 954–71.

D'Anieri, Philip. "A 'Fruitful Hypothesis'? The Regional Planning Association of America's Hopes for Technology." *Journal of Planning History* 1, no. 4 (2002): 279–89.

Dean, Jodi. *Democracy and Other Neoliberal Fantasies: Communicative Capitalism and Left Politics*. Durham, NC: Duke University Press, 2009.

Debord, Guy. *Society of the Spectacle*. New York: Zone Books, 1995.

DeLanda, Manuel. "Does Convergence Imply Homogenization?" Paper presented at European Media Master Forum, Stuttgart, Germany, April 1999.

Deleuze, Gilles, and Guattari, Felix. *A Thousand Plateaus: Capitalism and Schizophrenia*. Translated by Brian Massumi. Minneapolis: University of Minnesota Press, 1987.

Department of Civil and Environmental Engineering, Massachusetts Institute of Technology. "MIT 'Real-Time' Rideshare Research." http://ridesharechoices .scripts.mit.edu/home/2009/02/academic-public-agency-research/ (accessed January 12, 2015).

Diamond, Jared. *Guns, Germs, and Steel: The Fates of Human Societies*. New York: W. W. Norton, 1997.

Donald, James. "This, Here, Now: Imagining the Modern City." In *Imagining Cities: Scripts, Signs, Memories*, edited by Sallie Westwood and John Williams. London: Routledge, 1997.

Doxiadis, Constantinos A. *Architecture in Transition*. London: Hutchinson, 1963.
————. *Ecumenopolis: The Inevitable City of the Future*. With J. G. Papaioannou. Athens: Athens Center of Ekistics, 1974.
————. *Ekistics: An Introduction to the Science of Human Settlements*. New York: Oxford University Press, 1968.
Dueker, Kenneth J., Irwin P. Levin, and Brent O. Bair. "Ridesharing: Psychological Factors." *Transportation Engineering Journal* 103, no. 6 (November/December 1977): 685–92.
Durkheim, Emile. *Professional Ethics and Civic Morals*. London: Routledge, 1992.
Easterling, Keller. *Extrastatecraft: The Power of Infrastructure Space*. London: Verso, 2014.
Ellin, Nan. *Integral Urbanism*. New York: Routledge, 2006.
Farr, Douglas. *Sustainable Urbanism: Urban Design with Nature*. Hoboken, NJ: Wiley, 2008.
Featherstone, Mike. "The Heroic Life and the Everyday Life." *Theory, Culture and Society* 9, no. 1 (1992): 159–82.
Fennell, Lee Anne. "Crowdsourcing Land Use." *Brooklyn Law Review* 78, no. 2 (2013): 385–415.
Findlay, John. *Magic Lands: Western Cityscapes and American Culture after 1940*. Berkeley: University of California Press, 1992.
Flew, Terry. *New Media: An Introduction*. Oxford: Oxford University Press, 2007.
Florida, Richard. *The Rise of the Creative Class: And How It's Transforming Work, Leisure, Community and Everyday Life*. New York: Basic Books, 2002.
Foucault, Michel. *Foucault Live: Interviews, 1961–1984*. Edited by Sylvere Lotinger. New York: Semiotext(e), 1996.
————. "Space, Knowledge and Power." In *The Foucault Reader*, edited by Paul Rabinow, 239–56. New York: Pantheon Books, 1984.
Freas, Alyssa M., and Stuart M. Anderson. "Effects of Variable Work Hour Programs on Ridesharing and Organizational Effectiveness: A Case Study, Ventura County." Washington, DC: Transportation Research Board, 1991.
Fuchs, Christian. "Class, Knowledge, and New Media." *Media, Culture and Society* 32, no. 1 (2010): 141–50.
Fuller, Matthew, and Usman Haque. *Urban Versioning System 1.0*. New York: Architectural League of New York, 2008.
Gabler, Neal. *Walt Disney*. New York: Vintage Books, 2006.
Galison, Peter. "War against the Center." *Grey Room* 4 (2001): 5–33.
Gennawey, Sam. *Walt Disney and the Promise of Progress City*. New York: Theme Park Press, 2014.

Giddens, Anthony. *The Constitution of Society: Outline of the Theory of Structuration.* Cambridge, UK: Polity Press, 1984.

Goldberg, Ken, ed. *The Robot in the Garden: Telerobotics and Telepistemology in the Age of the Internet.* Cambridge, MA: MIT Press, 2000.

Gordon, Eric. *The Urban Spectator: American Concept Cities from Kodak to Google.* Hanover, NH: Dartmouth College Press/University Press of New England, 2009.

Gordon, Eric, and Adriana de Souza e Silva. *Net Locality: Why Location Matters in a Networked World.* Malden, MA: Wiley-Blackwell, 2011.

Goulder, A. "Sociology and the Everyday Life." In *The Idea of Social Structure: Papers in Honor of Robert K. Merton,* edited by Lewis A. Coser, 417–32. New York: Harcourt Brace Jovanovich, 1975.

Graham, Stephen. *Cities under Siege: The New Military Urbanism.* London: Verso, 2011.

———. *Telecommunications and the City: Electronic Spaces and Urban Spaces.* London: Routledge, 1996.

———. "Constructing Premium Network Spaces: Reflections on Infrastructure Networks and Contemporary Urban Development." *International Journal of Urban and Regional Research* 24, no. 1 (2000): 183–200.

———. "Telecommunications and the Future of Cities: Debunking the Myths." *Cities* 14, no. 1 (1997): 21–29.

Graham, Stephen, and Simon Guy. "Internetting" Downtown San Francisco: Digital Space Meets Urban Place." In *Sustaining Urban Networks: The Social Diffusion of Large Technical Systems,* edited by Oliver Coutard, Richard E. Hanley, and Rae Zimmerman, 32–47. London: Routledge, 2004.

Graham, Stephen, and Simon Marvin. *Splintering Urbanism: Networked Infrastructures, Technological Mobilities and the Urban Condition.* New York: Routledge, 2001.

Green, Nicola. "On the Move: Technology, Mobility, and the Mediation of Social Time and Space." *Information Society* 18 (2002): 281–92.

Greenfield, Adam. *Against the Smart City: The City Is Here for You to Use.* Helsinki: Do Projects, 2013.

———. *Everywhere: The Dawning Age of Ubiquitous Computing.* Berkeley, CA: New Riders, 2006.

Gruebele, Philip A. "Interactive System for Real Time Dynamic Multi-hop Carpooling." September 2, 2008. http://dynamicridesharing.org/resources/Multi_hop_social_carpool_routing_System.pdf (accessed January 12, 2015).

Gubbi, Jayavardhana, Rajkumar Buyya, Slaven Marusic, and Marimuthu Palaniswami. "Internet of Things (IoT): A Vision, Architectural Elements, and Future Directions." *Future Generation Computer Systems* 29, no. 7 (2013): 1645–60.

Guildi, Jo. *Roads to Power: Britain Invents the Infrastructure State.* Cambridge, MA: Harvard University Press, 2012.

Gwilliam, Ken, ed. *Cities on the Move: A World Bank Urban Transport Strategy Review.* Washington, DC: International Bank for Reconstruction and Development/ World Bank, 2002.

Hall, Randolph W., and Amer Qureshi. "Dynamic Ridesharing: Theory and Practice." *Journal of Transportation Engineering* 123, no. 4 (July 1997): 308–15.

Halpern, Orit, Jesse LeCavalier, Nerea Calvillo, and Wolfgang Pietsch. "Test-Bed Urbanism." *Public Culture* 25, no. 2 (2013): 272–306.

Hannam, Kevin, Mimi Sheller, and John Urry. "Mobilities, Immobilities and Moorings." *Mobilities* 1, no. 1 (2006): 1–22.

Hardey, Michael. "The City in the Age of Web 2.0: A New Synergistic Relationship between Place and People." *Information Communication and Society* 10, no. 6 (2007): 867–84.

Harvey, David. "Between Space and Time: Reflections on the Geographical Imagination." *Annals of the Association of American Geographers* 80, no. 3 (1990): 418–34.

———. *The Condition of Post-Modernity: An Enquiry into the Origins of Cultural Change.* Cambridge, UK: Blackwell, 1989.

Hawley, Amos H. *Human Ecology: A Theoretical Essay.* Chicago: University of Chicago Press, 1986.

Hwang, Keith, and Genevieve Giuliano. *The Determinants of Ridesharing: A Literature Review.* Berkeley: University of California Transportation Center, 1990.

Institute for Mobility Research. *Megacity Mobility Culture.* New York: Springer Verlag, 2013.

Jacobs, Jane. *The Death and Life of Great American Cities.* New York: Random House, 1961.

Jacobson, Sheldon H., and Douglas M. King. "Fuel Savings and Ridesharing in the US: Motivations, Limitations, and Opportunities." *Transportation Research Part D: Transport and Environment* 14, no. 1 (January 2009): 14–21.

Jameson, Frederic. *Signatures of the Visible.* New York: Routledge, 1992.

Jenkins, Henry. *Convergence Culture: Where Old and New Media Collide.* New York: New York University Press, 2006.

Jenkins, Henry, Sam Ford, and Joshua Green. *Spreadable Media: Creating Value and Meaning in a Networked Culture.* New York: New York University Press, 2013.

Jensen, Ole B. "Flows of Meaning, Cultures of Movements—Urban Mobility as Meaningful Everyday Life Practice." *Mobilities* 4, no. 1 (2009): 139–58.

———. *Staging Mobilities.* London: Routledge, 2013.

Jordon, Tim. *Hacking: Digital Media and Technological Determinism.* London: Blackwell, 2008.

Kaika, Maria. *City of Flows: Modernity, Nature, and the City.* New York: Routledge, 2005.

Kasarda, John D., and Greg Lindsay. *Aerotropolis: The Way We'll Live Next.* New York: Farrar, Straus and Giroux, 2011.

Katz, Barry M. *Technology and Culture: A Historical Romance.* Stanford: Stanford Alumni Assn., 1990.

Kellerman, Aharon. *Personal Mobilities.* London: Taylor & Francis, 2006.

Kelley, Kalon L. "Casual Carpooling—Enhanced." *Journal of Public Transportation* 10, no. 4 (2007): 119–30.

Kelty, Christopher M. "Culture's Open Sources: Software, Copyright, and Cultural Critique." *Anthropological Quarterly* 77, no. 3 (Summer 2004): 499–506.

Kent, Fred. Project for Public Spaces. http://www.pps.org/about/team/fkent/ (accessed April 26, 2009).

Kirk, Andrew. *Counterculture Green: The Whole Earth Catalog and American Environmentalism.* Lawrence: University Press of Kansas, 2007.

Kitchin, Rob, and Martin Dodge. *Code/Space: Software and Everyday Life.* Cambridge, MA: MIT Press, 2011.

Kollock, Peter, and Marc Smith. "Managing the Virtual Commons: Cooperation and Conflict in Computer Communities." In *Computer-Mediated Communication: Linguistic, Social, and Cross-Cultural Perspectives,* edited by Susan Herring, 109–28. Amsterdam: John Benjamins, 1996.

Koolhaas, Rem, and Bruce Mau. *S, M, L, XL,* New York: Monacelli Press, 1993.

Kostof, Spiro. *A History of Architecture: Settings and Rituals.* 2nd ed. Edited by Gregory Castillo. Oxford: Oxford University Press, 1995.

Kowshik, Raghu R., John Gard, Jason Loo, Paul P. Jovanis, and Ryuichi Kitamura. "Development of User Needs and Functional Requirements for a Real-Time Ridesharing System." Working paper. University of California, Davis: Institute of Transportation Studies, 1993.

Kowshik, Raghu R., and Paul P. Jovanis. "Real-Time Ridesharing: Does It Work? Results and Recommendations from the Sacramento-Area Field Operational Test." https://trid.trb.org/view.aspx?id=510994 (accessed May 15, 2016).

Kriem, Maya. "Mobile Telephony in Morocco: A Changing Sociality." *Media, Culture & Society* 31, no. 4 (2009): 617–32.

LaHood, Ray. "First Steps toward Livable Communities." *Fast Lane: The Official Blog of the U.S. Secretary of Transportation.* http://usdotblog.typepad.com/secretarysblog/2009/03/first-steps-toward-livable-communities.html#.VLPoWMo8gVk (accessed March 22, 2009).

Latham, Robert, and Saskia Sassen. *Digital Formations: IT and New Architectures in the Global Realm*. Princeton, NJ: Princeton University Press, 2005.

Latour, Bruno. *Reassembling the Social: An Introduction to Actor-Network-Theory*. Oxford: Oxford University Press, 2005.

———. *We Have Never Been So Modern*. Translated by Catherine Porter. Cambridge, MA: Harvard University, 1993.

Lefebvre, Henri. *The Production of Space*. Translated by Donald Nicholson-Smith. Oxford: Wiley-Blackwell, 1992.

Lennard, Suzanne H. Crowhurst, and Henry L. Lennard. *Public Life in Urban Places: Social and Architectural Characteristics Conducive to Public Life in European Cities*. South Hampton, UK: Gondolier Press, 1984.

Lessig, Lawrence. "In Defense of Piracy." *Wall Street Journal*, October 11, 2008.

Levofsky, Amber, and Allen Greenberg. "Organized Dynamic Ridesharing: The Potential Environmental Benefits and the Opportunity for Advancing the Concept." Transportation Research Board. http://dynamicridesharing.org /resources/Levofsky_and_Greenberg_Organized_Dynamic_Ridesharing.pdf (accessed January 30, 2001).

Levy, John M. *Contemporary Urban Planning*. 4th ed. London: Prentice Hall, 1997.

Little, Stephen E. "Networks and Neighborhoods: Households, Community and Sovereignty in the Global Economy." *Urban Studies* 37, no. 10 (2000): 1813–25.

Livingstone, Sonia. "The Changing Social Landscape." In *Handbook of New Media: Social Shaping and Social Consequences of ICTs*, edited by Leah A. Lievrouw and Sonia Livingstone, 17–21. London: SAGE, 2002.

Lynch, Kevin. *The Image of the City*. Cambridge, MA: MIT Press, 1960.

Mandiberg, Michael, ed. *Social Media Reader*. New York: New York University Press, 2012.

Manneheim, Steve. *Walt Disney and the Quest for Community*. Burlington, VT: Ashgate, 2002.

Marx, Karl. *A Contribution to the Critique of Political Economy*. 1859. New York: International Publishers, 1979.

Marx, Leo. "Technology: The Emergence of a Hazardous Concept." *Social Research* 64, no. 3 (1997): 965–88.

Massey, Doreen B. *Space, Place, and Gender*. Minneapolis: University of Minnesota Press, 1994.

Matsuda, Misa. "Mobile Communication and Selective Sociality." In *Personal, Portable, Pedestrian: Mobile Phones in Japanese Life*, edited by Mizuko Ito, Daisuke Okabe, and Misa Matsuda, 123–42. Cambridge, MA: MIT Press, 2005.

Maxwell, Joseph. *Qualitative Research: An Interactive Approach*. 2nd ed. Thousand Oaks, CA: SAGE, 2005.

McArthur, J. A. "Digital Subculture: A Geek Meaning of Style." *Journal of Communication Inquiry* 33, no. 1 (October 2008): 1–13.

McCullough, Malcolm. *Digital Ground: Architecture, Pervasive Computing, and Environmental Knowing.* Cambridge, MA: MIT Press, 2004.

McGetrick, Brendan, and Rem Koolhaas, eds. *Content.* Cologne: Taschen, 2004.

McLuhan, Marshall, and Bruce R. Powers. *The Global Village: Transformations in World Life and Media in the 21st Century.* Cambridge: Oxford University Press, 1989.

Meyerson, Martin. "Utopian Traditions and the Planning of Cities." *Daedalus* 90, no. 1 (1961): 180–93.

Meyrowitz, Joshua. *No Sense of Place: The Impact of Electronic Media on Social Behavior.* New York: Oxford Press, 1985.

Mitcham, Carl. *Metaphysics, Epistemology, and Technology: Research in Philosophy and Technology.* Toronto: Jai Press, 2000.

Mitchell, William J. *Beyond Productivity: Information Technology, Innovation and Creativity.* Washington, DC: National Academies Press, 2003.

———. *City of Bits: Space, Place, and the Infobahn.* Cambridge, MA: MIT Press, 2000.

———. *Me++: The Cyborg Self and the Networked City.* Cambridge, MA: MIT Press, 2004.

Mitchell, William J., Chris E. Borroni-Bird, and Lawrence D. Burns. *Reinventing the Automobile: Personal Urban Mobility for the 21st Century.* Cambridge, MA: MIT Press, 2010.

Morency, Catherine. "The Ambivalence of Ridesharing." *Transportation* 34, no. 2 (March 2007): 239–53.

Morton, Timothy. *Hyperobjects: Philosophy and Ecology after the End of the World.* Minneapolis: University of Minnesota Press, 2013.

Moss, Mitchell, and Anthony Townsend. "How Telecommunications Systems Are Transforming Urban Spaces." In *Cities in the Telecommunications Age: The Fracturing of Geographies,* edited by James O. Wheeler and Yuko Aoyama, 31–42. New York: Routledge, 1999.

Mostafavi, Moshen. *Ecological Urbanism.* Zurich: Lars Müller, 2010.

Mumford, Lewis. *Technics and Civilization.* New York: Harcourt, Brace and World, 1963.

Niles, John S., and Paul A. Toliver. "IVHS Technology for Improving Ridesharing." Proceedings of the 1992 Annual Meeting of IVHS America. Newport Beach, CA: 1992.

Offenhuber, Dietmar, and Katja Schechtner, eds. *Inscribing a Square: Urban Data as Public Space.* Vienna: Springer-Verlag, 2012.

Ortolano, Guy. "Planning the Urban Future in 1960s Britain." *Historical Journal* 54, no. 2 (June 2011): 477–507. http://journals.cambridge.org/action/displayAbstract?fromPage=online&aid=8273300 (accessed August 14, 2014).

Pagano, Celeste B. "DIY Urbanism: Property and Process in Grassroots City Building." *Marquette Law Review* 97, no. 2 (2013): 335–89.

Pariser, Eli. *The Filter Bubble: What the Internet Is Hiding from You.* New York: Penguin Press, 2011.

Phillips, Amy K. "The Image of the Simulated City: Sim City 2000 and Popular Perceptions of the City." Master's thesis, University of California, Berkeley, 1993.

Picon, Antoine. *Smart Cities: A Spatialised Intelligence.* Chichester, UK: Wiley, 2015.

Picon, Antoine, and Alessandre Ponte, eds. *Architecture and the Sciences: Exchanging Metaphors.* Princeton, NJ: Princeton Architectural Press, 2004.

Pisarski, Allan E. *Travel Behavior Issues in the 90's.* Washington, DC: USDOT, Federal Highway Administration, 1992.

Poole, Robert W., Jr., and Michael Griffin. *Shuttle Vans: The Overlooked Transit Alternative.* Policy paper no. 176. Los Angeles: Reason Foundation, 1994.

Popov, Luomir. "Architecture as Social Design: The Social Nature of Design Objects and the Implications for the Profession." *Journal of Design Research* 2, no. 2 (2002).

Poy, Cyrille. *La Ville Ecologique: Contributions for a Sustainable Architecture.* Brussels: Archives d'Architecture Moderne (AAM), 2009.

Prelorenzo, Claude, and Dominique Rouillard, eds. *La métropole des infrastructures.* Paris: Picard, 2009.

Procopio, Claire H., and Steven T. Procopio. "Do You Know What It Means to Miss New Orleans? Internet Communication, Geographic Community and Social Capital in Crisis." *Journal of Applied Communication Research* 35, no. 1 (February 2007): 67–87.

Protzen, Jean-Pierre. "Reflections on the Fable of the Caliph, the Ten Architects, and the Philosopher." *Journal of Architectural Education* 34, no. 4 (Summer 1981): 2–8.

Raban, Jonathan. *Soft City.* New York: Harvill Press, 1974.

Rabinow, Paul, and William M. Sullivan, eds. *Interpretive Social Science: A Second Look.* Berkeley: University of California Press, 1987.

Rand Corporation. "Autonomous Vehicle Technology: How to Best Realize Its Social Benefits." http://www.rand.org/content/dam/rand/pubs/research_briefs/RB9700/RB9755/RAND_RB9755.pdf (accessed January 12, 2015).

Reno, Arlee T., William A. Gellert, and Alex Verzosa. "Evaluation of Springfield Instant Carpooling." Washington, DC: Urban Institute, 1989.

Resnick, Paul. "SocioTechnical Support for Ride Sharing." http://pec.putney.net /files/docs/draft_ride_share.pdf (accessed March 30, 2016).

Ribeiro, Fabíola M., and Rejane Spitz. "Archigram's Analogical Approach to Digitality." *International Journal of Architectural Computing* 4, no. 3 (2006): 20–32.

RIDES for Bay Area Commuters, Inc. "Casual Carpooling Update, 1998." http:// www.nctr.usf.edu/wp-content/uploads/2011/04/Casual-Carpool-Report-1998 .pdf (accessed January 12, 1999).

Rittel, Horst W. J. "On the Planning Crisis: Systems Analysis of the 'First and Second Generations.'" *Bedrifts Oekonomen* 8 (October 1972): 390–96.

Rittel, Horst W. J., and Melvin M. Webber. "Dilemmas in a General Theory of Planning." *Policy Sciences* 4, no. 2 (1973): 155–69.

Robins, Kevin, and Frank Webster. *Times of the Technoculture: From the Information Society to the Virtual Life.* New York: Routledge, 1999.

Rosch, Eleanor. "The Environment of Minds: Toward a Noetic and Hedonic Ecology." In *Cognitive Ecology*, edited by Morton P. Friedman and Edward C. Carterette, 3–23. San Diego: Academic Press, 1996.

Rubyni, Kati. *The Car in 2035: Mobility Planning for the Near Future.* Barcelona, Spain: Actar, 2013.

Sassen, Saskia. *The Global City: New York, London, Tokyo.* Princeton, NJ: Princeton University Press, 2001.

———. "Identity in the Global City: Economic and Cultural Encasements." In *The Geography of Identity*, edited by Patricia Yaeger, 131–51. Ann Arbor: University of Michigan Press, 1996.

———. "Re-Assembling the Urban." *Urban Geography* 29, no. 2 (2008): 113–26.

———. *Territory Authority Rights: From Medieval to Global Assemblages.* Princeton, NJ: Princeton University Press, 2006.

Saxenian, Anna Lee. *Regional Advantage: Culture and Competition in Silicon Valley and Route 128.* Cambridge, MA: Harvard University Press, 1994.

Schivelbusch, Wolfgang. *The Railway Journey: The Industrialization of Time and Space in the 19th Century.* Berkeley: University of California Press, 1986.

Schön, Donald A. "From Technical Rationality to Reflection-in-Action." In *The Reflective Practitioner: How Professionals Think in Action*, 21–75. New York: Basic Books, 1983.

Sennett, Richard. *The Fall of Public Man.* New York: W. W. Norton, 1974.

Sharp, Willoughby. "Worldpool: A Call for Global Community Communications." *Only Paper Today*, December 1978, 8–9.

Sheller, Mimi. "Mobile Publics: Beyond the Network Perspective." *Environment and Planning D: Society and Space* 22, no. 1 (2004): 39–52.

Sheller, Mimi, and John Urry "The City and the Car." *International Journal of Urban and Regional Research* 24, no. 4 (2000): 737–57.

⸻, eds. *Mobile Technologies of the City.* London: Routledge, 2006.

⸻. "Mobile Transformations of 'Public' and 'Private' Life." *Theory, Culture, and Society* 20, no. 3 (2003): 107–25.

⸻. "The New Mobilities Paradigm." *Environment and Planning A* 38, no. 2 (2006): 207–26.

Shepard, Mark. *Sentient City: Ubiquitous Computing, Architecture, and the Future of Urban Space.* Cambridge, MA: MIT Press, 2011.

Shirky, Clay. *Here Comes Everybody.* New York: Penguin Press, 2008.

⸻. "Social Software and the Politics of Groups." *Networks, Economics, and Culture,* mailing list, and *Economics & Culture, Media & Community,* Open Source (March 9, 2003).

Sorkin, Michael. *Variations on a Theme Park: The New American City and the End of Public Space.* New York: Hill & Wang, 1992.

Spielberg, Frank, and Phillip Shapiro. "Mating Habits of Slugs: Dynamic Carpool Formation in the I-95/I-395 Corridor of Northern Virginia." *Transportation Research Record: Journal of the Transportation Research Board* 1711, no. 1 (1999): 31–38.

Stallabrass, Julian. "Just Gaming: Allegory and Economy in Computer Games." *New Left Review* 198 (March/April 1993): 83–106.

Tao, Chi-Chung. "Dynamic Taxi-Sharing Service Using Intelligent Transportation System Technologies." Paper presented at WiCom 2007, Shanghai, September 21–25, 2007. Published in *2007 International Conference on Wireless Communications, Networking, and Mobile Computing,* 3209–12. Piscataway, NJ: IEEE Communications Society, 2007.

Thorburn, David, Henry Jerkins, and Brad Seawell, eds. *Rethinking Media Change: The Aesthetics of Transition.* Cambridge, MA: MIT Press, 2003.

Thrift, Nigel. "Remembering the Technological Unconscious by Foregrounding Knowledges of Position." *Environment and Planning D: Society and Space* 22 (2004): 175–90.

Tierney, Thérèse F. "Disentangling Public Space: Social Media and Internet Activism." *Thresholds* 41 (Spring 2013): 82–89.

⸻. "In [Re]search of the Public: Reality and Representation in Online Social Sites." Pilot study conducted at Dalhousie University, Halifax, Nova Scotia, 2008.

⸻. *The Public Space of Social Media: Connected Cultures of the Network Society.* London: Routledge, 2013.

Tierney, Thérèse, et al. [as 510 Collective]. 2009. *Los Angeles RED_car*. March 21, 2009. Infrastructural Innovation Design Competition and Exhibition, Southern California Institute of Technology, Los Angeles.

Tsay, Shin-Pei, and Victoria Hermann. *Rethinking Urban Mobility: Sustainable Policies for the Century of the City*. Washington, DC: Carnegie Endowment for International Peace, 2013.

Toffler, Alvin. *Future Shock*. New York: Random House, 1970.

Townsend, Anthony. "Life in the Real-Time City: Mobile Telephones and Urban Metabolism." *Journal of Urban Technology* 7, no. 2 (2000): 85–104.

———. *Smart Cities: Big Data, Civic Hackers, and the Quest for a New Utopia*. New York: W. W. Norton, 2013.

Tschumi, Bernard. "Spaces and Events." In *Architecture and Disjunction*, 139–49. Cambridge, MA: MIT Press, 1994.

Tsagarousianou, Roza, Damian Tambini, and Cathy Bryan, eds. *Cyberdemocracy: Technology, Cities and Civic Networks*. London: Routledge, 1998.

Tsao, H.-S. Jacob, and Da-Jie Lin. "Spatial and Temporal Factors in Estimating the Potential of Ride-sharing for Demand Reduction." PATH Research Report UCB-ITS-PRR-99-2. Berkeley, CA: California Partners for Advanced Transit and Highways, 1999.

Ungemah, David, Ginger Goodin, Casey Dusza, and Mark Burris. "Examining Incentives and Preferential Treatment of Carpools on Managed Lane Facilities." *Journal of Public Transportation* 10, no. 4 (2007): 151–69.

Urban Consortium for Technology Initiatives. "The Coordination of Parking with Public Transportation and Ridesharing." Washington, DC: U.S. Department Transportation, Office of the Secretary of Transportation, 1982.

Urry, John. *Mobilities*. Cambridge, UK: Polity, 2007.

———. "Small Worlds and the New 'Social Physics.'" *Global Networks* 4, no. 2 (2004): 109–30.

———. "Social Networks, Mobile Lives and Social Inequalities." *Journal of Transport Geography* 21 (March 2012): 24–30.

Varnelis, Kazys. *The Infrastructural City: Networked Ecologies in Los Angeles*. Barcelona: Actar, 2009.

———. *Networked Publics*. Cambridge, MA: MIT Press, 2008.

Virilio, Paul. "Speed and Information: Cyberspace Alarm!" *CTheory*, 1995.

———. *The Vision Machine*. Bloomington: Indiana University Press, 1994.

Von Seggern, Hille, Julia Werner, and Lucia Grosse-Bächle, eds. *Creating Knowledge: Innovation Strategies for Designing Urban Landscapes*. Berlin: Jovis Verlag, 2008.

Wachs, Martin. "Can Transit Be Saved? Of Course It Can." *Proceedings of the Metro-politan Conference on Public Transportation Research*, 1–25. Chicago: University of Illinois, Urban Transportation Center, June 1992.

Wark, McKenzie. *A Hacker Manifesto [version 4.0]*. Cambridge, MA: Harvard University Press. 2004. http://subsol.c3.hu/subsol_2/contributorso/warktext.html (accessed August 24, 2007).

Wash, Rick, Libby Hemphill, and Paul Resnick. "Design Decisions in the Ride-Now Project." *GROUP '05 Proceedings of the 2005 International ACM SIGGROUP Conference on Supporting Group Work* (2005): 132–35. Sanibel Island, FL, November 6–9, 2005. ACM Digital Library.

Washbrook, Kevin, Wolfgang Haider, and Mark Jaccard. "Estimating Commuter Mode Choice: A Discrete Choice Analysis of the Impact of Road Pricing and Parking Charges." *Transportation* 33, no. 6 (November 2006): 621–39.

Webber, Melvin. "The Marriage of Transit and Autos: How to Make Transit Popular Again." Last modified January 16, 1998. http://faculty.washington.edu /jbs/itrans/webber.htm (accessed May 15, 2016).

———. "Order in Diversity: Community without Propinquity." In *Cities and Space: The Future of Urban Land*, edited by Lowdon Wingo, 23–54. Baltimore: Johns Hopkins Press for Resources for the Future, 1963.

———. "Planning in an Environment of Change, Part II: Permissive Planning." *Town Planning Review* 39, no. 4 (January 1969): 282–84.

———. "The Urban Place and the Non-Place Urban Realm." In *Explorations into Urban Structure*, edited by Melvin M. Webber. Philadelphia: University of Pennsylvania Press, 1964.

Weiner, Norbert. *The Human Use of Human Beings: Cybernetics and Society*. New York: Avon Books, 1986.

Weintraub, Jeff. "The Theory and Politics of the Public/Private Distinction." In *Public and Private in Thought and Practice: Perspectives on a Grand Dichotomy*, edited by Jeff Weintraub and Krishan Kumar, 1–42. Chicago: University of Chicago Press, 1997.

Weiser, Mark. "The Computer for the 21st Century." *Scientific American*, September 1999, 94–104.

Wellman, Barry. "Little Boxes, Globalization, and Networked Individualism." In *Digital Cities II: Computational and Sociological Approaches*, edited by Makoto Tanabe, Peter van den Besselaar, and Toru Ishida, 11–25. Berlin: Springer, 2002.

Wellman, Barry, and Bernie Hogan. "The Immanent Internet." In *Netting Citizens: Exploring Citizenship in a Digital Age*, edited by Johnston McKay, 54–80. Edinburgh: St. Andrew Press, 2004.

Wheeler, James O., and Yuko Aoyama, eds. *Cities in the Telecommunications Age: The Fracturing of Geographies*. New York: Routledge, 2000.

White, Lynn. *Medieval Technology and Social Change*. Oxford: Clarendon Press, 1963.

Whitehead, Alfred North. *Process and Reality*. Edited by David Ray Griffin and Donald W. Sherburne. Corrected ed. New York: Simon and Schuster, 1978.

Whyte, William H. *The Social Life of Small Urban Spaces*. Washington, DC: Conservation Foundation, 1980.

Wigley, Mark. *Constant's New Babylon: The Hyper-Architecture of Desire*. Rotterdam, Uitgeverij, 1998.

———. "Network Fever." *Grey Room* 4 (Summer 2001): 82–122.

Wiley, Stephen B. Crofts. "Rethinking Nationality in the Context of Globalization." *Communication Theory* 14, no. 1 (2004): 78–96.

———. "Spatial Materialism." *Cultural Studies* 19, no. 1 (2005): 63–99.

Winner, Langdon. "Do Artifacts Have Politics?" *Daedalus* 109, no. 1 (1980): 121–36.

Wolfe, Alan. "Public and Private in Theoretical Practice: Some Implications of an Uncertain Boundary." In *Public and Private in Thought and Practice: Perspectives on a Grand Dichotomy*, edited by Jeff Weintraub and Krishan Kumar, 182–203. Chicago: University of Chicago Press, 1997.

Woodworth, Park, and Robert Behnke. "Smart Jitney/Community-Enhanced Transit Systems." http://faculty.washington.edu/jbs/itrans/minerva31.doc (accessed January 12, 2005).

Zeiger, Mimi. "Urban Renewal." *Architect*, June 2009. http://www.architectmagazine.com/urban-development/what-is-the-future-of-american-urbanism.aspx (accessed January 17, 2015).

Zeisel, John. *Inquiry by Design: Tools for Environment Behavior Research*. New York: W. W. Norton, 1981.

Zucker, Paul. *Town and Square: From the Agora to the Village Green*. New York: Columbia University Press, 1959.

Zukin, Sharon. *Naked City: The Death and Life of Authentic Urban Places*. New York: Oxford University Press, 2009.

Contributors

Sven Beiker is a management consultant with specialization in product development and particular interest in the automotive industry and personal mobility. Until 2014, he was the Executive Director of the Center for Automotive Research at Stanford University, an interdisciplinary partnership between academia and industry to address the challenges of personal mobility in the twenty-first century. Prior to that he worked at BMW with responsibilities in technology scouting, innovation management, systems design, and series development. He holds MS and PhD degrees in mechanical engineering.

Kai-Uwe Bergmann is a partner at Bjarke Ingels Group (BIG) who brings his expertise to proposals around the globe, including work in North America, Europe, Asia, and the Middle East. He heads up BIG's business development, which currently has the office working in over twenty different countries, as well as overseeing BIG's Communications. Registered as an architect in the United States and Canada, he most recently contributed to the resiliency plan "The Dryline" to protect ten miles of Manhattan's coastline. He complements his professional work through previous teaching positions at the University of Florida, the New School of Architecture in San Diego, and his alma mater, the University of Virginia.

Alfredo Brillembourg founded Urban-Think Tank (U-TT) in Caracas, Venezuela, in 1993. Since 1994 he has been a member of the Venezuelan Architects and Engineers Association and has been a guest professor at the University José Maria Vargas, Simón Bolívar University, and the Central University of Venezuela. Starting in 2007, he has been a guest professor at the Graduate School of Architecture and Planning, Columbia University, where he cofounded the Sustainable Living Urban Model Laboratory (S.L.U.M. Lab) with Hubert Klumpner. He has over twenty years of experience practicing architecture and urban design and has lectured at conferences around the world. Since May 2010, he has held the chair for Architecture and Urban Design at the Swiss Institute of Technology (Eidgenössische Technische Hochschule, ETH) Zürich in Switzerland. In 2012, U-TT won the prestigious Audi Urban Future Award.

Jordan Geiger is an architect and educator whose work crosses architecture and interaction design, considering implications of human–computer interaction for social and environmental issues. He lectures, exhibits, and publishes internationally on theoretical research and on his projects, which frequently investigate globalization's design problems at many scales. He is editor of *Entr'acte: Performing Publics, Pervasive Media, and Architecture*, which explores ephemeral and interstitial formations of publics and of public space with the proliferation of new technologies. Geiger has taught at the University at Buffalo, at the Academy of Fine Arts in Vienna, at UC Berkeley, and at the California College of the Arts in San Francisco.

Bjarke Ingels heads the global architectural practice Bjarke Ingels Group (BIG). The firm incorporates innovative sustainable development and sociological concepts into their architectural and urban designs. Since 2009, he has won numerous architectural competitions and awards, including the prestigious Audi Q3 Urban Future Award and the *Wall Street Journal*'s Innovator of the Year for architecture.

Mitchell Joachim is a cofounder of Terreform ONE (Open Network Ecology). He is an Associate Professor at New York University and the European Graduate School, Switzerland, and a TED Fellow. He is the recipient of numerous awards including the Official Selection Venice Biennale 2014, the AIA New York Urban Design Merit Award, the Victor Papanek Social Design Award, the Zumtobel Group Award for Sustainability and Humanity, and the History Channel's Infiniti Award for City of the Future. His name appeared on "The Smart List: 15 People the Next President Should Listen To" (*Wired*, 2012) and "The 100 People Who Are Changing America" (*Rolling Stone*, 2009); and he was featured in *Time* magazine's "Best Invention: MIT Smart Cities Car" (2007).

Hubert Klumpner graduated from the University of Applied Arts in Vienna. He later worked with Enrique Miralles and Paul Rudolph before receiving a master of science in architecture and urban design from Columbia University in 1997. He is a member of the German Chamber of Architects, and since 2001 he has been an urbanism consultant of the International Program for Social and Cultural Development in Latin America (OAE and UNESCO). In 1998 he joined Alfredo Brillembourg as Director of Urban-Think Tank (UTT) in Caracas. Since 2007, he has been a guest professor at the Graduate School of Architecture and Planning, Columbia University, where he cofounded the Sustainable Living Urban Model Laboratory (S.L.U.M. Lab) and lectured at conferences around the world. Since 2010, he has held the chair for Architecture and Urban Design at the Swiss Institute of Technology (Eidgenössische Technische Hochschule, ETH) in Zürich, Switzerland. In 2012, U-TT won the prestigious Audi Urban Future Award.

Nashid Nabian is a partner at Shift Process Practice, an architectural design office on Tehran whose projects have received international recognition. Nabian holds a doctoral degree from Harvard Graduate School of Design. She also held a postdoctoral fellowship at MIT SENSEable City Lab, where her research focused on the digital augmentation of architecture and constructed landscapes, particularly public spaces, and how novel technologies impact the spatial experience by soliciting the needs and desires of inhabitants. Her work in the field of digital augmentation has been showcased in various venues, including the ACADIA, IEEE Digital Ecosystems Conference, the UCMedia Conference on User-Centric Media, the Mobile Multimedia Communications Conference, and *Seed* Magazine.

Christine Outram's research focuses on tackling problems of sustainability and livability in inner urban areas through harnessing the power of emerging technologies and distributed computing. She was a Research Associate with MIT's SENSEable City Lab, where she was project leader for the Copenhagen Wheel—a wheel that turns ordinary bikes into electric hybrids with regeneration and real-time environmental sensing capabilities.

Carlo Ratti trained as a civil engineer and architect and now directs the MIT SENSEable City Lab, which explores the "real-time city" by studying the way sensors and electronics relate to the built environment. Most recently, he opened a research center in Singapore as part of a MIT-led initiative on the Future of Urban Mobility.

Mitchell Schwarzer is a historian who writes on architecture and urbanism. He is Professor of Visual Studies at California College of the Arts, Oakland and San Francisco. On the subject of technology, he is the author of the book *Zoomscape: Architecture in Motion and Media* (2004) and the articles "A Sense of Place, A World of Augmented Reality," *Places* (2010); "Landscape Navigator: The Experience of Place on YouTube and Google Maps," *Harvard Design Magazine* (2013); and "Computation and the Impact of New Technologies on the Photography of Architecture and Urbanism," in *Visioning Technologies: The Architectures of Sight* (forthcoming in 2017).

Frederic Stout directed the Program on Urban Studies at Stanford University from 1973 to 1977 and has taught courses on urban history, urban culture, and urban planning theory ever since. He is the coeditor of *The City Reader*, the most widely adopted textbook/anthology in the field of urban studies (now in its sixth English-language edition, with a Chinese edition published in 2013).

T. F. Tierney is the founding director of URL: Urban Research Lab at the University of Illinois at Urbana-Champaign. URL focuses on the design implications of network technologies on cities, people, and infrastructure. In 2013, Tierney was a U.S. delegate to Smart & Digital Cities in France; she was selected for the quality of her research in the application of new technologies to build the next generation of cities. Tierney is the author of several books, including *The Public Space of Social Media: Connected Cultures of the Networked Society* (Routledge, 2013), which was a finalist for the Jane Jacobs Urban Communication Award (2014), and *Abstract Space: Beneath the Media Surface* (Routledge, 2007), and is coeditor with Anthony Burke of *Network Practices: New Strategies in Architecture and Design* (Princeton Architectural Press, 2007). Tierney holds a PhD in architecture with a designated emphasis in new media from the University of California, Berkeley, and a BArch from California College of the Arts. During 2006, she was a predoctoral researcher at the MIT media lab.

Anthony Townsend is a visiting professor at New York University in the Rudin Center for Transportation Policy and Management, where his research focuses on the role of telecommunications in urban development and design. He is also Research Director at the Institute for the Future, a nonprofit independent research group in Palo Alto, California. His earlier work with the wireless community networking movement is described in *Smart Cities: Big Data, Civic Hackers, and the Quest for a New Utopia* (Norton, 2013).

Chamee Yang holds a bachelor's degree and master's degree from the Department of Communication at Seoul National University in South Korea and was a visiting researcher at the University of Tokyo in Japan. Her multidisciplinary research interests include media and cultural studies, urban studies, critical theory, and science and technology studies. She is currently at the Institute of Communication Research at the University of Illinois at Urbana-Champaign, working on her doctoral thesis, "Networked Urbanization and the Birth of Creative Subjects: Ethno-historiography of the New Songdo City Project in South Korea," in which she critically examines discourses surrounding new media and technologies of governance, the influence of media and technology on urban landscape and architecture, and histories and politics of urban technological development in an East Asian context.

Index

accelerometers, 7

actor network theory (ANT), 8

aerospace, 50

agriculture, 45, 73, 97, 182; building integrated, 26n6; transformed by motor vehicles, 139; urban utopias and, 164

AGV (autonomous ground vehicle) technology, 17–18, 33n68

AHS technology, 33n67, 92

AIA (American Institute of Architects) San Francisco, 129

Airbnb, 68

air-conditioning, 57

airports, 30n35, 41, 58, 81n5, 116; Incheon International Airport (South Korea), 196; New York City, 49; U.S. Air Traffic Control System, 55, 61n45

Alexander, Christopher, 89, 119

Allen, Stan, 9, 18–19, 54

Ambasz, Emilio, 48

America in Ruins: Beyond the Public Works Pork Barrel (Choate and Walters), 51

"Among the New Words" (Russell, 1953), 44

Amsterdam, city of, 65, 67

Anthropocene, 57

antiquity, classical, 10

Apple corporation, 10, 35n78; Apple laptop, 150; App Store, 64; Siri, 65

Apple Watch, 8

Apps for Democracy, 63, 65, 66

Archigram, 46, 88

architecture, 4, 22, 45, 68, 164, 209; ecology and, 170; infrastructure in relation to, 47–48; infrastructure inseparable from, 39; landscape urbanism and, 9, 163; of movement, 102

Architecture Mobile (Friedman, 1958), 46

Architecture Mobile, l', 13

Armstrong, Ellis, 50

Arrival City (Saunders, 2010), 151

art history, 45–46

artificial intelligence, 95, 167; Artificial Intelligence Laboratory, 95

Ashlock, Philip, 64

Asphalt Nation (Kay), 143

atoms, 42

Audi, 10, 35n78; Urban Parangolè—Mobile Village (São Paulo), 184; Urban Future Initiative, 21, 101–4, 102, 103, 104, 182

Austin, city of, 117

Autolib' Paris, 20, 213

Automated Highway System, 17

automation, 88

Automobile and the Environment, The (children's book), 143–44

automobiles. *See* cars (automobiles)

autonomous vehicles (AVs). *See* driverless (self-driving, autonomous) vehicles

"autopia," 11, 88, 91
aviation, 144

baby boomer generation, 139
Banham, Reyner, 11, 47, 88
bank cards, 7
beaches, 30n35
Beihai (China), city of, 173
Beiker, Sven, 21–22
Bell Laboratories, 15
Bergmann, Kai-Uwe, 21
Berkeley, California, 23
Berlin: Potsdamer Platz, 163
bicycles/bicyclists, 101, 104, 106, 127, 149,
    152; bicycle paths, 102, 121; bike sharing,
    5; carsharing and, 128; free public bicy-
    cles, 193; movement away from autos
    in favor of, 135, 141; multimodality and,
    109, 118; public transit integrated with,
    182; shared bicycles, 112, 117
BIG (Bjarke Ingels Group), 21, 100, 210;
    Audi Urban Future Initiative and, 101–4;
    Denmark Pavilion, Shangai XPO (2010),
    106; Loop City project and, 104–7, 105
BigApps contest, 66
big data, 11
biology, 22, 43, 166
biometrics, 78, 81n6, 217
bioregionalism, 150
biosphere, 24
biotechnology, 160
BlaBlaCar, 212
blogs, 33n70
Bloomberg, Michael R., 115
bluejacking, 79
Blur building (Diller-Scofidio), 82n11
BMW corporation, 66
Bohr, Niels, 42
Bomb the Suburbs (Wimsatt, 2001), 143
border controls, 72, 73
Borroni-Bird, Christopher, 2, 90, 91

Borsodi, Ralph, 150
Boston, city of, 75, 212
Boston Institute for Contemporary Art,
    82–83n12
Boundary Waters Treaty (1909), 82n7
Bourgeois Nightmares (Fogelson, 2005), 143
Bratton, Benjamin H., 82n10
Brazil, 185
breakbulk freight shipping, 54
bridges, 30n35, 39, 73; New York City, 49;
    over Øresund Strait, 106
Bridj, 212
Brillembourg, Alfredo, 22–23, 177, 214
Britain. See United Kingdom
Broadacre City (Wright, 1935), 141, 144
broadband, mobile, 7, 28–29n25
Bronx River Parkway, 49
Brooklyn 2110, City of the Future (Terre-
    form ONE), 164–65, 165
Brooklyn Bridge (1883), 49
Brown, John Seely, 72
Bruegmann, Robert, 53
buildings: ancient, 44; lifespans of, 52–53;
    public, 50
building systems, 19
built environment, 9, 18, 34n77, 46,
    100; computing technologies and, 73;
    human-computer interactions in, 72–73;
    networked digital elements in, 116
bureaucracy, 64, 88
Burns, Lawrence, 2, 91–92
buses, 15, 98n11, 112, 138; bicycle transit
    integrated with, 182; bus rapid transit
    (BRT), 98n11; bus tracking, 63, 67; elimi-
    nation of fares, 115; multimodality and,
    109, 113, 116, 117, 118

cable cars, 49, 53, 174, 176
CabSense, 65
Callenbach, Ernest, 143
"calm technology," 72

Calthorpe, Peter, 150–51
Cambridge, Massachusetts, 23
Canada, U.S. border with, 72, 74, 76, 81nn6–7
canals, 30n35, 40, 53, 101, 141
capitalism, 144, 187, 188, 204
car2go, 5, 94, 98–99n13; microleasing and, 20, 213; multimodality and, 116, 117
Caracas, city of, 23, 181; cable cars in, 174, 176; Torre David office tower, 177, 178, 179, 180
carbon (greenhouse gas) emissions, 1, 9, 26n2, 80, 169; cities' efforts to reduce, 67; minimized carbon footprints, 175; urban rezoning and, 17; zero-emission cars, 95. See also climate change; fossil fuels
Carma, 129, 212
Carnegie Endowment for International Peace, 25
cars (automobiles), 4, 16, 49; accidents and injuries, 122, 138; car rental, 68, 128, 147, 153; carsharing, 34n74, 67–68, 127–28, 139, 147, 153, 188; combined with other transport devices, 109; commoditization of, 127–28; communication between vehicles, 126–27; on-demand vehicles, 109, 111, 116; electronic hitchhiking and, 15; etymology and history of, 121–22; Ford's "Universal Car" (Model-T), 140; fuel-efficient, 2; historical relationship with cities, 137–140; horses replaced by, 135; hybrids, 148; inefficiency of personal automobile, 91, 122; as instrument of personal freedom, 31n50, 121, 139; microleasable, 20; networked dashboards, 110, 111; as new transport alternative, 31n54; personal automobiles in future mobility, 21, 101, 121; at rooftop level in Motopia, 13; stackable car with solar recharge, 162; tollbooths

and automotive culture, 71; from utopia to dystopia, 140–45; Volkswagen project in Nazi Germany, 141. See also driverless (self-driving, autonomous) vehicles; electric vehicles (EVs)
Car Talk (NPR show), 145
Castells, Manuel, 16, 89, 97, 148
cathedrals, 39
CCTV (closed-circuit TV), 79, 192–93, 193, 196, 206n16
CDMA (Code Division Multiple Access), 28n25
cell phones, 29n26, 97, 116, 154
cellular networks, 5
central heating, 57
centralized networks, 47, 89
CFC Media Lab (Toronto), 35n82
Chairman Bao (mobile restaurant), 97
Challenge of the Slums, The (UN-HABITAT, 2003), 146
Champaign-Urbana metropolitan area, Illinois, 23
Charles, Prince, 161
Chicago, city of, 69, 142
Chin, Ryan, 26n6, 34n75, 95, 98n11, 215
China, 40, 146–47, 199
Choate, Pat, 51
Christaller, Walter, 116
Churchill, Winston, 44
circuitry, 48
Cisco Systems, 10, 68, 188–89, 198, 211; "Smart + Connected City" idea, 193; TelePresence HD video system, 190, 191
cities, 44–48, 56–57, 70, 153; city squares, 102; defined by social relations, 12; formal, 174, 175; fossil fuel–based energy systems and, 168; greenhouse gas emission reductions and, 67; growth of, 173; historical relationship with automobiles, 137–140; informal, 24, 174, 176–77, 179, 181–83; infrastructure

cities (continued)
inseparable from, 39; megacities, 140, 147, 162, 173; "network of cities," 148; polycentric, 17, 20, 91; skyscraper cities, 141; as sociotechnical processes, 4; vulnerability to catastrophic events, 51. See also smart cities

CityCar, 26n6, 95

City in History, The (Mumford, 1961), 47, 143

cityLAB, at UCLA, 23

City-less and Country-less World, A (Olerich, 1893), 144–45

Citymapper, 21

City of To-morrow and Its Planning, The (Le Corbusier), 186

City Science Initiative, 26n6, 34n75, 95, 98n11, 215

Ciudad Lineal (Soria y Mata, 1892), 141

Civic Commons, 64

civic hackers, 64

civic laboratories, 69

Clark, Shelby, 18

clean energy, 23

climate change, 1, 9, 24, 175; cities' efforts to reduce carbon emissions, 67; "new urban mobilities" and, 135, 136; urbanism as solution to, 151. See also carbon (greenhouse gas) emissions; fossil fuels

Clipper Card, 7

cloud computing, 5

Cloud of Things, 4

Code for America, 6

Cold War, 44

commerce, 4, 136, 179, 181, 189

Commissioners Plan (New York, 1811), 48–49

communication technologies, 5, 7, 11, 47, 154

community, 23, 30n35, 63, 136, 151; automobile and decline of, 143; communi-

cation technologies and, 53; defined by social overlay, 12; Disney's experimental prototype, 13, 14, 15, 17; environmental sustainability and, 24; human infrastructure and, 45; informal, 183; real-time information and, 114; reimagining of, 154; "smart" design and, 176; social media and, 6; sustainability and, 175; virtual, 148

commuting routines, 209

complexity theory, 168

Computer City (Crompton, 1964), 88

computers, 11, 48, 126; in automated vehicles, 125; "calm technology" and, 72; computer literacy, 213; high-throughput computation, 160; human-computer interactions, 3, 72–73; ubiquitous computing, 26n1

computer science, 74, 166, 203

conservative politics, 15, 32n61

Constructivists, Russian, 215

container shipping and ports, 54, 58

Contemporary City (Wright), 144

Contribution to the Critique of Political Economy, A (Marx, 1859), 42

COP21: United Nations Convention on Climate Change, 23

Copenhagen, city of, 105–6

Core Sample (Rueb, 2007), 82–83n12

Costa, Frank J., 40

"coupling" strategy, 215

Crack in the Picture Window, The (Keats, 1956), 143

"creative class," 136, 147

credit cards, 7

Crick, Francis, 43

crowdsourcing, 6, 28n19, 87, 160

Crowley, Dennis, 64

Cuff, Dana, 23

dams, 58

D'Anieri, Philip, 204–5

DARPA (Defense Advanced Research Project), 34n78; Grand Challenge, 95; LA_Redcar and, 93; Urban Challenge, 17

data collection, 7, 8, 10, 25, 216–17

DC Data Catalog, 65

De Architectura (Vitruvius), 40

decentralization, 89, 150, 183

Deleuze, Gilles, 116

Delos Summit (1958), 11

democracy, 10, 162

Democritus, 43

demographics, 22, 100, 136, 210

Deng Xiaoping, 146

Denmark, 105, 107

design/designers, 9, 19, 21, 101, 209; design theory, 89; ecological, 22; experimental, 11; incremental design, 183; "intelligent," 175; planetary designers, 169; scale and, 168

Detroit Digital Stewards, 6

developing world (emerging nations), 7, 15, 22, 148; emerging middle class in, 136, 140, 143, 146; informal transit (paratransit) in, 212; infrastructure as measure of modernization, 54; microgrids for, 211

Development of Large Technical Systems, The (Hughes and Mayntz, eds., 1988), 52

Digital City Design Workshop, at MIT, 114

Digital Humanitarian Network (DHN), 6

digital media, 80

digital modeling, 221n27

digitization, 55

diseases, tracking spread of, 63

Disney Realty Company, 13, 14, 15, 32n61

distributed networks, 89–90, 89, 94–95

DIYcity.org website, 63–64, 67

DIYtraffic service, 64

Dodge, Martin, 221n27

Doxiadis, C. A., 11

driverless (self-driving, autonomous) vehicles, 12, 33n68, 34–35n78, 125–26, 148; AGV technology, 17–18, 33n68; AHS technology and, 33n67, 92; Audi A2 concept car, 101; diagram of driverless traffic, 102; embedded sensors of, 8; integrated approach to personal urban mobility and, 129; LA_Redcar and, 92, 95; quiet and nonpolluting, 102–4

Dublin, city of, 65

Dupuy, Gabriel, 50–51

Eames, Charles and Ray, 168

EAR studio, 82n11

Easterling, Keller, 17, 82n10, 168, 172n16

ecograms, 163

École nationale des pont et chaussées (School of Bridges and Highways), 41

ecological urbanism, 9

ecology, 98n9, 160, 163, 169–170

economy, 10, 48, 136, 218; cars and economic development, 141; "creative economy," 199, 200; economic cycles, 52; FEZ (free economic zone), 195–96; fossil fuel–based energy systems and, 209; game theory, 74; informal economies, 176; "knowledge economy," 198; recession, 65; small-is-beautiful, 150; South Korean economy, 199

ecosystems, 57, 162

Ecotopia (Callenbach, 1975), 143

"Edge City," 149

Edmonton, Canada, 65

Edwards, Paul, 57

efficiency, 30n39, 52, 67, 128, 153, 200, 216; driving, 123; of electric vehicles, 123–24; facilitated by technology, 46; governance and, 191; improvement of, 129; individuals and, 113; optimization of, 130, 186; postwar systems and, 56; of road traffic, 126

Eisenhower, Dwight, 61n43, 145–46

Ekistics, 11, 30n43

Electric Networked Vehicle (EN-V), 20

electric vehicles (EVs), 107, 123–24, 129, 131n2, 148, 211, 214; limitations of, 124; mobility-on-demand systems and, 20, 26n6, 34n75, 95; stackable, 17

electronics, 72, 199; electronic mapping, 125; hand-held, 34; money card, 5

electrons, 41, 42

elevators, 32n57, 182; coordination of individual mobility and, 103; elevator shafts, 49; skyscraper without, 179; urban densities and, 140

Ellul, Jacques, 56

Emerson, Ralph Waldo, 145

Empire State Building (New York), 50

End of Nature, The (McKibben, 1989), 169

energy, 48, 106, 109; alternative sources of, 211; localized, 160; movement of, 46; renewable, 3, 92, 135, 164; sustainable, 182

Engels, Friedrich, 145

engineering/engineers, 9, 41, 47, 50, 152; automated vehicles and, 125; civil, 51; software engineers, 219; structural, 166; utopian ideals and, 202

E.P.C.O.T. (experimental prototype community of tomorrow), 13, 17

"equality among entities" (EaE), 8

evolution, 43

Exit Strategy app, 65

extraterritorial zones, 168, 172n16

Eyestop bus stops, 114

Facebook, 212, 217

facial recognition, 77, 175

Feiffer, Jules, 71

Feldman, Ben, 98n8

Fennell, Lee Anne, 7

Fill That Hole, 6

Firestone Tire, 137

Fishman, Robert, 143, 149

Five-Fingered Plan, in Copenhagen, 105–6

510 Collective, 90, 98n8

Fix My Street, 6

Flew, Terry, 25

flood control, 50

Florence, Italy, 114, 115

Florida, Richard, 147

folding vehicles, 175

Ford, Henry, 140

Fordism, 140–41

Ford Motor Company, 10, 35n78

Format Design, 90, 98n8

forts, 39

fossil fuels, 9, 168, 209, 214, 218. *See also* carbon (greenhouse gas) emissions; climate change

foundations, of buildings, 41, 44

Foursquare app, 5, 64, 67, 212

Fragile Foundations: A Report on America's Public Works (1988), 51

France, 13

free trade zones, 4

freeways, 12, 16, 32nn54–55, 90

Freud, Sigmund, 43

Friedman, Yona, 13, 46, 58

FriendFreight, 114, 115

fuel cell technology, 148, 175

Fuller, Buckminster, 11

"Futurama" exhibit (New York World's Fair, 1939), 142

Gabler, Neal, 32n61

game theory, 74

Garden Cities (Howard, 1898), 141, 144

Garreau, Joel, 149

GE (General Electric), 10

Geiger, Jordan, 20, 210

General Transit Feed Specification, 66

Gennawey, Sam, 13

Geography of Nowhere, The (Kunstler, 1993), 143

geo-location, 28n19

geology, 43

George Washington Bridge (1931), 49

geotagging, 213
Geraci, John, 63
Germany, 52, 69, 77, 141
Gernsback, Hugo, 113
Ghaziabad, India, city of, 173
Giedion, Siegfried, 47
Gilbertson, Nate, 64
GIS (Geographical Information Systems) data, 79, 117, 221n27
Glaeser, Edward, 150
Global Information Infrastructure (GII), 55
globalization, 19, 73, 145–49, 168
global warming, 67
GM (General Motors), 10, 31n54, 35n78, 145–46; Advanced Vehicle Concepts, 90; Electric Networked Vehicle (EN-V), 20; "transportation conspiracy" and, 137–38
Godelier, Maurice, 42
Gomez, Enrique, 177
Gone Tomorrow: The Hidden Life of Garbage (Rogers), 166
Google, 10, 66, 69, 95, 217; Car, 34n78; Earth, 79; Street View, 95; Wallet, 7; X lab, 18, 34n78
governance, 1, 10, 73, 201, 210; citadel functions of, 136; data collection and, 25; decision making about technology and, 218; e-government, 160; planning and, 12; transparency of, 188
Governance of Large Technical Systems, The (Coutard, ed., 1992), 52
GPS (Global Positioning System), 7, 19, 55, 188; autonomous vehicles (AVs) and, 95; carsharing and, 67; phantom (unstaffed) tollbooths and, 77, 79; smartphone apps and, 112; surveillance and, 216
Graham, Stephen, 4, 24, 187, 196, 204
Great Depression, 52
Greeks, ancient, 42
Green Brain Park Space, 161
Green Metropolis (Owen, 2009), 150
GreenWheel, 26n6

Griffith, Saul, 18
Grossman, Nick, 64
"growing house," 176
GSM (Global System for Mobile Communication), 28n25
Guattari, Félix, 116

hackathons, 5, 160
Haiti, earthquake in, 6
Handy, Katherine, 98n8
Hard Systems, 18, 22
Harleson, Chris, 66
Harman, Graham, 8, 29n30
Harrison, Wallace, 60n23
Harvard University: Graduate School of Design, 9, 173; Kennedy School of Government, 66
Harvey, David, 32n56, 203, 205n1
Haselmayer, Sascha, 68–69
Helsinki, city of, 34n76
Herzog & de Meuron, 181
High Line (Manhattan), 22, 163
high-speed networks, 1, 29n25
highways, 49, 51, 71, 106; autonomous vehicles and, 125; multimodality and, 113
History of Public Works in the United States, 1776–1976 (Armstrong, ed.), 50
Hitler, Adolf, 141
holistic ideas, 9, 25
home automation, 175
"Home Is Not a House, A" (Banham, 1965), 47
Hong Kong, 5
Hooke, Robert, 43
hospitals, 30n35, 191, 196
housing, 32n57, 49, 181, 182; as basic element of infrastructure, 45; modular design and, 176; multimodal approaches to, 152; suburban, 143; sustainable, 174
Howard, Ebenezer, 141, 144
Howells, William Dean, 145

Hughes, Thomas Parke, 51–52
human-computer interactions, 3, 72–73
hydroelectricity, 107

IBM corporation, 10, 68
ICTs (information and communication technologies), 2, 9, 10, 11, 97; disinformation and, 190; organization of mobility and, 90; social equity and, 25; Soft Systems and, 19; in South Korea, 199; urban form and, 22
IDEO, 25
imaginaries, cultural, 218
i-metro scalable prototype, 18
Inca Empire, 40
Incheon, South Korea, 23, 207n37; Global Fair and Festival (2009), 201, 207n36; IFEZ (Incheon Free Economic Zone), 195, 196, 198, 203, 204; New Songdo City, 190, 191, 192, 203, 206n14; Songdo Tribowl Gallery, 202. *See also* Songdo International Business District; U-City
India, 146
individuality, 46
industrial design, 22
Industrial Revolution, 48, 97
Indymedia, 6
information, 11, 30n43; city as "information system," 12; flows of, 17, 136, 168; "information superhighway," 190; realtime, 109, 112, 113, 119
infrastructure, 1, 26n1, 90, 168; in ancient societies, 40; efficiency of existing infrastructure, 118; etymology and history of, 19, 39, 41–48; fixed, 7, 28n23; hard, 24; "infrastructure crisis" (1980s), 39, 51; lifespans of, 52–53; mobility systems and, 2; multimodal transportation and, 113, 114, 118; New York as exemplar of, 48–50; personal, 9–10, 23, 93, 213; scale and, 19; sensory, 64; "soft," 210–11; VLOs (Very Large Organizations) and,

72–74; wireless, 4. *See also* intelligent infrastructure
"Infrastructures, Societies, and History" (Godelier), 42
Ingels, Bjarke, 21
innovation, 11, 69, 162, 175; large technical systems (LTSs) and, 52; mobile, 188; utopian ideals and, 23
intelligent infrastructure, 3, 5–8, 15, 18, 87, 219
Interactive Telecommunications Program (ITP) (New York University), 64
Internet, 11, 24, 49, 53, 217; access to information and, 16; activism and, 6; expansion to meet new demands, 211; generational differences and, 127; Global Information Infrastructure (GII), 55; information technologies of, 55–56; as infrastructure, 19; innovation and, 69; "Internet of cars," 126; Internet of Things (IoT), 4, 7, 26n1; Internet Protocol version 6 (IPv6), 7; invisible infrastructure of, 58; shopping and, 149; traffic and travel data, 92
"internetworks," 19
Interrante, Joseph, 144
Interstate Highway System, 54–55, 56–57, 61n43, 139
invention/inventors, 47, 50, 52
"iPhone revolution," 199
IT (information technology), 10, 16, 175, 177, 187
iTrans app, 65
i Ventures, of BMW, 66

Jackson, Commander Robert, 45
Jefferson, Thomas, 145
Jellicoe, Geoffrey, 13, 32n57
jitneys, 15, 16, 212
Joachim, Mitchell, 9, 22, 209–10
John F. Kennedy International Airport, 49
Juster, Norton, 71

Karasz, Arthur, 44–45
Katz, Barry, 25
Kaufman, Sarah, 64
Kay, Jane Holtz, 143
Keynes, Milton, 12, 16
Kimmelman, Michael, 49
Kitchen, Rob, 221n27
Klumpner, Hubert, 22–23, 214
Kogi BBQ (mobile restaurant), 18, 33n70, 96
Koolhaas, Rem, 172n19
Korea, South, 23, 187, 190, 195–96, 204; *chae-bol* companies, 198, 200; strategic dependence on science and technology, 199; unique form of modernity in, 200
Krieger, Alex, 159
Kubler, George, 45
Kunstler, Howard, 143
Kwitny, Jonathan, 137–38

LA_Redcar, 90, 91, 92, 97, 98n8, 129; apps for, 94, 94; replacement of conventional cars and, 95
labor, division of, 42
Lagos, city of, 69, 173
landscape architecture, 163
landscapes, 44, 57, 78
landscape urbanism, 9, 161–62
land use, 34n74, 72, 97, 216
Large Cities Climate Leadership Group (C40), 67
large technical systems (LTSs), 52
Latour, Bruno, 8
law enforcement, 71, 73, 77
Le Corbusier, 141, 144, 186
LED lighting, 175
Lehmann, Inge, 43
leisure, 88, 106, 195
Lenin, Vladimir, 141
libraries/librarians, 5, 153, 182, 215
lidar, 95
Living Labs Global Awards, 69
Local Motion, 18

locative media, 1
London, city of, 48, 142, 163
Loop City project, 104–7, 105
Los Angeles, 1, 12, 16; abandonment of street cars, 31n54; automobile dominance in, 143; Red Line transit system, 137, 138; regulation of food and alcohol in, 33n70; as test bed for urban transport design, 90–91
Los Angeles: The Four Ecologies (Banham), 88
Lubumbashi (D.R. Congo), city of, 173
Lyft, 5, 20, 92, 95, 129, 212
Lynch, Kevin, 160, 218

machines, 8, 48, 52, 113; historians of technology and, 50; integrated into assembly lines, 47; invisibility of, 41; regionally extended, 44, 46; urban studies and, 136
Manifesto of the Communist Party, The (Marx and Engels, 1848), 145
Manila, city of, 1, 2
Marshall, Tyron, 98n8
Marvin, Simon, 4, 24, 187, 196
Marx, Karl, 42, 145, 205n1
Mashed Systems, 18, 20, 21
mass transit, 51, 140, 141, 210; "first and last mile problem," 98n11; fixed-route, 142; historical relationship of cars and cities, 135; personalized, 152; polycentric city and, 91; "transportation conspiracy" against mass transit, 137–38. *See also* buses; subways; trolleys
matter, 18, 43, 48
Mau, Bruce, 172n19
Mayntz, Renate, 52
McHugh, Bibiana, 66
McKibben, Bill, 169
McLuhan, Marshall, 11, 154
McTavish, Dan, 214
Mechanization Takes Command (Giedion, 1948), 47
Meier, Patrick, 28n19

memory, 48

Metabolists, 46, 88

metadata, 10

Metrocable des Caracas (Venezuela), 174

Metropolitan Transit Agency, 64

Mexico, U.S. border with, 74, 76, 81n6

Mexico City, 1, 173

Meyerson, Martin, 201

Miami, city of, 181

microleasing, 20, 213

middle class, 139; in developing world, 136, 140, 143, 146, 153; utopian views of automobile and, 140–41

migration, 1, 172n20, 173

military installations, 50

military planners, 51

military science, 45–46

millennial generation, 136, 147

Milwaukee, city of, 12

MIT (Massachusetts Institute of Technology): Digital City Design Workshop, 114; SENSEable City Lab, 21, 114, 116–17, 234n77

MIT (Massachusetts Institute of Technology) Media Lab, 1, 3; City Science Initiative, 26n6, 34n75, 95, 98n11; Smart Cities Group, 17

Mitchell, William, 1, 3, 4, 17, 18, 148; on adaptation to fuel scarcity, 91–92; on the digital revolution, 97

mobile phones, 7, 54, 64, 116

mobile technologies, 4, 7, 24, 165; experimental prototypes, 18; urban globalization and, 145–49

mobility, 19, 46, 56, 87, 100; access to enabling infrastructures, 214–16; across scales and between nations, 77–79; "calm technology" and, 79–80; "communities of mobility," 148; emerging solutions in informal cities, 177, 178, 179, 180, 181–83, 181; between formal and informal cities, 174; in globally urbanizing world, 149–151; global mobility, 195–97; mobility assemblage, 210–14; "new urban mobilities," 135; overdependence on personal vehicles, 121; paradox of, 187, 188–190; social mobility, 189; speed and, 186; sustainable transport and, 20; virtual mobility and corporeal stasis, 190–91

Mobility & the City Colloquium (San Francisco, 2010), 129

mobility-on-demand (MoD) systems, 2, 5, 20, 26n6; City Science Initiative and, 95; on-demand vehicles, 109, 111, 116; flexible options and, 20–21, 34n76; LA_Redcar and, 93; sharing economy and, 34n75

mobility zoning, 24

modernism, 137, 162

modular constructions, 176

monorails, 12, 15, 16

Mörtenböck, Peter, 89–90

Morton, Timothy, 8

Moses, Robert, 49

Mostafavi, Mohsen, 9

Motopia: Glass City of the Future (Jellicoe), 13, 13, 32n57

Mulroney, Brian, 82n7

multimodal transportation, 18, 140, 149; Audi Urban Future Initiative and, 101; everyday commuting experience of, 110; reliability and flexibility of, 111–15; rhizomatic urbanism and, 115–18; ubiquitous, 109, 112

Mumford, Lewis, 47, 135, 143, 153

Municipal (Muni) Wi-Fi, 35n81

museums, 5

MyCityWay guide, 66

Nabian, Nashid, 21, 210

Nader, Ralph, 142

National Automated Highway System Consortium NAHSC/PATH I-15, 96, 99n17

National City Lines, 31n54
National Council on Public Works Improvement, 51
NATO (North Atlantic Treaty Organization), 19, 44
natural disasters, 51
nature, 56, 57, 154; as source of ultimate meaning and value, 169; transformed into society, 42
NDBs (nondirectional beacons), 55
near-field communication, 7
networked computing and control (NCC) systems, 4
networked technologies, 6, 10, 20, 214, 218
networks, 56–58, 91; linear, 44, 56, 57; "network society," 16; organization of, 89; reach of, 48
Networks of Power (Hughes, 1983), 51–52
New Songdo International City Development LLC, 190
New Towns Act (Britain), 31n52
New Urbanism, 149–150, 161
New York City, 22, 66, 67, 142; Central Park, 164; digital transportation systems, 114; as exemplar of infrastructure, 48–50; High Line, 22, 163; lack of underground mobile coverage, 65; as megacity, 173; public transit improvement in, 115; squatter communities in, 176; Times Square, 184–85; as utopian "City of Skyscrapers," 113; World's Fair (1939), 142
Next Bus app, 112
Nexus Cards, 72, 74, 77, 81n6
NGOs (nongovernmental organizations), 6
Nieuwenhuys, Constant, 88
9/11 terrorist attacks, 50, 81n6
nodes, 56–58, 96, 119, 152, 215; in central place theory networks, 116; of command and control, 41; linkages, 48; of mobility at national borders, 78
nuclear power, 1
Nunn, Samuel, 194

Obama, Barack, 146
object-oriented ontology (OOO), 8
Occupy movement, 6
"Octopus card" (Hong Kong), 5
OECD (Organisation for Economic Co-operation and Development), 7, 10
oil pipelines and refineries, 57, 58
Olerich, Henry, 144–45
Olmsted, Frederick Law, 144, 163–64
"Omnibuilding" (1968 article in *Progressive Architecture*), 46–47
Open Bike Share System, 117
Open Plans, 64
optical-fiber cables, 54
"Order in Diversity" (Webber), 88
Øresund Strait (Denmark-Sweden), 105, 106
organization theory, 74
Ortolano, Guy, 15
Otherlab, 18
Outram, Christine, 21, 210
Owen, David, 150, 151

Palo Alto, California, 23
paradigm shifts, scientific, 43
Paradox Engineering, 26n1, 29n29
paratransit, 212
Paris, city of, 5, 48; Autolib', 20, 213; Metro system, 142; Paris Region Entreprise, 213; Vélib,' 21, 213
Park, Geun-Hye, 199
parking, 33n68, 92, 121, 139; automated vehicles and, 126; mobile apps for, 68, 69; retrofitted parking garages, 179, 181–82, 181; smart parking, 188; ubiquitous mobility and, 117; urban land use and, 34nn74–75
parks, 9, 30n35, 49, 50; in Audi Urban Future Initiative, 101–2; automobiles and, 139
"peak oil," 99n16
pedestrians, 101, 104, 127, 149, 177. *See also* walking

People's Computer Company, 63, 64
Perera, Dinesh, 98n8
Persuasive Electric Vehicle, 26n6
phantom (unstaffed) toll plazas, 71–72, 80n3; border controls and, 74; land area of, 75; as VLOs (Very Large Organizations), 72–74
Phantom Tollbooth, The (Juster/Feiffer, 1961), 71
physics, 42
phytoremediation ponds, 162
pipelines, 30n35, 48, 57
pipes, 49
plate tectonics, 43
Plato, 43
playgrounds, 49, 104, 139
plumbing, 41
pollution, 74, 98n10, 103, 122, 136
population density, 11, 128, 150, 210
population growth, 1, 31n52, 136, 218
Portland, Oregon, 65, 66
ports, 116
poststructuralism, 9
"post-tuning," 167
Poundbury (Prince Charles, designer), 161
power grids, 5, 19, 47, 55; hydroelectricity, 107; microgrids, 211; public works and, 50; from small to large systems, 52; smart electric grids, 2; street lighting, 49, 53, 140; wind power, 107; wireless electricity, 113; wires, 48
power plants, 58
Powers of Ten, The (Eames and Eames), 168
pilgrimage, 39
privacy, 8, 10, 79, 192, 214, 216–17
product-service systems, 67
Progressive Architecture magazine, 46
Project X, 13–15, 14
psychology, 43–44
P2P (peer-to-peer) communications, 90
public space, 8, 30n35, 58, 102, 174, 181; smart cards and, 193; surveillance in,

196; wireless infrastructural integration and, 214
public works, 9, 30n35, 48; definitions of, 50–51; "infrastructure crisis" and, 51; in New York City, 49
Public Works Improvement Act (1984), 51

quantum mechanics, 42

radar, 95
radio, 7, 16, 50, 58
Rae, John B., 142, 148
railroads/rail lines, 12, 30n35, 41, 50, 53, 141; central rail systems, 113; formal cities and, 175; light rail, 105, 107, 149; as most sustainable mode of transport, 16; multimodality and, 113; telegraph wires and, 54
Rapid Re(f)use (Terreform ONE), 166–67, 171n13
Ratti, Carlo, 21, 34n77, 210
Reagan, Ronald, 82n7
Real Time Rome, 116–17, 117
"Redefining Cities" (Calthorpe), 150
Reinventing the Automobile (Mitchell, Borroni-Bird, and Burns), 2, 91–92, 148
RelayRides (Turo) app, 18, 68, 129
"Resistance in the Iron Curtain Countries" (Karasz, 1950), 44–45
restaurants, mobile, 96–97
"Rethinking Urban Utopias" (Joachim), 9
rezoning, 17
RFID (radio-frequency identification) technologies, 20, 68, 188, 194; New York City public transit and, 115; phantom tollbooth plazas and, 72, 74, 77; switch to GPS tracking, 79; in U-City (Incheon, Korea), 190, 192
ride sharing, 18, 20, 63, 153; integration of communication and commoditization, 129; limitations of, 91
right-of-ways, 17, 54, 55

Road and the Car in American Life, The (Rae, 1971), 142

Roadify app, 5, 18, 66

roads, 30n35, 41, 50, 73; in developing world, 54; formal cities and, 175; road safety, 4, 55; urban development and, 40

RoboScooter, 26n6

Rogers, Heather, 166

Rojas, Francisca, 66

Rome, ancient, 40, 59n2

rooftop farms, 162

Roosevelt, Franklin, 61n43

Roumeas, Vincent, 213

Rueb, Teri, 82n12

Russell, I. Willis, 44

Rutherford, Ernest, 42

S, M, L, XL (Koolhaas and Mau, 1995), 172n19

Saarinen, Eero, 49

safety, 25, 104, 127, 130, 141, 151, 214; automated vehicles and, 125, 129; commoditization of cars and, 128; as planning objective, 203; ride sharing and, 91; road safety, 4, 55; vehicle communication and, 126

Sandy, Hurricane, 6

San Francisco, 12, 29n29, 65, 128; car-sharing in, 68; Golden Gate Park, 75; Internet of Things (IoT) and, 26n1; "war against the automobile" in, 139

sanitation, 41, 174, 179, 181

São Paulo, city of, 175, 182, 184

Sassen, Saskia, 17, 146, 168

satellite technologies, 78

Saunders, Doug, 151

scalability, 64

scale, 19, 77–79, 159, 168–69, 170, 189

schools, 30n35, 183, 191

Schouwburgplein (Rotterdam), 161–62

Schwarzer, Mitchell, 19

Schwegler, Ben, 171n13

science/scientists, 14, 41, 167, 199; atomic structure, 42; industrial scientists, 47

self-driving vehicles. *See* driverless (self-driving, autonomous) vehicles

Selvadurai, Naveen, 64

semaphores, 53

SENSEable City Lab, at MIT, 21, 34n77, 114, 116–17

sensors, 1, 8, 21, 22, 92, 221n27; AHS sensors, 92; in cars, 126; cost of, 7–8; data collection and, 10; self-aware infrastructure and, 87; sensor topologies, 26n1; smart dust (networked microsensors), 112

SENTRI (Secure Electronic Network for Travelers Rapid Inspection), 81n6

Seoul, city of, 5

Seoul on Wheels (mobile restaurant), 97

Sert, José Luis, 160

sewage, 48, 49, 50, 58

Shannon, Kelly, 53

Shape of Time, The (Kubler, 1962), 45

sharing economy, 20, 34n75, 67, 87

Sherman Antitrust Act (1890), 138

Shirky, Clay, 64

Shore, James, 183

Short Message Service (SMS), 6

shrines, 39

shuttles, 16, 112

Sidecar, 20

sidewalks, 101, 102, 214

Siemens, 10, 211

Silicon Valley, 18, 65, 198

Singapore, 23

Situationist International, 88

skyscrapers, 50, 113, 144, 179, 182

slums (favelas), 143, 146, 151, 175, 185, 216; IT (information technology) and development in, 177; lack of infrastructure in, 23

smart cards, 193; as payment cards 5, 7

smart cities, 3, 10, 70, 209; civic hackers and, 63, 64, 67; growing, learning cities versus, 175–77; history of, 10–12

Smart Cities Group, at MIT Media Lab, 17
smart dust, 26n1, 112
Smart Growth movement, 149
smartphones, 5, 7, 19, 129, 160; automated
    vehicles and, 125–26; carsharing and,
    128; evolution into personal infrastruc-
    ture, 213; Internet of Things (IoT) and, 8;
    situated software on, 65; transportation
    apps, 112; virtual mobility and, 191; wide
    adoption of, 64
Smets, Marcel, 53
Snell, Bradford, 137
social media, 6, 24, 33n70, 64, 149
sociology, 2, 189
"Sociometry and Psychology" (Zazzo,
    1949), 43–44
sociotechnical system, 8
soft buses, 162, 164
S.O.F.T. Mobility, Blimp Bumper Bus (Ter-
    reform ONE), 164
Soft Systems, 18, 19, 20
software, 18, 98n9; location-based, 217;
    situated, 19, 65, 69; social software, 92,
    93–94
Soja, Edward, 1
solar power, 211
Songdo International Business District
    (Incheon, Korea), 23, 193, 195, 197–98,
    200, 201
Soria y Mata, Arturo, 141
soundscape, 78
Sousa, E. S., 219n6
Southeastern Wisconsin Regional Planning
    Commission (SEWRPC), 32n55
Soviet Union, 141
space: annihilation of, 186, 205n1; changed
    perceptions of, 54; code and production
    of, 218
"space of flows/spaces of places" dichot-
    omy, 148, 153
space programs, 73
Spaces of Hope (Harvey), 32n56

spatial practices, 77, 87, 96
Splintering Urbanism (Graham and Marvin), 24
Split-Level Trap, The (Gordon, 1961), 143
Sprawl Kills (Hirschhorn, 2005), 143
squatter communities, 173, 176, 179
Stalder, Felix, 217
Standard Oil, 137
Stanford Industrial Park, 13–14
Stanford University, 13, 18, 22, 147; Artifi-
    cial Intelligence Laboratory, 95; Center
    for Automotive Research, 21
start-ups, 23
Steadman, Philip, 54
storm runoff, 49
Stout, Frederic, 22, 210
streetcars, electric, 49
streets, 101, 102, 214
suburbs, 91, 98n10, 107, 218; automobiles
    and accessibility of, 135; as "bourgeois
    utopia," 143; "classic suburbs" of pre-
    automobile era, 149; social anomie in,
    137; suburban sprawl, 138, 141, 145, 147;
    as "technoburbia," 149
subways, 48, 49, 65, 98n11, 141, 184; formal
    cities and, 175; multimodality and, 113;
    New York public transit improvement
    plan and, 115; user experience of, 214
superstructures, 42, 46
Superstudio, 88
surveillance, 29n29, 115, 175, 193–96, 200,
    216
sustainability, 8–9, 21, 24–25, 91, 130, 152,
    186; apps contests and, 66; of cities, 3;
    community involvement and, 175; dense
    cities and, 150; of ecological design, 22;
    ecological design and, 165; of electric ve-
    hicles, 124; energy production, 182; flex-
    ible transportation infrastructure and,
    90; housing, 174; integrated approach
    to personal urban mobility and, 129;
    multimodality and, 109; "new urban
    mobilities" and, 135, 136; of rail transit,

16; ride sharing and, 20; smart power grid and, 107; solutions to problems of automobiles, 123; suburban sprawl as threat to, 141; "truth windows" and, 169; of urban land use, 34n74

Sweden, 105, 106, 107

systems theory, 11

Taipei, city of, 69

Taken for a Ride (PBS documentary, 1996), 138

Tange, Kenzo, 46

Tarr, Joel, 50–51

taxis, 15, 112, 142, 149; employment opportunities and, 139; merged with public transit, 152; motorcycle, 179, 183; multimodality and, 116, 117; taxi apps, 21, 65

Technological Society, The (Ellul, 1964), 56

technology, 14, 22, 48, 88, 159; technological determinism, 198–201, 218; transfer of, 52; urban planning's predispositions toward, 197–98; "value-neutral," 195

Technology and the Rise of the Networked City in Europe and America (Tarr and Dupuy), 50–51

telecommunications, 8, 19, 40, 48, 53, 148

telegrams, 53

telegraph, 53–54, 205n1

telephone systems, 48, 57, 140; invention of the telephone, 53; privatized, 50

television, 16, 48, 50

Terreform ONE (Open Network Ecology), 22; Brooklyn 2110, City of the Future, 164–65, 165; Rapid Re(f)use, 166–67, 171n13; S.O.F.T. Mobility, Blimp Bumper Bus, 164

Tesla corporation, 10

text messages, 54, 64

Thompson, J. J., 43

311 systems, 64

Thrun, Sebastian, 18, 95

Thün, Geoffrey, 214, 215

Tierney, Gerald, 98n8

time, changed perceptions of, 54

T-money card (Seoul), 5

TOD (transit-oriented development), 91, 96, 150, 215–16

Tokyo, city of, 46, 173, 196

Torre David office tower (Caracas, Venezuela), 177, 178, 179, 180

tourism, 114, 189, 195

Townsend, Anthony, 5, 19, 192, 212

traffic congestion, 98n10, 106, 122, 136, 138; automated vehicles and, 125; carsharing and, 128; centralized traffic management and, 127; driverless cars as solution to, 103; historical relationship of cars and cities, 137, 141

traffic flow, 4, 121, 129; Audi Urban Future Initiative and, 102, 103, 104, 104; carsharing and, 128; optimization of, 17; vehicle communication and, 126

trains, 15, 41, 55, 67; elevated, 49; Loop City project and, 105, 106; Monorail, 16; multimodality and, 112, 118

tram systems, 98n11, 183

trans-Atlantic cables (1858), 53

transit apps, 5, 20, 66–67

transportation, 1, 4, 12, 39, 47; adaptation to fuel scarcity, 91–92; automobiles integrated with public transportation, 130; cars and street space, 31n54; dynamic hubs, 117–18; expansion of transportation webs, 48; fixed physical hubs, 109, 116, 118; free public transport, 5; impacts on the environment, 26n2; informal, 212; as infrastructure, 19; LA_Redcar prototype design, 90; major problems of, 121, 123; organization of mobility and, 90; public works and, 50; sensors and, 8; sustainable, 20; tactical system components, 91–96, 92–93, 94, 96; "transportation conspiracy" against mass transit, 137–38; transport infrastructure, 30n35. *See also* multimodal transportation

Traveler from Altruria, A (Howells, 1894), 145
Tricart, Jean, 220n15
Tri-Met transit authority (Portland, Oregon), 66
Triumph of the City (Glaeser, 2011), 150
trolleys, 53, 135, 138, 141, 142
Tsay, Shin-pei, 25
tunnels, 49
Turo (RelayRides) app, 18, 68, 129
TWA Flight Center (Kennedy Airport terminal; Saarinen, 1962), 49, 60n23
Twelve Tables of Roman law, 59n2, 220n11
Twitter, 18, 63, 96–97

Uber, 5, 20, 21, 65, 129, 212; LA_Redcar compared with, 92; mobility-on-demand (MoD) and, 95
U-City (Ubiquitous City; Songdo district, Incheon, Korea), 187, 201, 202; illusory liberty and ubiquitous control in, 192–95, *193*; paradox of mobility in, 190–91
U-Life Solutions, 190–91
unemployment, 174
UNESCO World Heritage sites, 114
United Kingdom (UK; Great Britain), 11, 12, 52, 137
United Nations: as extraterritorial zone, 172n16; Human Settlements Programme (UN-HABITAT), 146; Relief and Rehabilitation Administration (UNRRA), 45
United States, 11, 52, 212; Air Traffic Control System, 55, 61n45; border controls, 72, 74, 76, 81nn6–7; Interstate Highway System, 54–55, 139; land-use patterns and transportation in, 98n10; as leading generator of waste, 166; Project X, 13–14, *14*; urbanization in, 137
University of California, Berkeley, 88; College of Environmental Design, 11; Partners for Advanced Transportation Technology (PATH), 17, 33n67

University of California, Los Angeles, cityLAB, 23
Unsafe at Any Speed (Nader, 1965), 142
urban design, 18, 159, 160
Urbaneering, 159–160, *160*; background of, 160–63; methodology, 163–66
Urban Future Initiative, 21, 101–4, *102*, *103*, *104*, 182
urbanism, 4, 153; DIY (do-it-yourself), 6, 20, 23, 218; ecological, 9; "green urbanism," 151; informal, 173; landscape, 9; performative, 9; rhizomatic, 115–18; spatial urbanists, 87
Urbanism in the Age of Climate Change (Calthorpe, 2011), 150–51
urbanization, 40, 136–37, 144, 151, 188, 211; auto-centric perspectives and, 210; impact of machines and systems, 47; Interstate Highway System and, 57
"Urban Mobility in the Smart City Age" (Schneider Electric, Arup, and the Climate Group), 186
Urban Mobility in the Smart City Age (Schneider Electric, Arup, and the Climate Group), 188
urban planning/planners, 9, 11, 12–13, 22, 135, 204; adaptation to changing conditions, 149; Audi Urban Future Initiative and, 101; dominance of private automobile and, 210; expanding urban population and, 173; "infrastructure crisis" (1980s) and, 51; multimodality and, 101; predispositions toward technology, 197–98; visions of continuity with the past, 15
Urban Research Lab (URL), at University of Illinois, 98n9
urban studies, 3, 136
Urban-Think Tank (U-TT), 23, 176, 182, 183, 214–15
user preferences, 91

Ushahidi, 6
U.S. Highway System (1920s), 54
UShip, 114, 115
utopias, 13, 32n56, 159, 187, 189, 204–5;
  automobiles and, 140–45; "degenerate,"
  203; discourse of the future and, 201–3;
  populist objectives, 162; "pragmatic
  utopianism," 100; technological determinism and, 198; utopian visions of New
  York City, 113

Vélib' (Paris), 21, 213
Velikov, Kathy, 214
Venezuela, 177
ventilation, 181
Verrazano Narrows Bridge (1964), 49
viaducts, 49
Vietnam War, 44
Ville Spatiale (France), 13
Ville Spatiale (Friedman, 1958–62), 46
Virilio, Paul, 8n5, 190
Vitruvius, Marcus Pollio, 40
VLOs (Very Large Organizations), 20,
  72–74, 81n6
voice recognition, 65
Voisin Motorcar Company, 141
volunteers, 6, 28n19
VORs (VHF omnidirectional range find-
  ers), 55

walking, 105, 112, 140, 149, 152; movement
  away from autos in favor of, 135, 141;
  space freed for, 128, 130; "walkable"
  neighborhoods, 200; walking-city
  values, 138; walking distance to public
  transportation, 98n10; walkways, 121. *See
  also* pedestrians
WALL-E (film, 2008), 171n13
Walt Disney Imagineering, 171n13
Walters, Susan, 51
war, 51

Washington, DC, 63, 65, 95
waste management, 19, 106, 176; public
  works and, 50; Rapid Re(f)use (Terre-
  form ONE), 166–67, 171n13; waste-to-
  energy, 211
waterbuses, 101
water systems, 19, 40, 47, 174; Croton Aque-
  duct (New York), 49; "growing house"
  and, 176; pipes, 48; public works and, 50
water taxis, 101, 200
Watson, James, 43
Waze, 5
Web 2.0, 4, 23
Webber, Melvin, 11, 12, 15, 31n50, 88
Weiser, Mark, 72, 79, 194
Werthmann, Christian, 173
West, Geoffrey, 70
West 8, 162
Who Framed Roger Rabbit? (cartoon movie,
  1988), 138
Whole Earth Catalog, The, 150
Wi-Fi, 5, 35n81, 147, 192, 215
Wilson, Charles, 145–46
Winter, Maximilien, 42, 44
Wireless Access Zone, 35n81
wireless network systems (WNS), 97n1,
  210, 212; data collection and, 30n39,
  216; fourth-generation, 219n6; mobility-
  on-demand (MoD) and, 93; Municipal
  Wireless Networks, 35n81, 65
wires, encased, 49
Woolworth Building (New York), 49
World Bank, 65–66
World Trade Center (New York), 50
World War, First, 44
World War II, 40, 44, 54
Wright, Frank Lloyd, 141, 144

Yahoo, 64
Yang, Chamee, 23, 214
YouTube, 33n70

Zaragoza, Spain, 5
Zazzo, René, 43
Zellner, Peter, 98n8
Zielinski, Sue, 214
Zimride, 18

Zipcar, 67–68, 94
zoning, 24, 91, 187, 189; changes disallowed in frozen city, 114; FEZs (free economic zones), 195–96; rezoning, 17
Zurich, city of, 23